Praise for *Unpacking My Father's Bookstore*

"This beautifully rendered work brings readers into the lush spaces of a beloved Jewish bookstore in midcentury Los Angeles. Moving gracefully between memoir and a larger story about the world of Jewish books, bookstores, and American Jewish readers, Roth unpacks his father's bookstore. In so doing he rearranges the books to tell his own story."

—Laura Levitt, author of *The Objects that Remain*

"Roth ushers us into the history of Jewish books in a way no other literary scholar could. This remarkable book gives us an insider's tour while offering an intimate, moving portrait of one American Jewish family as well as a sharp, detailed, and thought-provoking account of how books move through and transform our lives."

—Josh Lambert, author of *The Literary Mafia: Jews, Publishing, and Postwar American Literature*

"*Unpacking My Father's Bookstore* is a brilliant family memoir and history of American bookselling. Attractively written and always compelling, this provides both an intimate, child's-eye view of the world and a profound understanding of the nature of cultural transformation."

—Bryan Cheyette, author of *The Ghetto: A Very Short Introduction*

"This isn't only a paean to the legendary Los Angeles bookstore, where browsing was a hermeneutical activity, but a eulogy to a father-and-son relationship and a map of how Jewish knowledge circulated in America in the second half of the twentieth century. Kudos to Roth for hearing the call of memory. Bookstores are where our minds feel grounded and our hearts find meaning."

—Ilan Stavans, editor of *How Yiddish Changed America and How America Changed Yiddish*

"When I was a child, my family flew to Los Angeles to see Grandpa Cal and Grandma Florence every year. On these trips, we visited the Huntington Library, the La Brea Tar Pits, the Los Angeles County Museum of Art, and, of equal importance, J. Roth Fine and Scholarly Judaica.

This spacious store was a treasure house overflowing with every kind of Jewish book. *Seforim*, novels, history, memoir, and children's books lined the shelves. Here, we would stock up on resources unavailable in Honolulu. Scholarly books, cookbooks, even Aleph-Bet coloring books for my sister and me. *Unpacking my Father's Bookstore* serves as poignant testimony to the value of old-fashioned bookselling, a family business, and the transmission of Jewish knowledge through the generations—*l'dor vador*."

—Allegra Goodman, author of *Isola*

"J. Roth Bookseller was a literary and cultural institution in Los Angeles's Jewish community. *Unpacking My Father's Bookstore* is testimony to the proposition that there is more to a bookstore than books. Roth describes the multi-generational journey that affixed this storefront's imprint on America's second-largest Jewish community."

—Zev Yaroslavsky, former Los Angeles County supervisor

Unpacking My Father's Bookstore

Unpacking My Father's Bookstore

Laurence Roth

RUTGERS UNIVERSITY PRESS
NEW BRUNSWICK, CAMDEN, AND NEWARK, NEW JERSEY
OXFORD AND LONDON

Rutgers University Press is a department of Rutgers, The State University of New Jersey, one of the leading public research universities in the nation. By publishing worldwide, it furthers the University's mission of dedication to excellence in teaching, scholarship, research, and clinical care.

Library of Congress Cataloging-in-Publication Data

Names: Roth, Laurence, 1960– author.
Title: Unpacking my father's bookstore / Laurence Roth.
Description: New Brunswick : Rutgers University Press, 2025. | Includes bibliographical references.
Identifiers: LCCN 2024050425 | ISBN 9781978836600 (hardcover) | ISBN 9781978836617 (epub) | ISBN 9781978836624 (pdf)
Subjects: LCSH: J. Roth Bookseller of Fine & Scholarly Judaica. | Roth, Jack (Bookseller) | Roth, Laurence, 1960—Family | Bookstores—California—Los Angeles—History—20th century. | Independent bookstores—California—Los Angeles—History—20th century. | Jewish booksellers—California—Los Angeles—Biography | Jews—California—Los Angeles—Intellectual life—20th century. | LCGFT: Biographies.
Classification: LCC Z473.J16 R68 2025 | DDC 381/.45002092 [B]—dc23/eng/20250203
LC record available at https://lccn.loc.gov/2024050425

A British Cataloging-in-Publication record for this book is available from the British Library.

∞ The paper used in this publication meets the requirements of the American National Standard for Information Sciences—Permanence of Paper for Printed Library Materials, ANSI Z39.48-1992.

rutgersuniversitypress.org

לאחים היקרים שלי, אהרון אלכסנדר ובנימין יחזקאל

For Alan and Benjamin

For what else is this collection but a disorder to which habit has accommodated itself to such an extent that it can appear as order?

—WALTER BENJAMIN,
"Unpacking My Library"

Contents

Unpacking My Father's Bookstore

Sotheby's, Manhattan, 1985

"Dad, the guy you bought the Copenhagen Haggadah from, did he come back Monday or Friday?"

"He came in Friday, and we waited for him all day Monday."

"Really? I remember he came on Monday, and then we waited Friday for him to come back. We were totally sweating whether he'd be back before we closed at four for Shabbos."

"No, we waited Monday, right? Yes."

How does this story go? Whom should I trust? My fallible memory, or my father's now failing one?

"I think he came *in* on Monday, Dad. It was fall of '82, before Ben came home the next year, and I was still at the store full-time."

"Was it '82?" Jack looks down at his hands folded neatly in his lap as he leans back on the red sofa in my den in Selinsgrove, Pennsylvania. His still trim eighty-eight-year-old frame rests easily on the cushions, and he's dressed in his usual outfit: dark brown tailored slacks, a brown-and-tan checked sport shirt from Brooks Brothers, tan silk socks, and russet brown tasseled loafers. We're at work again this afternoon trying to clear up details from his past about the Jewish bookstore he owned and operated in Los Angeles for twenty-eight years, and I'm tired, though not from our conversation. Almost twenty inches of snow is piled up on the front lawn, but the walkway and sidewalk in front of the house are clear after I'd spent all morning in the cold struggling to dig them out with my cheap shovel. Jack had watched me work from behind the glass storm door at our entryway, his arms behind his back and neatly combed white hair crowning his head. He occasionally flashed me a thumbs-up to signal what a fine job I was doing. Judging again, I said to myself, but I couldn't tell whether he approved of my progress or I had shoveled the snow in what he deemed was the correct way.

"Let's say it was '82 for now," I continue. "He came in on Monday and walked up to the front counter where I was sitting, and I thought he was just another person, not Jewish, from the bus stop out front, who confused the Pico store for a regular bookshop. But then he said he had a book he wanted to sell. It was wrapped in something, paper or maybe cloth, and when he unwrapped it, I knew I had to get you. You came out, and I saw immediately from how you talked that he had something really valuable."

"I had to be careful," Jack cuts in, "but I didn't want him to get away. He got it from his mother. They were gentiles, and she worked for a rich Jewish family in Hungary. She was their maid, I think. They gave it to her, he said, as a token of appreciation for her work when they had to let her go, you know, when the Nazis came in. Maybe it was really for safekeeping and she just told him that, or she stole it—whatever. They all died, and then she came to the U.S. after the war. I offered him $1,200, but I didn't want to seem too eager, so I told him he could take his time and think about it."

"Yeah, and you started freaking out after he left, because you didn't think he'd be back, or that he'd go over to Fairfax."

"What are you talking about, 'freaking out'? I didn't 'freak out.'" Jack's look of disgust at my description warns me to tidy my memory, just as I did my walkway, making it neat and spotless in the way he likes; otherwise we'll just start arguing and I'll get nothing out of him.

"You were concerned, I meant to say, right?"

"Sure I was concerned. He could have gone somewhere else. But he came back, and I gave him the $1,500."

"It was $1,500?"

"Right, and he came in just as I was ready to close, and I gave him a check. The Haggadah was done in 1779, just beautiful. It was illuminated, and I kept it in a safe-deposit box at the bank. I'd go and look at it, but it wasn't good to keep it there. So I sold it at Sotheby's."

"You made a good profit on it."

"Well, I bought it for $1,200 and it went for $150,000 at auction, so I guess I did okay."

Jack says he needs to lie down for a while, and as he climbs the stairs I put in my notes that $1,200 is probably the right amount since he repeated it twice, but this is the game I play with him, and with myself. I'm improvising, because I've never done this before, and, instead of recording him, I find it easier to write everything down, which is, I'm sure, exactly what I shouldn't be doing. It's just that I hate putting a recorder or microphone between us. I prefer to jot down what he's saying when he says it. Yes, I'm a professor and I know how this should work, but I'm also the only son asking him to tell his stories, so I'm doing this my way. I get to decide.

"Bullshit!" says Elana, Jack's second wife, when I later tell her about his version of the Sotheby's story. It seems that $1,500 really is what Jack paid for the Haggadah, because she was there and has the tax returns to prove it. And no, he didn't write a check either, because she told him not to use the store's checking account for the purchase so that the Haggadah wouldn't be part of the store's inventory. He paid the guy in cash.

I quickly run through the rest of Jack's story with her: that he called Sotheby's to begin arrangements, and they put him in touch with one of their affiliated appraisers in L.A., who said the Haggadah was worth only $15,000 (obviously too low), so then he called George Snyder, Sotheby's Judaica specialist at the time, who recognized its real value. Elana laughs. $15,000 was the amount a customer in Hancock Park offered Jack for the Haggadah, and he was considering taking it. She and her business colleague had to sit him down and explain what a bad idea that was. It was they who convinced him to take it to Sotheby's for auction. They even had to talk him into setting a reserve on the sale, the confidential minimum price below which a lot won't be sold. It was $150,000, precisely the amount it sold for, she says.

Jack had previously sent me the Sotheby's catalog for the sale, so I'd already seen the sale results and a sale confirmation notice. They were both tucked into the page where Lot 19 is listed in *Important*

Judaica: Books, Manuscripts and Works of Art, New York, Monday, November 25, 1985:

> HAGGADAH. Seder Haggadah Shel Pesach . . . [in Hebrew, instructions and various passages in Judeo-German] written in the letters of Amsterdam, in Copenhagen, Rosh Chodesh, Nissan, 1779 by the scribe Yehuda Leib Ha'Cohen.
>
> Manuscript on vellum, 20 leaves including one blank, 8½×7½ inches (21.5×19 cm.). Written in a fine square Ashkenazi Rabbinic and cursive Hebrew script, pointed and unpointed, illuminated with decorative vignettes and panels. Slight staining, some portions smudged. Contemporary panelled calf gilt; rubbed. In a tapestry cloth container.

The notice reveals that the reserve was indeed $150,000, which was also the low estimate. The high estimate was $200,000. The sale results say that the Haggadah sold for $165,000, so after Sotheby's took its 10 percent commission, Jack walked away with $148,500, or about $460,000 in today's money.

This was the most important purchase and sale of my father's bookselling career. His reclamation of a nearly lost work of European Judaica was to him a great mitzvah—he helped preserve a remnant of Israel, a testament to the economic and cultural clout his generation of American Jews wielded after the Holocaust. And its auction put him over the top as a financial success, confirming in his mind that he was, at last, the sophisticated, upscale bookseller that he aspired to be. It was the gold nugget of his California dream, and he cashed it in.

For me, though, it was all vicarious, which is why I'm less concerned with pinning down an exact and verifiable version of Jack's purchase and sale than I am with exploring all the avenues of meaning in his or, rather, in *our* story. Don't mistake my concern about control as the entire picture here. I also found a few small grains of bullion back in the Golden State, but mine are merely a metaphor for another kind of value. Sure, I'm grateful that Jack sent me photos of every page in the Copenhagen Haggadah, and if I simply wanted to document his good taste, they'd be crucial. No, for me the most precious items in these stories about his bookstore are those details in the background or just off camera in major scenes like "The Sale of the Haggadah." That's where I was, that's where my brothers were, all three of us bit players, extras. And having been there, having witnessed those scenes, I can imagine myself into my father's world.

Like this scene, his procession to Sotheby's in the early afternoon of November 25: It's a cool day, mid-forties outside, with a few clouds in the mostly sunny sky above the Waldorf Astoria, my father's favorite hotel in New York. I see Jack in a silk scarf and tan corduroy trench coat, bought from Saks Fifth Avenue, exiting from the glass revolving doors on Park Avenue, following Elana, who's wearing her fur coat. Jack pulls out a money clip from his right pocket, peeling off a few dollar bills for the doorman, who rushes to get them into one of the Yellow Cabs lined up at the curb.

As they head uptown to Sotheby's new flagship building and world headquarters at 1334 York Avenue, a former cigar factory and Kodak warehouse, Jack is excited, perhaps thumbing through the sale catalog, whose frontispiece is a reproduction of his Haggadah's title page. Photos of two other pages from the Haggadah are included in the overleaf following the lot listing, and though no estimate is included in the listing ("Estimate on request"), Jack knows that it's the most expensive item up for auction. It's worth more than any of the Isidor Kaufmann paintings, the Ilya Schor silver Sabbath candelabra, or even the "Important German Carved and Painted Wood Circumcision Ceremony Box, late 17th century" featured on the cover of the catalog.

Jack and Elana are whisked upstairs to the private seating area above the bidding room ("windowed sky boxes," as the *Financial Times* calls them), where other sellers with high-value lots wait for the auction to begin at 2 P.M. promptly. When it does, Jack watches the action below with fascination; here he is, the kid from Corona, Queens, the youngest son of an immigrant *shochet*, a ritual slaughterer, finding himself gratifyingly elevated in more ways than one. The crying of Lot 19 begins. Jack tries to keep track of who's bidding, but a number of potential buyers are calling in by phone to preserve their anonymity, so he can only guess who's on the line. The Israel Museum? The Jewish Historical Museum in Amsterdam?

It's all moving quickly now. He feels a jolt of excitement when the bids rise above the reserve, he tries to interpret the auctioneer's movements, and then suddenly he hears the familiar refrain, "Going once, going twice . . . sold." Jack turns to Elana and smiles, rolling his eyes the way he usually does when his face registers surprise or wonder. He thinks the Haggadah was bought by the owner of a chemical company who's noted for his Judaica collection, but that's just a hunch. Soon he's caught up in the flurry of activity after the sale—signing forms, shaking hands—though he can't help trying to keep an eye on what's happening with the other lots. After all, he's a collector too.

Can I imagine his daydreams as well on the way back to the Waldorf?

This is where I pause, right where I picture the future about to unroll in front of my father, like some celestial red carpet that I can only walk backward. I'm writing this, after all, from where it leads, tired after digging out my property from a night of snowfall and still trying to be the good son (or at least the only one willing to weather his endless criticism), remembering that I grew up in a town where red carpets always look better on camera than they do in real life. Is my version of the story any better than anyone else's in the family? Is it any less true? Maybe I'm just playing a private round of three-card monte, where there's no honest shuffling, only a sleight of hand meant to confuse the mark—me, trying to outsmart myself. But my father's story is as much mine as it is his, in a certain sense, and I need to tell it as I experienced it, as I lived it with my family, and as I remember it.

Looking up from my notebook, I watch Jack return from the guest bedroom and quickly inspect my sofa to see if it's still clean enough for him to sit on. I'll never know exactly what he was thinking that day at Sotheby's. But always I wonder: Between the books and the art and the well-appointed Jewishness in which he clothed himself, what else did he want to do with all that money? What was that man trying to purchase?

Why can't I let *that* question go?

CHAPTER 1

Grand Opening (*objects*)

If I'm looking for answers, I should start here, in June 1979, when my father moved his bookstore from 1070 South La Cienega Boulevard, southwest of Carthay Circle in Los Angeles, to a larger, more upscale space at 9427 West Pico Boulevard in the Pico-Robertson neighborhood. That's when he and the store reached what I consider their retail maturity, and I helped him prepare for that bar mitzvah. Thirteen years earlier he had bought M. Harelick Books, a small Yiddish-oriented bookshop that Michael Harelick founded, and renamed it Harelick & Roth Booksellers. By that summer it was well on its way to becoming one of the premier Jewish bookstores in America, a unique and celebrated bastion of Jewish literature and learning whose inventory of books was the largest west of the Mississippi and perhaps the most Jewishly diverse in the United States at that time. Yet, unlike Shakespeare and Company, Gotham Book Mart, or City Lights, few people today know of it outside the dwindling number of its former customers and kibitzers. It's a sad truth that over the past two hundred years most independent bookstores like my father's, whether family-run or quirky sole proprietorships, disappear from history, even though these retailers often had outsize effects on their communities.

But at that celebratory moment in 1979, my father's bookstore was at its most visible and vibrant. Jack had finally retired Harelick's name, and the store officially became J. Roth / Bookseller of Fine & Scholarly Judaica. Having outgrown the prior location's already once-expanded space and flush with a line of credit from his banker, City National Bank, my father was ready to scale up and claim ownership of his success. It would be his "real" grand opening, as he called it. Jack remembered that he chose the location on Pico because it was fresh territory with clean streets and neat storefronts, located at the farther, western edge of the neighborhood's fast-growing Jewish population. It was free of the clutter and Jewish kitsch he associated with the aging Fairfax Avenue neighborhood, the previous center of Jewish retailing in L.A.

To be sure, it was still a Jewish neighborhood; B'nai David–Judea Congregation, founded in 1948, anchored the center of Pico-Robertson at 8906 West Pico, and Beth Jacob Congregation, located since 1954 on Olympic Boulevard, marked the northern border between Pico-Robertson and Beverly Hills. Both were Orthodox synagogues. But the retail businesses there were mostly dry cleaners, upholstery stores, appliance repair shops, and sundry non-kosher restaurants. One of the oldest stores in the neighborhood was (and still is) Sonny Alexander Florists, established by New York cab driver Alexander Friedman in 1929 after the stock market crash convinced him to head west and start over at 9330 West Pico. The Jewish-owned food shops at that time—like Beverlywood Bakery, established in 1946 at the corner of Pico and Oakhurst Drive, or Factor's Famous Deli, opened in 1948 across the street from the 9427 building, or Label's Table Delicatessen, which started in 1974 at 9226 West Pico—had no kosher certifications, and they catered mainly to nonobservant Jews and to non-Jewish customers. The arrival of J. Roth Bookseller and Yeshiva University High School of Los Angeles, which also opened in 1979, even farther west, on 9760 West Pico Boulevard, augured a new phase in the neighborhood's development in which it would eventually displace the Fairfax District, just as Fairfax had displaced Boyle Heights, as the Jewish center of Los Angeles. My father's grand opening celebrated that as well.

Come June, then, the new store was refurbished and readied. The chocolate brown gusseted bags with twisted paper handles and the store's logo and address printed on them in gold, a sophisticated touch that Jack helped to design and of which he was immensely proud because it evidenced that his was a quality shop, were stacked and ready to be filled. Invitations to customers and the press had been mailed out, and the books had been transported, sorted, alphabetized, and shelved. My father wanted a space big enough to serve the sprawling variety of Jewish literary tastes in Los Angeles. As he said in a feature story about him later that summer in the industry magazine *Judaica Book News*, "I worked towards the goal of making this store a part of the history of Jewish L.A., to expand with it and reflect its growth." The writer of the story, David A. Haskell, made a point to connect my father to that history, to the "eight hardy Jewish pioneers" who established the Jewish community in 1850 and to the city's rapid expansion and its "pursuit of business and culture." J. Roth Bookseller's success as the preeminent Jewish bookstore in the western United States reflected a boom not only in Los Angeles Jewish life but also in Jewish publishing nationwide. "I would hope," my father told Haskell, "that I have brought a sense of dignity and a bit of honor to the Jewish book that it has always deserved."

Jack assigned my older brother, Alan, to musical entertainment for the big day, outfitted in a white jacket and black bow tie. Despite the near-constant friction between the two, the day signaled a truce. For Jack, thirteen years of violin lessons would finally be put to good use in showing off his talented son. Al, as he liked to be called, just loved to perform. Muscled up under his formal attire from years as a high school gymnast and with his thick black hair drawing a dark halo over his violin, he roamed the sales floor, playing Bach selections, the theme from *Fiddler on the Roof* (at Jack's request), and Grigoraş Dinicu's "Hora Staccato," a fiery and difficult piece made famous by Jascha Heifetz. Al eventually stationed himself at the entrance like some pied piper of Jewish customers. My younger brother, Benjamin, a sophomore at Beverly Hills High School, was there too. He was Ben to us, the socialite of the family, the kid with the full cheeks and glossy auburn hair who when he asked strangers on the street for a nickel people actually fished one out of their pockets and purses for him because he was such a charming little boy. He helped out behind the sales counter. My mother wasn't there. She and Jack were divorced by then, so there was no official hostess, though I recall that a number of Roth relatives volunteered to play a supporting role in this family production.

And me? I was in charge of photography. Why hire a professional when I'd commandeered Jack's old Canon Rangefinder and taken photography courses in high school for three years straight? By senior year I even had two photographs on the classroom's wall of fame, both imitations of Duane Michals's black-and-white work from the early seventies. Mr. Arst, shaggy and dark-bearded, his eyeglass pouch sticking up out of his short-sleeve shirt pocket, was a champion of Michals's style. Which I thought of as a knack for cerebral arrangements of naked people caught alone in small, dimly lit rooms, their faces blurred or lost in shadow, with each photo's rich tonal palette reproduced in technically superb prints. My takeaway was reductive; I simply became enamored of photographing objects with visually striking surfaces: aluminum siding, doorways, blighted trees. On a family visit to see my aunt in Philadelphia that winter, I took along my camera and decided to try color film: churches and tombstones and snow.

So you see, I knew that my father had it wrong. I couldn't shoot the grand opening, because I didn't know how to shoot dignity and honor, much less people socializing at a commercial event. I wasn't any good at that kind of photography. When I soaked up photography books on Weegee, Diane Arbus, Brassaï, and Robert Frank, I didn't focus on the people in their prints. I scrutinized all the objects in the background: the greasy-looking bedspreads and cheap wallpaper in New York tenements, glimpses of Central Park in the 1960s, the foam rings on the inside of a beer glass, a diner sign for "Hot Dog 18¢." I was fascinated by their surfaces and substance. What was it like to touch those things, to live with them in their place and time? What's *their* story?

I called my friend Eddie, who'd been a regular on Mr. Arst's wall, and asked him to do the job instead. I'm looking at his black-and-white photographs now. There's the front of the new bookstore with the half-moon store sign above the entrance, designed and constructed by Josef Pelzig, an artist and Polish refugee of the Holocaust who kept himself afloat on that kind of work. There's Al playing the violin on the sidewalk outside the open glass doors, my father behind him talking to a customer, and me with my uncle Cantor Jacob Konigsberg backs to the camera and chatting near the curb. Yet what really captures my attention are the bits of other store signs jutting out in receding distance down Pico Boulevard, "Shoe Repairs," "—ociates," "—estate," "—ndry." And the streetlights, which I notice are of two types, the thirties-style dual torch model and the sixties-style overhanging beacon. It's forever mid-century America in that stretch of boulevard. I can almost feel the slight breeze that blows against the skirt of the middle-aged woman walking down Elm Street away from the entrance, and the warmth of that June day as I gaze into the aging paper of Eddie's print. In another photo, taken inside the store from the second-floor loft where the art was displayed, Eddie captured the crowd at its height, my father surrounded by a mob of friends, relatives, employees, and browsing customers. Still, what I see most clearly as I examine the print, here in my office at a small liberal arts college in central Pennsylvania, are the covers and titles of the books in the paperback racks: *Call It Sleep*, *The Fixer*, *The Joys of Yiddish*, *The Chosen*, *The Rise of American Jewish Literature*, *World of Our Fathers*.

I'm drawn to these photos not because of any longing to speak to the people in them but because the objects in them still speak to me and still inform my conception of how Jewishness looks. And not just the books. Even the racks are of a particular vintage, that combination of wire and wood you don't see anymore, and the same goes for the rectangular waist-high display tables with storage space beneath holding stacks of books, the five narrow oblong fluorescent light fixtures dangling from the ceiling, and the apparel the people wear—polyester blouses and wide lapels, Sansabelt slacks and bulky white purses. This is what a Jewish bookstore looked like—what one *should* look and feel like—one where I see only two men wearing a kippah, one of whom is Avrum Schwartz, cantor at Congregation Beth Kodesh in Canoga Park and Jack's longtime employee and resident intellectual.

Growing up in a Jewish bookstore spotlighted material things for me and provided the premise for my education in literature: books are objects that summon both accounting and interpretation. For my father, books were both a business and an intellectual responsibility. His attitude toward these things that required financial investment and moral attention, careful cataloging and analytical thought informs my tally and explanation of the lessons in books and reading that he drilled into me. On the one hand, there was the business of bookselling: it suffused the life of my family. At the end of the day, if my father was home for dinner (and he rarely was), the table conversation was about the ludicrous demands of New York Jewish publishers or, most likely, the outrageous behavior of customers—rabbis at the top of the list, followed by bar mitzvah–gift shoppers, *Yekkes* (those snooty German

Jews), and sundry Yiddish-speaking oddballs. On the Sabbath and holidays, my father would sometimes take us to an Orthodox synagogue, sometimes a Conservative synagogue, occasionally even to a Reform synagogue. It was good for business. At social events, he would often go so far as to take orders or promise to track down a hard-to-find book. It was also good for business.

On the other hand, literature shaped our upper-middle-class American Jewish perspective; books flooded into our home. Signed first editions of Isaac Bashevis Singer, oversize Jewish art and photography books, rare and new printings of prayer books and Hebrew Bibles, fiction by Sholem Aleichem, Cynthia Ozick, Isaac Babel, and Jerzy Kosinski, anthologies such as *A Treasury of Jewish Poetry* by Nathan and Marynn Ausubel and *The Golden Peacock* by Joseph Leftwich, nonfiction by Hannah Arendt, Amos Oz, Ben Hecht, Trude Weiss-Rosmarin, and Martin Buber. And not just Judaica; our library included Tolstoy, Dostoyevsky, Zola, Theodore Dreiser, William Dean Howells, Charles and Mary Lamb's *Tales from Shakespeare*, multiple biographies of the Kennedys, the entire Time-Life series on countries of the world, the *Encyclopaedia Britannica*, and Lewis Carroll's *Alice's Adventures in Wonderland*, illustrated by Salvador Dali in a series of twelve heliogravures, which my father framed and hung in the long hallway of our ranch house in Encino, an affluent L.A. suburb in the San Fernando Valley.

Little wonder, then, that I see my father's business and his love of books—his love of their look and feel—through the prism of Walter Benjamin's famous essay about the passion and tactics of book collecting, "Unpacking My Library." For Benjamin, taking ownership of a book is to bring it into the "magic circle" of one's library, to give it consciousness as an extension of the existential and intellectual order within one's mind. Do you separate the books you own into your own idiosyncratic categories, as I do with my "really Jewish" books, "sort of Jewish" books, and "not Jewish" books? Or walking into someone's home, seeing the way their books are neatly arranged or carelessly strewn about, even the way the spines look next to each other on a shelf, doesn't that conjure a glimpse into the owner's sense of self? "You don't even need to have read them," Jack once told a friend of mine. "Books say something about the status of a person." A collector is also a wily tactician of the book business who must outwit the dealers and auctioneers who hold books captive. To the collector, Benjamin recognizes, "ownership is the most intimate relationship that one can have to objects. Not that they come alive in him; it is he who lives in them."

I've always appreciated the humor and the subtle theorizing of Benjamin's essay. It so aptly describes my father and his store. Despite the fact that his collection was a commercial venture—a "regular bookstore," as Jack put it—the way its stock was bought, sorted, and displayed reflected the mind and habits of a book collector. The two times that I witnessed the store's books packed up and moved, first to Pico-Robertson and eventually to Beverly Hills, will always color my reading of the quotation that is the epigraph for my unpacking of Jack's business and pedagogy. There on his spotless floor in weighty boxes and on wooden pallets all around was Jewish literature in heaps: children's books, reference books, *sifrei kodesh*, cookbooks, fiction, nonfiction, *musar*, history, women's literature and *nidah* manuals, biography, humor, books in Yiddish and Hebrew, textbooks, used books, antiquarian and limited editions—the grand disorder of a Jewish bookstore where the religious and the secular, the patriarchal and the feminist, the popular and the arcane were all shelved under one roof.

But to Jack Roth, whose habits as owner and salesclerk were many and ironclad, the store exemplified his belief that a clean, well-lighted place and the salutary order of clearly labeled subject categories could help remake the Jewish bookstore in America and lift it out of the chaos and grubbiness that blighted those he used to shop in as a kid on the Lower East Side. He construed those categories, however, and that of Jewish literature itself, as widely as possible. This was so because for him Jewish cultures and Jewish identities were multifaceted, complex, and often surprising, and he was always glad to be solicited for publication advice by authors looking to expand Jewish collections with volumes like *The Beautiful People of the Book: A Tribute to Ethiopian Jews in Israel*. More people in more books meant more customers and more business as the market discovered, as he had, that Jewish literature was larger and more diverse than imagined. In the end, of course, he could interpret those subject categories as he saw fit because the books were his, and the store his magic circle. My story is about growing up in that circle, about the ways my father's bookstore taught me how to understand books and Jewishness, collection and family, and the history of Jewish bookstores in the United States. I watched and learned and slowly discovered through the objects of my father's profession how bookstores and identities are assembled.

Inklings of this knowledge arrived early. I came to language not in a classroom or through a toddler's board book, but through those alluring objects lining the wood shelves in the store's dark chocolate–colored bookcases, larger versions of the three-shelf-high, glossy-finished cases at home in our living room. Playing in front of them one day, I suddenly realized that the figures decorating all the narrow spines were letters. If this was an "L" and that was an "O," then the jaunty-looking black letters on the white background would sound out as *wit-heh lo-vee*, which after a few more stabs at pronunciation I finally figured into *With Love*. Only much later did I wonder at the presence of the French singer Maurice Chevalier's autobiography in my parents' collection, and how of all the books there it was the first whose title I could read. But that was an essential part of my education, learning how ink and paper could not only speak *to* me but also *for* me, as well as for my family and for others with both love and an unexpected strangeness.

A few years later, I was seven years old and Jack was having an IBM computerized billing machine installed in the La Cienega store. Jack had just expanded into the renovated space of the old beauty shop next door, which was where the billing machine had been set up in a corner that he'd turned into his new bookkeeping office. To my eyes and ears, it seemed as if the reels of hole-punched tape magically ran the loud, clacking typewriter. The salesman explained the system as I walked the linoleum's black and white tiles in rhythm to the keystrokes while they drummed across the carbon paper—long burst, long burst, short, short, short. And in my child's mind, like alchemy, these objects became the sound of bookselling to me.

Then in 1971, a pivotal moment. I was ten or eleven, and for some reason I was alone in the small room at the back of the store where my father kept his office supplies and sometimes ate lunch at an old wooden table shoved against the wall. I was bored sitting there, so I wandered out to the sales floor to find something interesting to read. Somehow, I discovered a few copies of Philip Roth's controversial *Portnoy's Complaint*, which, because of customer complaints—*Jack, this is how the goyim should see us?*—my father had moved from the new-book table, where they had been displayed face up, and shelved them, yellow spines out, in the literature section. Did I really find them by accident? Did I know they were there? Had they been moved, in fact, because they were no longer new? What I recall is that I took a copy back to the lunch table and something changed, something that had to do with cored apples and my confusion about a character named the Monkey, for sure, but also with reading and Jewishness. What was *this* doing in the store? What did it *mean*?

Books, I discovered, spell out the stories of individuals and families, indeed of peoples, like mass-produced Rosetta stones, each a potential key for translating the languages of our personal and social experiences, and even the sounds in our world, into communicable form. Growing up in a bookstore was all the evidence I needed to agree with the sociologist Bruno Latour when he explains in "Why Has Critique Run Out of Steam?" that "a thing is, in one sense, an object out there and, in another sense, an *issue* very much *in* there, at any rate, a *gathering*." Objects like books are not just something we collect, mere stuff added to the collection of consumer goods that encumber our shelves, closets, and living spaces. As reflections and extensions of our intellectual and emotional lives, such objects of our passions, such "things," also help to sound out—haltingly, sometimes without real comprehension—the vocabulary of our relationships with other people, especially when we speak about, fight over, and market those objects.

To me, possessions are as valuable and vulnerable as the people drawn into their orbit. The model airplanes I built that were parked on top of my dresser, which my brothers knew to damage if they really wanted to hurt me. The bedroom set from my mother's childhood, three pieces with inlaid wood, decorative brass pulls, molding, and scrolled legs passed down to Al, who sold them during his punk phase to our good friend Jeffrey for quick cash, although Jeffrey knew well enough to sell them back to me. The narrow-plank oak floors in my house, which I'd prefer remained unblemished and stained as dark as they were on the day the last bucket of varnish was laid on them. I cringed at every wound they suffered. My guitars, always stored carefully in their cases, strings wound no more than three to four turns on each tuning peg, and when I play them I'm careful not to nick their finish even if it already shows years of wear. I like my silver kiddush cups and Shabbat candlesticks to gleam, all the menorahs, family photos, and knickknacks neatly arranged on the sideboard and tables, and all the paintings on the walls squared up and hung at just the right height.

And, naturally, I shelve my books a certain way, not so much in neat rows and in alphabetized order but in artful piles and with attention to their physical look—they must be placed in a way that reflects the order in my own mind. All the poetry books go in the glass-fronted lawyer's case in my campus office. The right half of my office bookshelves is for Jewish books, the left half for gentile books, except for the second shelf from the top, which holds Jewish fiction and assorted comic books all the way across. At home, the linear translation of the Pentateuch, the Soncino Books of the Bible, the *Kitzur Shulchan Aruch*, and all the siddurim and mahzorim, the everyday prayer books and the High Holiday ones, must go in the right side of the bookcase on the north wall of my study. Of all the books I own, only Philip Roth's and Michael Chabon's are shelved together as complete collections; other writers are on their own.

The boxes containing what's left of my father's bookstore, wedged under the chairs in my office, join this long line of objects in my life. To say that they all just manifest a particular type of fetish is understandable, and I admit the likelihood—my son has accused me more than once of liking things more than people. But to leave it at that would reduce objects to only one level of private meaning. Just as my son will look back at me, for good or ill, I look back at my father through those photographs from June 1979 and I want to remember more than the pied texture of the linoleum floor, the parquet wood of the checkout counter, the flood of light through the plate glass windows at the front of the store, the stacks and spines of English, Hebrew, and Yiddish titles, or the names of long-forgotten customers. I'm provoked now—perhaps all too predictably in late middle age—by a desire to recall an intersection of time and place and things whose meanings both compel and escape me, as when I'm trying to retrieve a word whose shape and sound flits just in front of my thoughts. What did it mean to grow up in a Jewish bookstore in Los Angeles amid that intersection? How did that space, that business, and all those books affect the people who whiled a few or countless hours there? And how did those people affect that space, that business, and all those books, even the very meaning of "literature"? How is it that Jewish literature seems to me not a golden chain, a venerable and self-evident tradition, but a particularly mortal set of goods?

The answers I offer to those and to other questions I raise in this book admittedly won't be definitive. As much as I want to be the professor here, it's impossible for me to treat this as a purely objective account. I can only meditate on the insights suggested to me by my memories of life in the store, interpreting them with the help of work by critics and writers that explores the intellectual, commercial, and cultural interconnections brought into being through our relationships with people and objects. That crowd at the Pico store's grand opening, for example, brings to mind Ray Oldenburg's concept of "third places." Jack's bookstore was an informal community anchor open to everyone, Jewish or not, in which customers were treated as guests equal in importance despite their varying social status. The conversations in and inspired by the store nourished public life by promoting communal affiliation, conversation, and education. The grand opening also sends me back to a classic work of cultural criticism, Gloria Anzaldúa's *Borderlands/La Frontera*. Her theorizing about the personal costs involved in trying to do justice to multiple identities—Chicana, lesbian, English speaker, Spanish speaker—and in making sense of the people and objects that make those identities tangible struck a chord when I first read it, though I knew my own situation was far less fraught than hers. Was J. Roth Bookseller a commercial borderland of Jewish and American cultural ownership? It was, after all, a space in which "theirs" could become "ours" could become "mine," a place where books were both merchandise and collectibles that allowed customers and me—but also, and perhaps especially, my father—to work out various and sometimes conflicting identities.

Perhaps another way to put this is to follow the Spanish writer and critic Jorge Carrión in his *Bookshops: A Reader's History*, where he depicts bookstores as "archeological sites or junk shops or archives that resist revealing to us the knowledge they possess." Their layered and manifold property, their abundance and variety of goods, is part of their nature and why it's sometimes a challenge to find exactly who or what we're looking for in their aisles and crossroads. They're also and often politically or socially suspect, their day-to-day operations a confounding balancing act between what's legally available or approved and what fickle readers want. I see how Lewis Buzbee in his memoir *The Yellow-Lighted Bookshop* could easily imagine their proprietors as pirates on the seas of modern commerce, or how the journalist Åsne Seierstad could suggest a similar characterization (albeit one far less idealized and more worryingly patriarchal) for Shah Muhammed Rais, owner of the Shah M. Book Company in Kabul, Afghanistan. I see how the booksellers of Hong Kong seem to be losing their battle to keep available the many stories that the Chinese Communist Party doesn't want told, much less for these same store owners to smuggle in any unauthorized or purportedly subversive information.

Their example reminds me that J. Roth Bookseller, like all bookstores, was also a place where the objects in its inventory were curated. Which is to say that my father had both the good fortune and the power—social, cultural, economic—to determine what books were available in his particular borderland. Back when I first started thinking about the 1979 grand opening, I was teaching a class on bookstores in which I assigned an article by the book historian Michael Winship on the mysteries of book distribution in the United States from the mid-nineteenth century to the middle of the twentieth. Its argument and title were inspired by a quote from O.H. Cheney's famous *Economic Survey of the Book Industry, 1930–1931*, which excoriated the irrational nature of the business—that its ambivalently professional workforce, hard-to-standardize products, and improvised delivery systems made the industry a striking example of how to lose money during the Depression. But worst of all, the absence of accurate information about how books actually got into buyers' hands was "the tragedy of the book industry." Winship extends Cheney's lament about book distribution to publishing studies scholarship, writing in "'The Tragedy of the Book Industry'? Bookstores and Book Distribution in the United States to 1950" that "book historians and literary critics appear to have assumed that the books written by authors and issued by publishers reached their readers seamlessly and without mediation; they have paid next to no attention to the mechanisms of book distribution or to how these mechanisms determined the availability of books and thus the kind of reading that the American public engaged in."

As my students and I parsed that sentence in Winship's introduction, I found myself talking about my father's bookstore and the grand opening, about the ways it was both a family celebration and a hard-nosed marketing ploy, about the money my father spent ordering the wide variety of titles he was sure his customers expected to see filling the new shelves. I reminisced about the hours we spent that day, and in the days following, talking up and selling one book at a time, a delivery system in which my father was both curator and matchmaker, a trend spotter and taste maker.

This firsthand perspective on cultural and retail mediation always lurked behind my teaching and scholarship over the past two decades, courtesy of the letters, and then packages, and then boxes of recollections and store memorabilia that my father began sending me after the store closed in 1994. These were the unexpected notes for this book's take on the concerns that first bothered me into writing.

At my inaugural meeting with my dean to discuss my research schedule as a fledgling assistant professor, I presented two possible first book projects: a revised version of my dissertation on American Jewish poets or, chucking all that, an entirely new book on American Jewish detective stories. Her eyes lit up. "That sounds like a book I'd want to read," she said. "Tell me more about it." Thinking on my feet, I spoke the first truth that popped into my head. "I was raised in a Jewish home, but I really grew up in a Jewish bookstore." My father, I explained, carried all types of Jewish books, not just religious texts, and I had watched as year by year he stocked more and more detective novels written by Jews, published by the major houses, and featuring proud-to-be-Jewish detectives. They sold very well. There must be something there, I guessed, something about the mixture of that formulaic story with contemporary American Jewish cultures that resonated with both Jewish and non-Jewish consumers.

Settling into the project, I mused about all those customers interested in histories and works of fiction that explained Judaism and Jewish life in an entertaining way. I called the type of literary and cultural innovation I saw in those stories "kosher hybridity." *Kosher* translates as "fit" or "proper," but it also connotes a desire for separation and restriction. I used it as a shorthand for Jewish difference in the stories, for a resistance to fitting in with mainstream cultures. I thought of it also as designating a kind of agreement struck by readers with these stories—that their author's depictions of Jewishness are kosher, are okay by them. Since I'd grown up in a bookstore, I recognized that readers were equally involved in this process; they have a choice of whether or not to purchase, literally and figuratively, the interpretation of Jewishness on display in a story. By putting *kosher* with *hybridity*—which implies remixing cultures, mating peoples, and mashing up art forms—I wanted to mirror the unique, often jarring, and sometimes confused fusions I discovered in American Jewish detective stories. Kosher hybridity is, as I meant it to be, an oxymoron reflecting the ironies and contradictions of a mostly voluntary Jewish life in America.

Or, more precisely, *my* life. Kosher hybridity described not just Harry Kemelman's Rabbi Small and his innovative use of the laws regarding *shatnes* (mixing linen and wool in a garment) to solve a synagogue architectural dispute—and to explain to his congregation how they should tailor proper American Jewish combinations. It also described my own perplexed reactions to selling books on Hasidism to the actor Jon Voigt, or Leo Rosten's *The Education of H*Y*M*A*N K*A*P*L*A*N* to students in a conversion class, or the Orthodox ArtScroll siddur to a customer who then asked me if I knew of Yashua the Jewish messiah.

It described, too, an indelible scene from my years working at the bookstore, when in the winter darkness of an early evening, just after closing, my father hurriedly opened the door for an elderly, stooped-over Hasid in an elegant black caftan and large black velvet yarmulke, followed by a young assistant, who stationed himself just inside the entrance. Speaking in Yiddish, the old man made his way to the philosophy section and to the university press books, asking my father questions about the new titles, and my father responded in a way I never saw with any other customer—deferential, solicitous, somewhat awestruck. The books my father packed up for him and carried outside to his waiting car were clearly secular works, on topics that other ultra-Orthodox customers would never even look at, much less purchase. When it was all over, my father told me that I couldn't tell anyone that

Rabbi Abraham Kahaneman—the Rosh Yeshiva of the Ponevezh Yeshiva in Bnei Brak, Israel, the premier institution of Lithuanian Jewish Orthodoxy—had been there and bought such *treyf*, non-kosher, books. It was a promise he made me repeat every year for three years running, after each of Rabbi Kahaneman's surreptitious visits.

How to explain *that* example of kosher hybridity? The more I thought about such behaviors and tastes among buyers of Jewish literature, the less satisfied I became with my purely textual readings of American Jewish detective stories, comic books, zines, and cookbooks. I realized that I was studying the very books that historically, and for complex reasons, elicited the same kind of social reaction that my father had to the Rosh Yeshiva's selections, that it's best not to talk about or admit to reading books whose purchase might be spurned by others as not literary, or serious, or kosher enough. The reason for those reactions can't lie simply in the books themselves. It can't be found merely in the success or failure of their aesthetic effects.

Literary value and literary innovation are a shared product of many interested actors and institutions; of an array of personal, social, and archival spaces; of the permission or ability to enter those spaces; and of the cultural, economic, and political forces buffeting a particular time and place. They're a dynamic result, too, of tens if not hundreds of small acts of internal and external negotiation among ourselves, other people, and technologies: holding a book, setting it down, picking it up again, and then passing it to a salesclerk, who punches a register before returning it to our hands; clicking to an online sales page, navigating the links to related pages, returning to scroll up and down again, and then clicking on the digital shopping cart to await the book's delivery to our homes or devices.

Touching and being touched by these material objects, we're also processing numerous cues for how to interact with them, cues given through both sales instructions and social expectations. Does the store's service prompt small talk with the salesclerk or a purely business demeanor? Does an Internet purchase prompt two-step verification or just a password with which to reaffirm a legal self and archive its commercial history? These cues, the historian Robin Bernstein says, offer a script that guides our performance of their social and cultural meanings, that guides how people knowingly or unknowingly "dance with things" and with them construct an understanding not only of literary value but also of identity, citizenship, race. How do our innermost desires, idiosyncrasies, and contradictions get caught up in this dance via the exchanges that connect books with readers, bookstore objects with owners, bookish things with people?

After twenty years of keeping my personal experiences private, I realized that the personal is not only political but also material, commercial, spatial, gendered, collectible, designable, audible, and networked. These are the theoretical themes that I explore in this book, using them to frame and then consider in each chapter an aspect of the bookstore's physical presentation so as to recall a particular period in its history. The stories I tell about my dances with things roughly follow that history in chronological order, although I often move back and forth in time to reflect on how I made my discoveries and to trace my own coming of age and coming to terms with my father and his business. I touch on beginnings in the first few chapters, both literally and figuratively, of my father, New York Jewish bookstores, Michael Harelick, and bookstores both Jewish and general in Los Angeles. In the middle chapters I tally the entwined emotional and material costs incurred by my father's beliefs and obsessions, and in the last chapters I recount how I found myself once again behind Jack's sales counter just in time to be a witness to the bookstore's final act. Each theoretical theme, each phase of the bookstore's history, each armful of recollections and the objects to which they're attached jointly set the scene in every chapter, but also, in a philosophic sense, for understanding the ways that bookstores help us gather together as the complex individuals we are and as living communities. All these things raise questions for me that blur the distinction between private and public, participant and observer, subject and object. Are you with me?

Yet it was Al, not Jack, who taught me how objects can also pull us apart, how by instantiating a rival magic circle or manifesting a different consciousness of American Jewish identity they can unravel even family ties. That unhappy knowledge also shaped how I interpret the interplay of people, Jewishness, literature, and things at J. Roth Bookseller. Al was my original interpretive model.

Back in 1979, the reception for the new bookstore wound down, friends made their final good-byes, and Eddie went home. After my brothers and I helped clean up, my father closed for the day. Did we celebrate somewhere else? I don't remember, but likely Ben and I stuck with my father, since Ben couldn't drive and, as usual, I had no plans. But it's summer, so I imagine that Al took off for a party in Westwood, where his friends Eric, Ted, and George were renting rooms at one of the UCLA fraternity houses. The previous year he'd been enrolled at Chico State University, where he discovered Pioneer Week, the university's Old West gold rush celebration and all-purpose bacchanalia—a major reason why *Playboy* would later crown Chico the nation's number one party school—as well as the rapidly expanding roster of post-punk musical groups, courtesy of a redheaded young woman who played him new albums by Elvis Costello and The Police. Disinterested in specifically Jewish things, Al began to collect records and other objects that staked out his own identity as a secular, unobservant Jew. Somewhere between the episode where Al damaged the axle on his yellow Fiat 128 by off-roading it around the Sierra foothills and the one where he introduced Jack to the town of Chico by taking him to the local head shop to compare water pipes, my father realized he was paying for an extended education in revelry. He stopped paying Al's tuition and board and forced him to come home and go to work.

But Al refused reentry into Jack's magic circle. A few months after the grand opening, and despite the compliments he received from the customers he'd serenaded at the store, Al sold his violin, bought an acoustic guitar, and started busking on the streets of Westwood Village. That exchange of instruments, common enough among Jews of our generation, was in his case also a declaration of independence from the Jewish literature and music making of my father's bookstore and from his role as the next Jascha Heifetz, an acceptable Jewish musical identity in Jack's mind. By the time I realized that Al was on to something—I'd picked up the guitar, too, my freshman year in college, and by senior year I wanted desperately to play with a band, any band—he'd already found out about the emerging music scene in Hollywood, driving himself and his buddies to an illegal after-hours club, the Zero, at West Cahuenga north of Hollywood Boulevard, and then later to its next incarnation as the Double Zero at Wilcox and Hollywood. Maybe that's also when Al started wearing his 1980s uniform: tartan pants, red sleeveless ribbed undershirt, black leather motorcycle jacket, and purple mohawk. Clothing was yet another set of objects that helped Al claim affiliation with an identity more in keeping with the personal collection that reflected the existential and intellectual order within his own mind.

By 1986, Jack's bookstore was at the apogee of its success and his magic circle was serving the widest possible diameter of tastes and religiosities among Jewish Angelenos. Yet there was little room left for Al, who by then had added to his collection an astonishing number of parking tickets, some of which he simply tossed on the sidewalk given how many others had accumulated on the floor of whatever car he managed to hang on to after the Fiat succumbed to its injuries. When he was finally picked up by the sheriff's department for outstanding parking tickets and hauled off to the L.A. County Jail, he found himself on the sheriff's bus shackled to a wiry-looking long-haired fellow. Al asked him what he did for a living. "Music," he said. Al said he played too.

"Well," he replied, "I don't give a shit about being on the bus to County, because as soon as I'm out, my band's gonna release an album."

"What's the name of your band?"

"Guns N' Roses."

Al recognized the name. He'd seen it a few times on the Whiskey marquee up on Sunset Boulevard. After they were both processed Al lost track of him, partly because Al was overwhelmed by how bad things were in County. It was so crowded he didn't get a bunk until his second day, and it took all his wits just to go to the bathroom without getting picked on or punched.

After he was released a few days later, he spotted a headline in the *L.A. Weekly* and saw that the jail was being sued for its cruel and inhumane conditions. "Damn right!" he blurted out, realizing he'd been part of a larger drama roiling the city that week, though he couldn't see all that from the inside. That was true in more ways than one. He also didn't know that I'd been on the phone with my father and that he'd made clear to me that Al had finally crossed the line. He'd bail him out, but after that Al would be cut off. He wasn't welcome in my father's home or at the store. Finished.

I'd been the middleman for years, shuttling messages and money between my father and Al, but in August 1986 Al had booked himself into an identity beyond the ken of my father's broad definition of Jewishness, one with far too close a connection to L.A.'s dysfunctional prison system. That wasn't kosher with Jack. As witness to all this, I saw close-up that there were limits to the objects and ideas my father would allow into his magic circle and that ultimately Jewishness was as subjective a category as "literature"—or "family." I don't recall if I told Al that he'd screwed up, but he wouldn't have bought that anyway. He wanted nothing to do with my father's world.

A week or so later Al was walking past the rear of the Whiskey when he recognized the guy loading in at the back door and waved hello. It was his bus mate. Slash waved back.

I continued to be in touch with Al. If I wouldn't exit the magic circle of my father's Jewish bookstore, I was just as unwilling to untether myself from my brother. I wanted both Jewish books and electric guitars in my collection. Much later I'd be able to apply a score of critical terms to Al's cultural and musical disaffiliation from the bookstore and my father's understanding of Jewishness. I might say that the social and artistic connections he discovered describe the mercurial way people create meaning in their lives. The relationships engaged or undone as a consequence of curiosity, accident, or desire, or the metal, plastic, and psychic cuffs of state power, are how we assemble our apprehensions of reality.

Except that's not the way I would have put it in those days, certainly not in the summer of 1979. I wouldn't have known then how quickly a new store begins to feel old hat, how quickly and inevitably the pristine objects I loved could be damaged, lost, or repossessed. I would have said that what was happening between my brother and father didn't feel like they were both playing it by ear, riffing on their own life choices, because I was sure they could keep things together if they really wanted to. I would have believed this because my father's bookstore had, in fact, provided my first lesson in the power to retell a story more to my liking and to bend reality into a shapelier form through the gravity of my own ego. That article in *Judaica Book News*? The one about Jewish pioneers and what my father hoped he'd contributed to the Jewish book? I wrote that. I'm David A. Haskell. Sure, I peppered the article with a few quotes and details that my father wanted to include. But mostly it was my creation. I saw a chance to get into print finally, a national publication at that, a way to do my father a favor even while staking out my future as a writer in a world of my own where I was neither my father's retail heir nor my brother's keeper.

My real role at the grand opening was not photographing the event but narrating it. I put it into a suitably honorable historical context and borrowed the feature form and the pseudonym as a convenience for public consumption. I took my middle name and my brothers' middle names and cobbled together my middle-child's version of the bookstore's grand opening, the version that most people read, the one where my father was "proudest of two things: one is having raised 'three of the finest boys in the world'" and only second to that "the expansion and move of his store to a spacious and elegant location adjacent to Beverly Hills." We were the family Roth, rising together against all odds. Success.

That's certainly one kind of American Jewish story. As the article's "adjacent" suggests, however, that narrative is also emblematic of another kind of story I was learning to write, a sort of picaresque whose meanings converge as each disparate episode is laid down one after another like books on a shelf or subject categories on a wall. Or like the various strategies a child might employ trying to negotiate a parent's magic circle, evident in my mediation between Al and Jack and in that *Judaica Book News* article by the way I tried to adjoin, connect, and arrange Jewish things with the particulars of my own time and place.

Which is to say that in that article I learned how to draw in and draw out my own relationship to the store and its reputation, to make it mine by comparison, juxtaposition, and invention. The trick was to begin by telling a story about my father that was secretly about myself and that was double-plotted from the first: American Jews, bookstores. And so, in the pages that follow, I return to a technique I know well in a final attempt to make sense of these two lifelong fixations. Both face resurgent forms of hostility that batter anew this country's enduring myths about the value of free markets, whether of ideas or of products. They're examples of assimilation and creative destruction, say the pundits and business leaders, each a patchwork enterprise in the purchase of new readings. Yet both persist, even thrive in certain locales and guises, in part through individual stubbornness and in part through the mysteries of association, of a human desire to find connection, dignity, love.

What about success? Well, not for J. Roth Bookseller. That space is gone, its collection of literature scattered or lost. No matter how vivid my memories are of the stock that filled the shelves in 1979, I can no longer hold, much less pass on, that collection in its entirety. The vitality of books within a magic circle, says Walter Benjamin, is also bound up in the recognition that they're a kind of inheritance—they're passed down from someone equally enamored of and invested in them. Ownership therefore implies a duty to preserve such a valuable legacy for future transmission, "For a collector's attitude toward his possessions stems from an owner's feeling of responsibility toward his property." My father's bookstore offered his customers an opportunity for such safekeeping, to possess the personal recollections, creative works, and scholarly interpretations attesting to past and present varieties of Jewish identity and historical experience. It offered them, in other words, an opportunity to create their own magic circles and so define and be defined by their own Jewish collections. The bookstore's appeal, and what made it viable for over twenty-five years, was that it retailed the building blocks for constructing Jewish memory and for making a Jewish literature of one's own, just as American Jews were looking to do both.

All that remains for me, though, are photographs, boxes of memorabilia, a few shelves' worth of books, and a copy of *Judaica Book News*, Spring/Summer 1979/5739, testaments to the rise and fall of a particular kind of American Jewish bookstore. It thrived in the glow of the Jewish ethnic pride movements of the sixties and seventies but was unable to market its uniquely broad definition and collection of Jewish literature after the resurgence of Orthodox Judaism and the assimilation of Jewish writing into the corporate book superstores during the late eighties and early nineties.

If you're wondering, I'll tell you right now how this American Jewish story ends. My father didn't retire; the store failed. His Orthodox competitors undercut his prices for traditional *sforim* and stripped off his religious customers, while the book superstores undercut his prices for new Jewish publications and lured away his secular customers. While Benjamin believed "inheritance is the soundest way of acquiring a collection," here's the final thing this book is about: There are limits to what one generation can will to the next. Memory easily goes bankrupt. Jewish literature—any literature—is an impermanent collection belonging, like all property, to those wealthy and passionate enough to claim ownership. Such a purchased inheritance is, in fact, a disorder to which each generation gives the appearance of order by unpacking and arranging it on shelves of their own making.

Let me show you what ours looked like.

CHAPTER 2

The Inventory (*commerce*)

Every year toward the end of December, in anticipation of closing the books on that tax year, my father would take inventory. It was an all-day affair, one that required him to lock the doors and lose a day of sales. In later years he'd try to do it at night, but it was too much work for him to go it alone, so he ended up relying on Avrum, his chief clerk, to help him finish it as quickly as possible. It was, Jack told me, "a horrific job," especially in the early days when it was just him and a pencil. Taking inventory required that he go to each section and laboriously count the number of books—History, 142 books, Hebrew Grammar and Dictionaries, 73 books, and so on. Since he was only interested in numbers, he didn't bother recording titles, except in the textbook section, where he needed the titles in order to complete his yearly consignment reports for the Jewish publishers back East. This doesn't sound difficult until you take into account that, over the course of its life, the bookstore's subject headings expanded from about a dozen to around twenty-five, doubling the number of categories the store featured. So each section presented scores and often a hundred or more books that needed counting. It was mindless but exacting work.

It didn't help that my father was a perfectionist whose preferred method of counting required him to touch each spine or cover so that he wouldn't lose track of the count, and he would sometimes start over to make sure his first pass was correct. He hated every tedious aspect of the job, yet seemed to thrive on the intimacy it fostered between him and his books. Tapping each one was almost like patting their backs and saying, I see you as I count you. Numbering them was also naming them in a way, for then each subject category became a patronymic for the books in them—Bibleson, O'Bible, Bibleovich—that communicated family resemblances. And as I listened to Jack's story, I thought it also said something about commerce and identity, about the relation of a business to the owner's sense of self.

Still, when I asked my father why he took inventory and why he only recorded the number of books themselves and not their titles, he paused. Was it for inventory control? To figure out if he met his sales goals? To advertise the number of books in his store? "Why the hell *did* we take inventory?" he said. I laughed, but only because this secretly confirmed a suspicion I had as a child, when I wondered what my father was really doing when he spent all night at the store, that maybe the whole thing was a convenient excuse to not have to deal with his personal inventory: a home in the San Fernando Valley, three raucous boys given to punching each other on the upper arms to see who could raise the darkest bruise, various housekeepers that during the week lived in the bedroom next to the laundry area, a neglected poodle, an epileptic German shepherd, and a wife none too happy at having to manage all this alone plus help run the store. When guests came over, like the young Chabad rabbi, sent by the Lubavitcher Rebbe to supervise his new outposts and to spy out the land, everything was arranged carefully and displayed in its proper place—the dogs in the backyard, the housekeeper in the kitchen, the wife in a hostess dress, the three boys in matching outfits and under strict orders to retreat to their rooms should they prove unable to control their fists. Looking at the art on the walls, the fine china on the table, and my brothers and me, the rabbi exclaimed, "All this from books?"

He knew how to take inventory. His quick survey of the things in our home revealed them as secret sharers in the commercial life and times of my father's business. Each was an extension of the other. So while my father may very well have forgotten his exact reasons for taking inventory, if how he counted when he did it and the home we lived in were any clue, they were likely related to his tightly curated exhibition of self and business—not that there was any real daylight between the two. My father's clothes closet was nearly mathematical in its symmetry, the suits hung up by color, each pair of shoes lined up in military precision with shoe trees to maintain their shape, shirts meticulously buttoned and hung, his army uniform as crisp and clean as the day he stowed it away as a final souvenir of his service. His store was the same: free of clutter, the shelves arranged in even rows and dusted regularly, each pile of books on the show tables around the shop arranged so that one book's spine faced right, the one above left, thereby ensuring a perfectly level and proportionate stack. Knowing exactly how many books were in each section of the bookstore, without concern for their title, was a once yearly summation of my father's daily routine: sweeping the sidewalk in front of his store, squaring up the books on the shelves and tables, counting the cash drawer, fussing over his world and its financial record, making them presentable to others.

Inventory, you see, is not just a business practice; it's a cultural one, too. It's not only how we tally what we own, learn what's in or out of stock, and discern what counts or doesn't count in the marketplace. It's also how we winnow existential worth from our piles of things, a way to order, control, and make meaning out of the random stuff of our lives. It's a type of identity formation. If we don't think about the myriad ways we regularly check our possessions, or tick off what others have, it's because these maneuvers have become habit and such a pedestrian part of our modern routines. As my father showed me, inventorying can be as idiosyncratic as the person doing the counting. Its true value, says Jeffrey Shandler in "Keepers of Accounts," "ultimately lies not in its contents but in how it is created and to what end."

I should admit here that, like my father, I dislike taking inventory, even though I know I'll have to do one if I want to sell you on the commercial American Jewish identity that Jack devised for our family business. How did he put it together, where did its parts come from? And how did I learn its import so well that I couldn't help feeling that the Chabad rabbi was just another customer who needed to be served, satisfied, and then sent away primed to extoll our good name?

It's Sunday sometime around 1970. I'm nine or ten and sitting behind the work desk / sales counter in the old store at 1070 South La Cienega reading *The Wise Men of Helm* by Solomon Simon when I hear a customer ask my father for a title that Jack isn't sure he has. I watch my father cross his arms and allow his eyes to scan the shelves and tables, as if sight alone could conjure up the book he was looking for. This is his strategy. My father first tries to jog his memory of a book's whereabouts by visual inspection. He then heads off to the corner of the store most likely to yield the culprit and begins a laborious search of a shelf's contents, running his finger over the spines as he glides through the alphabet of that section. I watch as my father rubs his other hand over his chin, his back to the customer but his voice gently humming "uh-huh" and "no" and "where . . . ?" I glance down and pick at the first sentences of a story where the people of Helm see the moon reflected in a barrel of water. Then my father announces with palpable satisfaction, "Here it is," quickly checks the title and copyright pages, and turns around offering the book to the customer. As I learn watching this trick again and again, the triumphant moment is sometimes accompanied by a quick biography of the author or a history of the press or some other little tidbit that brings the almost lost item back into being.

What my father was doing is called "hand selling." I like that term, although it's misleading. It's a metonymy, where "hand" stands for a human being creating a personal relationship with the customer and bringing all three into material relation with one another—where "hand" also implies conversation, touching, transaction, memory. This was how my father taught me about the relationship between customers and our stock and that the connection between the two was obviously a form of marketing, but what we were marketing wasn't just a book. We were also, like the villagers of Helm, trying to create a container for the uncontainable, using the business to capture and then retail various expressions of Jewishness, especially the store's own. That took more work than I realized at first.

I'm in the Pico store this time, loafing behind an actual sales counter: a three-sided wood structure in the center of the store with shelves on the exterior for featured books and loss leaders, an electronic cash register, and a parquet countertop. Now I'm reading Lionel Davidson's *The Menorah Men*, or maybe Leon Uris's *QB VII*, and a customer comes in and asks if we have *Jewish Feasts and Fasts* by Julius Greenstone. I point him toward the Life Cycle and Introduction to Judaism sections and return to my book. My father quickly intercepts him and joins the hunt, and when the older gentleman leaves I get an earful. "Don't just tell the customer that the book is 'over there,'" my father says with a desultory wave of his hand toward the bookshelves, in a fairly good imitation of the bored college students he sometimes hired over the summer as part-time clerks. "You get up off your *tuchus*, and you take the customer by the hand and lead him to the section where the book is. You find it for him." As a reasonably bored student myself, I had a vision of literally clasping hands with one of our regular middle-aged customers and, like two kindergarteners, skipping over to the Life Cycle section to see where yet another dull book about the Jewish holidays might be.

Yet my father's advice was not just about customer relations. What he meant was that I had to touch the books, speak to the person beside me, create a history and meaning for the inventory that would make it understandable and, hopefully, a desirable purchase, though like any form of communication it required nimble editing skills.

"Where do you have the Soloveitchik books?" asks a young man in black slacks, an open-neck white shirt, and a black velvet yarmulke.

"Uh, they should all be in the Philosophy and Jewish Thought section on that far wall. Here, follow me. Right, see *Lonely Man of Faith* that we have face out there—that's it."

"You sell Yeshayahu Leibowitz?" He nods toward the display table in front of the section. "The guy who called Zionists 'Judeo-Nazis' and attacked the Rishon LeZion?"

"Well, he was referring to the settlers, but you know he and Soloveitchik admired each other . . ."

"Where's the ArtScroll section?"

Later that day it's a different story. A young woman with a hamsa amulet on her necklace walks straight toward me.

"I'm looking for *Standing Again at Sinai*."

"Women's Studies section, follow me. And . . . are there any left? . . . Ah, here you go."

"Is there anything else on the Bible from a feminist perspective?"

"Not really. This has been out for about a year now, and the only other book similar to it is this, *Four Centuries of Jewish Women's Spirituality*."

"*A Hedge of Roses*? What's this one?

"That's a book about marriage from an Orthodox perspective. Though what he says about the ritual bath . . ."

"Is the *Spirituality* book good?"

"Very. Are you familiar with Glückel of Hameln or Grace Aguilar, Ray Frank, Zelda, maybe Marcia Falk?"

"Oh right, she did *The Song of Songs*. Do you gift wrap?"

This wasn't simply selling a book or merely ticking off a list of relevant facts and authors, or just having a chat. Hand selling is a way to humanize the books by framing them in a narrative. It puts the stock's order into words, revealing how its arrangement and worth is calculated. Hand selling is also how a salesclerk keeps the inventory in mind, by rehearsing the books' biographies and allowing the customer to consider, compare, commend, collect. This became habit with me; I could no longer just point out a book. I had something to say about each, too. I realized that keeping track of the inventory is not only knowing whether a book is in stock but also remembering the story that makes it desirable and then calibrating its effect on the customer. So I became proficient in cataloging the stock's relationship to the past and the present, to the businesses that circulated the stock, and, especially, to a Jewish bookseller whose story begins not in Southern California but in New York City, and who's already halfway across the store and signaling that we should follow.

My father was born in the borough of Queens in 1932, the youngest of six children. My grandfather, Isaac Roth, had immigrated to the United States in 1926 from what was left of the Austro-Hungarian Empire, having served in that army, along with his father and uncle, during the First World War. ("I aimed above the enemy's head," he assured my brothers and me when we asked him about it.) My grandmother Pepi, née Weberman, followed him three years later, arriving in 1929 with the three oldest children, Michael, Gee, and Harry. My grandfather received his *semicha*, or rabbinic ordination, from the chief rabbi of Érmihályfalva, the small town where he'd met and married Pepi, which then was a commercial hub and center for Jewish life in the area and now lies in northwestern Romania. While sometimes introduced by others as "Rabbi" or "Reverend," he made his living as a *shochet*, a ritual slaughterer. Nobody else I knew had a *zeyde* with that kind of job, so I liked to brag about it in Hebrew day school. When he came to Los Angeles for my brother's bar mitzvah I asked him to show me how to slice a chicken's jugular according to Jewish law. He took a kitchen knife and illustrated the proper way to grasp the blade, and then, with what seemed surprising dexterity for an old man struggling with Parkinson's, he flicked it in three deft strokes across an imaginary bird's throat.

Later I discovered that Isaac was also an amateur poet. He translated the Book of Esther into rhymed Yiddish couplets, and it was published in 1928 as a *shalach monos*, a festival gift for the holiday of Purim, by a yeshiva that taught both traditional Jewish subjects and vocational skills. While there were a great many religious books in my grandparents' home, my father can't recall seeing any books by secular Jewish writers. Isaac and Pepi were strictly Orthodox, admirers of Satmar Hasidism though not adherents themselves.

My father was named after Yaakov Yosef Guttman of Preshov, a Hasidic rebbe considered a *ba'al mofes*, one who performs miracles, who died the year my father was born. Yaakov Yosef Roth, Jack in English, attended Yeshiva Torah Vodaath in Brooklyn, but rather than go on to rabbinical school, as his three older brothers had done, he chose to enroll in the City College of New York, take a few classes in Russian literature, and work part-time for Jonathan David, a Jewish publishing company and wholesaler. No overriding reason drove all these decisions. As the youngest of six children, there was less pressure on him to prove his religious devotion. And it was the late forties and early fifties after all; New York's urban cosmopolitanism was a powerful lure. Between Frank Sinatra and the New York Jewish intellectuals—Philip Rahv, Alfred Kazin, Lionel Trilling, Daniel Bell, and Irving Howe—lay a world that my father found irresistible. As a teenager he used to play hooky from Torah Vodaath and ride the subway into Manhattan to visit the Jewish Museum on Fifth Avenue. Once, as he was loitering in Grand Central Station, he saw Joe DiMaggio dressed in a beautiful gray cashmere suit and matching overcoat and heading for the exit. Thinking quickly, he pulled out his Torah Vodaath student identification card and asked Joltin' Joe to sign the blank reverse side. Years later he had it framed and hung it on his bedroom wall until the old ink oxidized and the signature faded, then disappeared.

What remained vivid for Jack is why he wanted a job in Jewish bookselling. When he was a boy my grandfather took him shopping among the Jewish bookstores on the Lower East Side, and he was appalled at what a mess they were. "One day," he announced, "I'm going to have a Jewish bookshop no one will be ashamed to walk into." I heard this story a few times over the years, but never with any details. Then one day a package arrived in the mail, and I opened it to find a copy of a talk Jack gave at the Association of Jewish Libraries conference in 1992. It included this version of the story:

> Some 53 years ago, my father took me to a Jewish bookstore for the very first time and the memory of it has lingered ever since. On that day in 1939 we went shopping at M. Lipschitz Hebrew bookstore on Rivington Street, one of many dotting the Lower East Side at that time. It was loaded with brass—brass candlesticks, brass menorahs, and brass mortar & pestle sets, used in European-Jewish homes for preparing foods or for making charoseth on Passover.
>
> While my father browsed for his treat—a traditional sefer—I wandered through the store mesmerized by this disarray of trinkets, talesim, tephilin, yahrzeit candles, and Rabbinic and cantorial robes and caps. I recognized siddurim and machzorim; I was impressed with the many books in Yiddish translation, books with the imprints of famous Hebrew publishers in Eastern Europe such as Joseph Schlesinger of Vienna, Reuben Maas of Berlin, Levin Epstein of Poland, and W. Heidenheim who published the famous Rodelheim siddur.
>
> Yet, looking back on it, Lipschitz was not what we would call today a "literary" bookstore. The emphasis in the store was definitely on religious objects and needs. And all the other stores—M. Wolozin & Co., Zion Tallis Company, J. Levine & Co., Zeigelheim's Jewish Books, Reznick, Menschel & Co., Rabinowitz Hebrew Bookstore—all of them had the same folksy appeal; they were Jewish bazaars.

The word "literary" jumps out as a telling description of my father's ambition and his judgment of what these booksellers emphatically were not. But "bazaar" should have been in scare quotes, too, since it was his antonym for "literary" and shorthand for a kind of cultural failure. Somewhere between Torah Vodaath and Manhattan he came to see storefront religion and the folklore business as unsophisticated and untidy, and no doubt that Rodelheim siddur was embarrassed by the low company it was forced to keep.

Yet the mixed merchandise my father describes, which punctured his notion of the ideal Jewish bookstore, had appeared in non-Jewish form in most U.S. bookstores since the 1700s. John Tebbel, in his short history of American bookselling, notes that the vast majority of bookselling establishments during the eighteenth and nineteenth centuries sold stationery, cards, candy, tobacco, coffee, dry goods, fancy goods, calendars, pamphlets, and erotica (under the counter), in addition to books. By the late nineteenth century, the most popular and aggressive book retailers were department stores, such as Wanamaker's and Macy's, followed closely by the publishers themselves, many of which—Brentano, Scribner, Doubleday, and E. P. Dutton, for instance—boasted lavish bookstores that offered their own nonliterary guilty pleasures for sale. So what my father thought was a parochial business model was, in fact, a common and long-standing one in the United States. I eventually understood that while Jack grew up steeped in the great family histories of European Jewish publishing, those tchotchke-filled bookstores he visited as a boy were a legacy of a less celebrated story, the rise of Jewish book retailing in America.

The first Jew to open a bookstore in the United States was Benjamin Gomez, scion of a famously wealthy Sephardic family who made their money in the early modern Atlantic trade networks. The American branch, led by Luis Moses Gomez, specialized in buying beaver pelts from the Algonquin peoples along the Hudson River and selling them in return for West Indian sugar and other unspecified goods from the Caribbean, which in those days, and for those trading for and with the Dutch West India Company, meant both enslaved people and salt.

Grandson Benjamin opened his bookstore in 1791 at 32 Maiden Lane in Manhattan and made his name importing fine editions of English works. He also sold stationery, Christian tracts, and historical and scientific works and published American editions of *Pilgrim's Progress* in 1794, *The Sorrows of Werther* and an abridged *Robinson Crusoe* in 1795, and James Cook's *A Voyage to the Pacific Ocean* in 1797. In 1794, he also published and distributed the first American edition of Joseph Priestley's *Letters to the Jews: Inviting Them to an Amicable Discussion of the Evidences of Christianity* and David Levi's *Letters to Dr. Priestley, in Answer to Those He Addressed to the Jews.*

Yet a dedicated Jewish book trade didn't emerge in the United States until near the middle of the nineteenth century. Before then, most Jews brought their own books with them when they arrived in America or sent for them through relatives or dealers back in Europe, and no doubt some Jewish merchants in this early period imported a few Bibles and prayer books as a courtesy to their fellow congregants in Newport, New York, Philadelphia, Baltimore, Richmond, and Charleston. One of these, Isaac Pinto, a Sephardic Jew from the British West Indies, paid a non-Jewish printer to print the first Jewish prayer book in the American colonies, an all-English translation published in 1766 for the members of Congregation Shearith Israel in New York. And a burst of activity occurred around 1820 when the first Jewish printer producing Jewish material appeared in New York, Solomon Henry Jackson. He published the first Haggadah, Hebrew-English prayer book, and Jewish periodical (*The Jew*) in the United States.

But it isn't until Isaac Leeser and Isaac Mayer Wise, founders of the Reform movement in the United States, begin writing and self-publishing their own work in the 1830s, '40s, and '50s—defenses of Judaism as congruent with Enlightenment philosophical and political ideas, newspapers, novels, prayer books edited for American Reform congregations, and an English translation of the Hebrew Bible—that Jewish publishing and bookselling coalesced into a recognizable trade. The first Jewish publishers in America appeared soon enough: the American Jewish Publication Society in Philadelphia in 1845, the Jewish Publication Society in New York from 1871 to 1873 and then Philadelphia in 1888, the Bloch Publishing Company in Cincinnati in 1854, and the Hebrew Publishing Company in New York in 1901. Still, before the First World War they all serviced a very limited market. In addition to prayer books and Hebrew Bibles, these new publishers primarily issued liturgical reference works and school texts, and, acting as agents for European Jewish publishers, they imported, reprinted, and/or translated various titles of Hebrew, Yiddish, German, Russian, and British Judaica.

And where was the first specifically Jewish bookstore in America? No one really knows. In the mid-nineteenth century there were no hard-and-fast distinctions between a print shop, a publishing house, a stationer, a lending library, and a bookstore. Publishers made and marketed their own books and sold others they bought locally and abroad, or for which they claimed distribution rights. The front room of their establishments were often reception areas, offices, stock rooms, and bookstores all in one. In New York, it seems the first of that sort of publisher with an extensive Jewish retail selection was Henry Frank from Bavaria, a printer-publisher of Hebrew books. One of thousands of German-speaking Jews who came to America to escape the violence of the German revolution in 1848, he set up a printing business that same year on Houston Street, where Katz's Deli stands today. According to Madeleine B. Stern's short biography of him, he printed, published, and sold Hebrew-German and Hebrew-English Haggadahs, prayer books, devotional books, and reference works bought by customers from Temple Emanu-El and the B'nai Jeshurun and Anshei Chesed synagogues. In 1864, two of Frank's sons opened a branch of the family business in San Francisco, but business directories there list them as stationers, not booksellers. True, the line between these two occupations was as porous as that between publishing house and bookstore, as witness their father's business. Yet Frank's Hebrew Book Store, by the late 1860s the biggest Jewish bookseller in the city, is still best known for its contribution to German Jewish publishing in America.

Around the same time, however, a small group of Eastern European Jewish immigrants noted the success of retail operations like Frank's and combined that setup with their versions of the *moykher sforim* (bookseller) stores, stalls, and peddlers' carts ubiquitous in Central and Eastern Europe. Here the story becomes more ambiguous and certainly less tidy. Sholem Abramovitsh's famous narrator-character, Mendele Moykher-Sforim—whose persona nearly supplanted the real identity of his maker, one of the creators of modern Yiddish literature and Jewish storytelling—is modeled in part on the rogues who were drawn to this mercurial business back in the old country. As a literary invention, Mendele is a notorious ironist. We shouldn't mistake him for an accurate portrait of his bookselling peers, as the literary scholar Dan Miron warns. But look at how that freewheeling raconteur inventories his stock in Abramovitsh's 1869 novel *Fishke the Lame*:

> Oh, and about my living? Well, now, I make that by colportage. That's to say I deal in sacred books. Which in our business means Pentateuchs and Prayerbooks, mostly. . . . Oh and storybooks. I carry all sorts of

> storybooks, and even some of your modern-type books, now and again. Only I must say I turned my hand to a lot of different trades in my day. When I left off boarding with my in-laws, why I set up first as a money changer, and then as a grocer, a taverner, a corn factor, a broker, and a schoolmaster. . . . Till finally I took to books. And managing quite nicely by it, thank you. Though, besides books, I've also took to carrying Prayershawls, too, and Bershad-wove "Four-corner" weskits; as also prime Eight-threaded show fringes for the fastidious, Phylactery straps, Ram's horns, Goodspells, Mezuzahs, Wolfstooth teething-dummies, Amulets, Woolly knitted combination Baby Bootees, and Toddlers' Yarmulkes. As a sideline, I also trade in brass and copper kitchenware, sometimes. Mind you, even I haven't worked out how the pots and pans got in with books.

Seems similar to the American version, no? Except here Mendele is the retail bookseller as hapless cultural middleman. He brokers and exchanges things and ideas, and, as that last line suggests, he's not too scrupulous about mixing religious, novelty, domestic, and literary goods. As Mendele would tell you, he's just a decent, hardworking Jew trying to keep his head above water amid the social and political turmoil of Tsar Alexander II's Russia. As Abramovitsh would have you understand, Mendele, that arch figure of the Jewish Enlightenment, is himself an inventory of the jumbled Jewish commerce between the traditional and the modern type, the sacred and the mundane.

I try to imagine my father as a young boy of six or seven just becoming aware of this jumble, of the distance as well as the cultural trade between his neat, well-scrubbed Jewish home in Corona, Queens—my grandmother was a fastidious housewife, my grandfather made it an honor to polish his shoes—and the grime of the Lower East Side's commercial district. I see him sitting on the floor in front of the family radio listening happily to Jack Benny; I see him a few years later frozen in his seat as his rebbe teaches a particularly slow student how to chant a difficult trope in the haftarah by yanking his ear in time to the melody, ripping the boy's ear half off (an ambulance had to be called). I think about his Italian childhood friend and how my father could still play street games with him even though Dicky would join the gentile kids in taunting my father with "Matzos, matzos, two for five, that's what keeps the Jews alive!" When Jack told my brothers and me about that he'd laugh too. We learned to see these experiences as funny, but they don't seem humorous now. Rather, they leave me to wonder if the story he told about the mess on Rivington Street wasn't also a story, similar to Mendele's, about bookselling as a way of explaining and marketing oneself, of claiming a place in an occupation where one's name *is* the trade—J. Roth Moykher-Sforim—and facing the world as if it were a precarious retail business and all the people in it just some very tough customers.

This symbiotic relationship between trade and identity, and the role-playing it often entailed, was both developed by and crucial to the booksellers who opened their doors south of Houston Street in the mid- to late nineteenth century. This includes one of the first to appear in a U.S. bookstore directory, Dingman's *Directory of Publishers, Booksellers, Stationers, Newsdealers, and Music Dealers and List of Libraries in the United States and Canada; Complete to November 1st, 1870.* Alongside Benziger Bros., August Brentano, E. P. Dutton & Co., M. W. Dodd, Harper Bros., J. W. Schermerhorn & Co., Leggat Bros. ("Cheapest Book Store in the World!"), and Charles Scribner & Co., there was also a lone, self-identified Jewish bookseller: Hyam Sakolski, at 53 Division Street.

You likely won't find Sakolski in any Jewish or American history books. He would have vanished into obscurity if Montague Lawrence Marks hadn't written a short profile of his bookstore for *Harper's New Monthly Magazine* in 1878, although without identifying Sakolski by name. Shnayer Z. Leiman, over a hundred years later, connected the location of Marks's stroll through the "Jewish quarter" of New York on Division Street with his observation in "Montague Lawrence Marks: In a Jewish Bookstore" about the bookseller's "characteristic 'ski' at the end of his name over the door." It had to be Sakolski's shop that Marks was writing about with such cheerful condescension, as he describes the Russian and Polish Jewish immigrants on the east side of the Bowery "keeping together in self-imposed ostracism, living very much as they lived in the squalid Ghettos of Europe." In their "fanatical" orthodoxy they're "the Pharisees of the Pharisees," and the judgments that their rabbinical courts dispense "are often absurdly whimsical." The good news is that the second generation is soon Americanized. "Their children attend the public schools," Marks notes approvingly, "are comely, and have lost that half-eager, half-frightened expression of countenance, born of the Ghetto and its centuries of cruel humiliation, which one often sees in the Jewish face of the lower type."

Sakolski's bookstore, which must have appeared to Marks as the most prominent in the neighborhood, beckons with its "queer cabalistic-looking letters painted on the windows," the "strange articles" in its show window, and the "rows of shelves filled with great folio volumes labelled in Hebrew." Do the "poor, squalid-looking people" surrounding him actually read, and in Hebrew? Stepping into the store, our American *flâneur* and intrepid explorer spies Sakolski in gold-rimmed glasses, "an elderly, intellectual-looking man, with a sallow complexion and a profusion of thick curly black hair and beard, both well streaked with gray." He's arguing with a "poorly clad, shrivelled-up little old Polish woman" over the price he'll pay her for the scrolls of the Five Megilot—Esther, Ruth, Ecclesiastes, Lamentations, and the Song of Songs. The woman finally relents and takes Sakolski's offer, and as the bookseller "takes out a greasy-looking wallet," Marks observes that Sakolski "doubtless has got a bargain."

You get the picture. Even I'm a little embarrassed by this scene, despite the distinctly sour smell of antisemitism wafting off the page. Sakolski comes across as a pure product of the Jewish bazaar, a hard-boiled book dealer. He admits to Marks that as more Jews have done well and moved uptown to hobnob with their Reform cousins, the price of Torah scrolls and religious books has dropped, and sales of prayer shawls and ritual goods are way down. Nevertheless, he still manages to sell a good number of individual volumes of the Talmud by offering them on weekly installment, and he keeps a copy of Joseph Johlson's 1831 German translation of the Pentateuch in stock, ostensibly in case any uptown German Jews should come calling. Marks thinks Sakolski a shrewd judge of the market when he mentions that his customers include Christian clergy with a taste for recent titles like Laemlein Buttenwieser's translation of Aaron Zebi Friedman's *Tuv Ta'am*, a defense of Jewish ritual slaughter, or William Henry Burr's translation of *Sefer Toledot Yeshu*, titled *Jesus of Nazareth*. Marks buys these last two as a "souvenir" of his adventure.

What amazing patience Sakolski shows trying to serve a writer-customer who has a pretty firm and sordid idea about the kind of Jewish product he wants to buy. That *Sefer Toledot Yeshu*? It's a notorious medieval Jewish retelling of the Jesus story, in which Joseph rapes Mary and Jesus is depicted as an evil magician and a liar. So what's so unsophisticated about Hyam Sakolski? Because it turns out that he was pretty good at playing other types of Jewish roles in different professional contexts. He was the reader and then the president of Beth Hamedrash Hagadol, the first and most prestigious Russian Jewish Orthodox congregation in the Lower East Side. Trow's New York City directory lists him as the successor to L. H. Frank, Henry Frank's son Leopold who took over his father's business when the elder Frank retired, which means Sakolski bought Frank's retail operation and inventory, likely making him the largest and wealthiest Jewish bookseller in the city. He was also an engraver, whose Biblical scenes are in the collection of the College of Charleston. He was certainly more of a sophisticate than Marks could imagine; in June 1869 his name appears in the list of patients taking the cure at Bad Kissingen, a fashionable and expensive spa town in Bavaria. All this from books.

When I tell my father this story he fails to see the connection; he's more interested in the titles that Sakolski carried and in trying to recall if he remembers them. He's not as fascinated as I am by Sakolski's sly performance in the article, his quick switches from the bazaar to the literary, from being Jewish to being the Jew. Perhaps I'm reading too much into a portrait Sakolski had no control over, but his solicitude for this gentile customer and cool explanation of his trade and titles feels familiar to me. He was code-switching, the way we signal our cultural or commercial affinities differently to different audiences, trying to meet their expectations. We all do that. But as my father's son, I also see what Sakolski was doing as another version of hand selling, similar to the type I learned in the store, and also to the literal version that Jack learned from my grandfather.

The way my father tells it, he and my *zeyde* Isaac were walking along the streets of Corona one afternoon when a gentile woman from the neighborhood approached them. "Reverend Roth," she exclaimed, reaching out her hand to shake his, "it's so nice to see you." My father watched dumbfounded as his *Tatte* took her hand in his and shook it, just like a regular goy. When they finished their little chat and the woman had walked on down the street, my father asked, "Ta, why did you shake her hand?" Because for punctilious Orthodox Jews, whose social interactions are governed by strict rules of gender segregation, touching your wife in public is highly unusual; touching a woman other than your wife is absolutely forbidden; touching a non-Jewish woman is unthinkable. "Yussi," my grandfather answered, using my father's Yiddish name, "sometimes you have to pretend that every day is Purim."

Given his translation of the book of Esther, I have to assume this must have been one of my grandfather's favorite holidays. It celebrates, of course, the triumph of Persian Jews over Haman, King Nebuchadnezzar's evil prime minister, who schemed to exterminate them. It's a carnivalesque holiday, with revelry accompanying communal recitations of the Scroll of Esther, the use of gragers, or noisemakers, to drown out the name of Haman when it's read, and the tradition of children dressing up as Queen Esther or her cousin, the righteous Mordecai, or—these days—as Disney characters and comic book superheroes. Moreover, the Talmud famously enjoins observant Jews to drink to excess on Purim, until one can't tell the difference between "cursed is Haman" and "blessed is Mordecai." So, on another level, Purim is carnivalesque as the Russian philosopher Mikhail Bakhtin used the term. The holiday promotes a ritualized subversion of the normal order of things—rationality, singular identity, the strong prevailing over the weak—that helps celebrants imagine their liberation from the social rules and roles imposed by the dominant culture. It eases speaking their truth to power.

What Isaac was telling my father was that in New York's streets, where danger lurked if you ran afoul of gentile social conventions, it's sometimes necessary to slip into those customs as if they were just another carnival costume. My father believed this a type of Orthodox *noblesse oblige*, related to the Jewish ethos of not embarrassing a person publicly. It's a way to excuse minor deviations from observance for the sake of Jewish public relations. Which points to why the handshake becomes the telling detail. It's the appropriate symbol of my father's New York world, where his behavior was fashioned through personal touch, doing business face-to-face, and showing great tact in the presentation of oneself and one's inventory to strangers. As a boy, hearing my grandfather's story in my father's voice, I couldn't help but grow up thinking the comic spirit of Purim in America was as much sales pitch as cultural ruse. And the more I thought about the story, the more I thought of Isaac as a buyer too, purchasing admission into the neighborhood's public squares.

Now I see him as both a proprietor—who one needs to be in order to sell oneself—and a customer—who one needs to be as a form of buyer protection. I doubt Isaac would see it this way, but my image of him holding two opposed identities in mind at the same time still explains for me a number of contradictory items in my father's inventory, like Jack's palpable nostalgia for the Jewish bazaar despite comparing it unfavorably to the literary, a far more respectable business.

That image of my grandfather prompts me to wonder, too, how, in the words of Ira Katznelson, "the contours of modern Jewish life have been shaped by living within the ambit of capitalism," as he writes in his essay "Two Exceptionalisms." In my father's case, it's not just that the rise of the type of Jewish bookstores he visited on the Lower East Side occurred at an important phase in the development of modern American consumer culture, or that those late nineteenth-century shops were molded by cityscapes newly geared to the entertainments of shopping, commercial spectacles, and ready-made fashion. As Katznelson points out, it's that capitalism also offered Jews a path to greater personal freedom, wealth, and ambition—as witness the terms of my father's declaration of occupation—even as it called up the sort of defensive fiction my grandfather relied on for his own peace of mind. Because once Isaac starts bending the rules of Jewish communal life to ease his way through gentile concerns, how long before that community breaks?

Is there any good way to balance that? This too is a personal choice. In my father's book business, you make a little story, you establish a relationship, you do what you have to do to move your stock. Out on the sales floor between the new and used books, the front list and the remainders, you have to believe that every deal is negotiable and every identity is under negotiation. That's how I learned to do business in America. It's how I imagine the Jewish booksellers in the Lower East Side learned it, too. I decide to take a visit.

It's a warm summer morning and I'm standing in front of 53 Division Street. The current occupant, Bill's Health Product, is advertising Ocean Dragon dried seaweed, BH7, and Brazil No. 1 Bee Propolis, while next door the staff at Yi Mei Gourmet Food and the Golden Bowl Restaurant are preparing for the lunch rush. A roar of voices and cars surrounds me, but across the street all's quiet inside the Yung Wing Public School, where the next generation of immigrant children seem to be hard at work too.

The nondescript four-story brick building I'm looking at stands at the intersection where Market Street, which runs parallel to the Manhattan Bridge, dead-ends into Division, and it's certainly not the same one that housed Sakolski's store almost 150 years ago. In fact, 53 is technically the address over the door next to the health food store entrance, which leads to the apartments upstairs. Yet it's apparent that Sakolski had a corner store, an anchor business and highly desirable retail space. The Manhattan Bridge didn't open until 1909, so from the 1870s to 1889, when Lewine and Rosenbaum bought out Sakolski and took over the store, through the turn of the twentieth century, this part of the Lower East Side was an especially busy warren of commercial streets. Not hard to imagine. Division, a block up from East Broadway, is an important east-west artery that today runs under the bridge and offers easy access to crowded Jewish tourist sites like the Eldridge Street synagogue, only a block and a half away.

By the time that synagogue was built, in 1887, the great wave of Russian Jewish immigration was well underway. Jewish bookshops had spread up to Canal and Ludlow Streets near the intersection where Canal, East Broadway, and Essex Streets meet, now called Straus Square. That was the commercial and social center of the Lower East Side. By the 1890s it was also the literary center, thanks to the Seward Park branch of the New York Public Library and the Yiddish journals and newspapers whose editorial offices dotted the area, including that of *The Jewish Daily Forward*. I walk past the marble-columned Forward Building on East Broadway and look for the famous bas-relief images of Karl Marx and Friedrich Engels on its facade. Instead, my eye catches the discrete signs advertising the building's current product, luxury condominiums.

I'm no fool. I know that every deal is negotiable until it isn't, or until the terms of the deal get changed in ways that were beyond the control of the Jews who worked in this neighborhood at the turn of the last century. So I'm taking another inventory this day, looking to understand better the geography of those deals and to remember how the Jewish booksellers down here managed them and their own commercial identities. I turn into Canal Street and see that 30 Canal is now a back door to Weilgus & Sons hardware store. This is where Asher Lämmel Germansky had his bookshop. I remember that Germansky helped the New York Public Library (NYPL) significantly expand its Hebrew and Yiddish book collection. One of the original trustees of the Rabbi Isaac Elchanan Theological Seminary in 1897, he's described in the NYPL's 1913 *Bulletin* as the "oldest of the local dealers," and he's acknowledged even before Ephraim Deinard, the revered Hebraist, collector, and publisher and one of the most famous Jewish bibliophiles of the modern era. Unlike Deinard, Germansky didn't limit his dealing to just literary materials. Six years before being lauded by the library, he and his business partner were sued for copying the labels of the Carmel Wine Company and placing them on bottles of wine that may or may not have come from Palestine, but definitely did not come from Baron de Rothschild's cellars.

A half block over, facing the asphalt triangle where Division and Ludlow intersect with Canal, there's a small coffee and juice bar where a tattooed young woman parks her bicycle and takes a seat at one of the outdoor tables. She pays no attention to me or the group of young students and their guide marching by on a tour of their own, and no one seems interested that across the street toward the middle of the block is an ornate building that used to be Loew's Canal Street Theatre, one of the last movie palaces from the 1920s still standing in New York. My attention, though, is drawn to 37 Canal, former home of Skal Icelandic Bar and, earlier last century, Joseph Werbelowsky's bookstore, just at the time he founded the Hebrew Publishing Company. I notice that it's a corner building too. Charles A. Madison, in his history of Jewish American publishing, paints Werbelowsky as one of the most successful booksellers on the Lower East Side. His practice of republishing Yiddish works from Russia and Poland in the United States without the authors' permission, however, or bothering to pay royalties, earned him the wrath of the Yiddish press. Which, as I look toward Straus Square just a few hundred feet away, actually sounds dangerous since those writers probably walked past this store all the time. Good thing Sholem Abramovitsh lived nine thousand miles away. He was livid when he discovered that his collected works, Mendele stories and all, had been pirated by Werbelowsky and were selling in Russia for less than the editions he'd authorized.

I walk up Ludlow with these stories in my head, past the Boe Fook Funeral Home, whose building began life in 1892 as the Kletzker Brotherly Aid Association, a *landsmanshaftn* (immigrant society) for Jews from Kletzk, Poland. Not long after, Max Kobre bought it to house his bank. Jews were starting to save their money, building up for the future. Just a few doors up I stop in front of 19 Ludlow, Meyer Chinsky's bookstore. Chinsky became the first treasurer of the Hebrew Publishing Company when it was formed in 1901, so I'm amused at his proximity to Kobre's bank. I realize Chinsky's store is off the intersection, in a less imposing location; it makes sense that he was subordinate to Werbelowsky. And then it dawns on me that, of course, all the booksellers on these blocks must have known one another. Working in such close quarters, they had to see one another every day, compete with one another, likely buy and sell to one another, landsmen in their own little book shtetl. Even the current version of the neighborhood, with its bars and condos, follows the same pattern today: crowds love crowds in retailing, and six or ten or a dozen of the same kind of business attracts more customers and more capital.

They also attract more attention from the authorities. In October 1897, Chinsky was arrested on the order of Anthony Comstock, the controversial United States postal inspector. The 1873 Comstock Law made it illegal to send through the mail any material deemed obscene or promoting abortion and contraception. As the self-described "weeder in God's garden," Comstock was also on the lookout for material he deemed sacrilegious to Christianity, and Chinsky's mailing of "Massa Tolo," as it was reported in the *New-York Tribune*, got him hauled into court. No doubt this was *Ma'aseh Talui*, *Deeds of the One Who Was Hanged*, a variant title of *Sefer Toledot Yeshu*, the very same book Marks purchased, clearly a dependable backlist title popular with a certain clientele. The story doesn't say if Chinsky was convicted. It's clear, though, that the days of dealing openly in books disturbing to gentile sensibilities were over.

I head back to Canal looking for Judah Meir Katzenelenbogen's bookshop, only a block and a half away. Katzenelenbogen, yet another founding partner of the Hebrew Publishing Company, was from a family of publishers and booksellers in Vilna, and the historian Eric Goldstein places him at the center of the boom in popular American Yiddish literature reaching Russia during the 1890s. It was he who sent his brother Mordechai the sensational, serialized Yiddish novels being published in the United States, which were then distributed in Russia both legally and illegally, the latter in order to avoid the scrutiny of Russian censors. I'm momentarily confused when I reach the address, because I'm standing under construction scaffolding in front of the S. Jarmulowsky Bank Building, which is undergoing major renovations. Then I recall that Sender Jarmulowsky was another banker, far larger than Kobre (Jarmulowsky helped finance the Eldridge Street synagogue and was its first president), and this, the first skyscraper on the Lower East Side, was testament to his success. So it seems fitting that an entrepreneur like Katzenelenbogen was a neighbor—doesn't hurt to have a business where people have money in their pockets.

And now that I've walked the book dealers' main drag, it seems fitting too that a 1906 magazine article about all these bookstores lining Canal, "musty with the smell of books and soup," insists that every one of them is part of a Jewish "trust," a single corporation with "a chain of some fifty book stores" throughout the Lower East Side. I'd always dismissed that, reading it as the anonymous reporter's antisemitic joke. Ah, those hustling, self-concerned Jews downtown—they're so obsessed with their own profit that they naturally have no sympathy for the sort of monopolies that agitated the reform-minded Progressives of the time. Yet they so love the book they're willing to put up with a single, exceptional monopoly, the "National Hebrew Publication Society." Now I wonder: Did someone try to explain to our uncomprehending correspondent the curious retail structure of Werbelowsky's new venture? Apparently, none of the partners had yet abandoned their separate retail operations in the five years since they'd incorporated. So the joke is that there really was a trust. Much smaller than suspected, but still large enough that its impressive volume of sales and variety of stock—from the ritual items in their stores' show windows to the Yiddish stories, plays, and translations of Shakespeare they kept in the back—hinted once again at something these early tourists of New York's Jewish ghetto couldn't see.

Which is that these bookstores were more than just advertisements for the cultural quirks of a bookish people. Katzenelenbogen's obituary says that his bookshop was a gathering place for Jewish scholars, and no doubt it was. But it was also, and more importantly, a safe house for his personal deal making and stratagems of American Jewish commercial expansion. All the partners' bookstores—in fact, all the bookstores here, including Sakolski's—were a resource and a refuge, command and control centers for their owners' negotiations with one another and the gentile authorities. No wonder none of them gave up their own shops. In the fast-changing marketplace of book distribution in the United States, spurred by the rise of a literate population, mechanized transportation, and the global flow of capital, bookstores like theirs were no longer simply an extension of an existing printing, publishing, or wholesaling business. Each was a personal bookstore, as this new type was called, a retail expression of their owners' style of commerce and of the role they wished to play in the literary marketplace, a wheelhouse for the boss's ventures that often included but wasn't limited just to publishing.

In other words, these bookstores weren't oddities; they were mirrors. They were street-level reflections of a business less genteel than supposed, and just as messy, individualistic, even cutthroat, as the American book industry itself during the Gilded Age, when New York publishers sought to control the market, when booksellers and department stores undercut those publishers' list prices (in what was known as the net price wars), and when copyright piracy was rampant.

At least that's what it was like in the big leagues down on Canal. Up on Rivington it was a different story. There, the booksellers served Jews who held jobs in light manufacturing and the service industries, and as I hurry over in search of the store my father visited I can see how its distance from the Yiddish press and the banks made this a tougher retail scene. Pinchas Friedman was probably the most well-known of the booksellers in this part of town, and in 1903 Clegg's *Directory* lists two other Friedmans running bookshops too, Joseph on Stanton and Gerson back on Ludlow. So perhaps there was another, smaller trust here too. Yet aside from his inclusion with Germansky in that 1913 NYPL *Bulletin* and being arrested for selling contraband sugar during the First World War, Pinchas Friedman leaves no other trace of his life's work.

Also vanished is any trace of M. Lipschitz's bookstore—in its place at 92 Rivington is a tailor shop and next door is a bistro specializing in all-organic southern French cuisine. So I head east, past the old Streit's matzo factory, looking for the location of one last bookstore, Chone Jaffe's at 247 Rivington.

I discovered Jaffe in a 1908 issue of *The Publishers' Weekly*. On his way to synagogue one Saturday morning, Jaffe passed by his shop and saw that a gas nightlight was still burning. He unlocked the door, but not wanting to violate the Sabbath by turning it out himself, he looked for a gentile to help him: "An Italian was passing and Jaffe beckoned to him. He told him what he wanted and they entered the store. They were followed closely by two other Italians. The three suddenly pounced upon him and ordered him to open the safe in the store. He refused, he says, and they knocked him down and kicked him as he lay on the floor. Then they threatened to kill him if he did not open the safe. When he refused they shoved him into the bookcase, where his wife found him." Some deals just can't be negotiated. And compounding that problem, Jaffe had mis-scripted his hand selling and played the wrong role in a rough, working-class neighborhood. He was lucky they left him alive. Not surprisingly, he went bankrupt two years later. Fast-forward a dozen more and the *American Book Trade Manual* of 1922 lists him as still in business at another nearby location on Stanton. Good for Jaffe.

But I can't get there. That end of Stanton is gone, demolished in the late 1930s to make way for the Grand Street Settlement expansion. Standing in front of the Our Lady of Sorrows School, I watch a group of children board their school bus, chattering and laughing, and tell myself that some deals simply disappear. Also, that Jaffe's store was a different kind of mirror. It reflected how tenuous the personal bookstore's defenses are against the mixed fortunes of urban development and redevelopment as each hungry generation treads down and then builds up the neighborhood surrounding it. Time to head home.

All these booksellers were long gone when my father and *zeyde* browsed the shelves at M. Lipschitz. Jack vaguely remembers Max Maisel, on Grand Street, still hanging on, but Jacob Druckerman, Louis Rothstein, Jerome Kantrowitz, Henry Hirsch, and Alexander Wasserman—who remembers them? The bookstores of my father's youth were, as he recollects, established during the 1920s, when the expansion of Jewish publishing offered new opportunities for retailing, especially in servicing niche markets: S. Goldman–Otzar Hasefarim specialized in Hasidic books, Schenker Books sold sheet music, and M. Vaxer specialized in Yiddish books. The J. Levine Company, which began at the turn of the century as a distributor of European ritual items, expanded into book sales only in the 1920s when the selection of traditional books, Hebrew textbooks, and English-language titles increased, although, as the store's now defunct website noted (the business closed in 2019), "the entire stock required only a few shelves."

By 1939 Jews had migrated to the outer boroughs, the market for Yiddish books and newspapers had dried up significantly, and competition for publishing Jewish writing increased among new mainstream publishing companies founded by Jews—such as Alfred A. Knopf and Boni and Liveright—and among established houses like Macmillan and Harper. New Jewish commercial publishers like Behrman House and KTAV catered to the growing demand for Jewish textbooks, scholarship, and reprints of older, European Jewish materials; organizational publishers such as the Union of American Hebrew Congregations, the Central Conference of American Rabbis, and United Synagogue of America developed new curricular materials for Jewish religious schools affiliated with those movements.

Jack was a teenager just after the Second World War, when a wave of new Jewish writing in English arrived for Jewish and general bookstores to sell. Jonathan Sarna, the preeminent historian of American Judaism, contends there was strong market demand: American Jews were in search of religious and cultural affirmation after the war, partly in response to the dire news from Europe and partly in response to their own rapid climb up the social ladder. They had a keen appetite for writing that defended, explained, celebrated, or chronicled the passage of Jews into the American mainstream. The Jewish Book Council of America even put out a manual, *The Jewish Book Shop: Its Organization and Operation*. They hoped to kick-start the opening of more Jewish bookstores that would help distribute Jewish books outside the large metropolitan areas. Literary voices such as Muriel Rukeyser, Arthur Miller, Grace Paley, and, of course, Saul Bellow and

Bernard Malamud already had national distribution. But there was an untapped audience, according to Sarna, for noncontroversial introductions to Jewish theology and observance (what the religion scholar Rachel Gordan calls "Introduction to Judaism" literature); fiction about Jews struggling with their heritage, like Jo Sinclair's *Wasteland* or Milton Steinberg's *As a Driven Leaf*; children's books that focused on ethics, morality, and American settings; and books that tracked the lesser-known arcs of Jewish success in America, like Harold Ribalow's *The Jew in American Sports.*

So my father felt, in ways his father didn't, that he belonged, that his Jewishness was urbane, cosmopolitan, and equal in ambition to the world-class city in which he lived. That's why he wanted to work part-time at Jonathan David, one of the new Jewish publishers. The company aspired to the same worldliness and cultural uplift; Alfred Kolatch started it in 1948 as an imprint for his book *These Are the Names*, explaining for English-speaking readers the history and meanings of Hebrew and Yiddish first names. As just a part-time student at the City College of New York, however, Jack had left himself open to the draft. Like the protagonist of Bellow's *Dangling Man*, my father seemed to need the help of larger historical circumstances to push him across the threshold into his future. In 1953 he found himself headed to Korea. "It is strange to believe that my ears, still ringing with the sweet discourse of Abaya and Rava should today be silenced by the unpalatable execution of military authority," he wrote in a letter he sent to the Queens Jewish Center newsletter. "Nevertheless, such it is. Perhaps, I feel, this experience will help me to better understand and know the true value of life when I meet it." The war ended as his troop ship crossed the Pacific, and he spent the remainder of his time there as a mail clerk. The high point of his service was getting a citation for bravery after jumping into the cab of a moving, driverless two-and-a-half-ton truck and stopping it before it plowed into the mess tent. When he returned to New York as a civilian he bought a new Chevy Bel Air, and in 1956 he landed a job as general manager of Behrman House.

Working at the company's office near the Empire State Building, he viewed the old booksellers down on the East Side as colorful, but out-of-date. They still clung to the "bazaar." When Bernard Morgenstern—whose bookshop was a hole-in-the-wall with mostly worthless Judaica and Hebraica—saw Jack at Behrman House, he'd always open his jacket and show him the spot in his trouser waist where he kept his cash hidden. The humor was that he kept it there in case he suddenly discovered for sale "a piece of incunabula," using the highfalutin gentile term for the very first printed books, which Morgenstern always hoped he'd stumble across going from bookstore to bookstore looking to buy anything old, rare, and Jewish.

That wasn't Jack's style though. He didn't want to sit in front of a Jewish bookstore the way Mr. Biegeleisen did, with a pile of index cards in hand listing his *yekar ha-m'tziyut*, his worthiest finds, the most valuable books he carried, just in case a collector should come by. Jack preferred an inventory that was properly listed, advertised, and circulated in printed catalogs, just like regular book dealers. Neat and professional. Had I absorbed that attitude? Is that why I disliked the way the Chabad rabbi inspected our home, as if he were looking at our private index cards? What kind of collector did he think *he* was? We ran a different kind of Jewish operation, employed a more sophisticated hand-selling script, and perhaps I picked up not just my father's desire for control over our inventory but also his liking for a more fashionable presentation of it. He'd call it more dignified. I'd call it his Jewish version of midcentury Madison Avenue, the sleek yet clubby style of modern commercial identity that dressed up consumer goods with the trappings of privilege. It was a White masculinist mainstream business aesthetic that beguiled my father, and me, and a rising American Jewish middle class.

You could say that was Jack's personal bookstore brand, which at that point just needed a family and a brick-and-mortar location for its full flowering. In 1957 my father married Rochelle Theilheimer, whose parents had fled Germany in the mid-thirties and owned a house in a respectably upper-middle-class section of Forest Hills. In 1958 their first child, my brother Alan, was born. Working for Behrman House, Jack learned the fine details of the Jewish book trade, more through careful watching than through any mentoring. As the product of a thorough Jewish education, conversant in the ideas, personalities, and historical trends of the Orthodox and Yiddish-speaking worlds, he seemed a ready-made employee to his boss, Jacob Behrman. Left to his own devices, my father used the position to further another kind of education. He noted the expansion of Judaica lists at the general publishing houses and the growing trade in Jewish textbooks. And he discovered—via phone calls and business trips to conferences for organizations like the National Association of Temple Educators—a growing network of Jewish synagogues, schools, and bookstores across the country. Then, on an especially torrid day in May 1966, trapped in the steamy confines of a New York City subway car, my father swore to himself that this was the last year he'd suffer through such an unbearable commute. Without telling Behrman, he flew to Los Angeles and made a deal with a Jewish bookseller he'd met back in 1960 when the National Association of Temple Educators convened in Los Angeles. Michael Harelick was happy to sell his store to his new young friend. But that's a story for the next chapter in my father's career.

At the end of this one, in August, a Mayflower moving truck pulled up in front of our apartment in a building just off the Long Island Expressway in Queens, a block over from Junction Avenue. My parents double-checked the list of family belongings and personal effects, took one last look around the bare apartment, and then packed their three boys, ages three, five, and seven, into a new 1965 powder blue Valiant. It rode low because of all the weight. We headed south out of New York, driving through the Shenandoah Valley to pick up U.S. 40 to Oklahoma City and then following parts of old Route 66 into Arizona. No time for constant bathroom breaks; my brothers and I peed into an empty juice bottle. We dropped down U.S. 15 to U.S. 10 and came into downtown Los Angeles on the Golden State Freeway, all of us craning our heads this way and that, amazed at the multi-level on-ramps and connectors rising above us.

A police siren sounded, and we turned as one to see a highway patrolman on a motorcycle behind us signaling my father to pull over. Jack rolled his window down and the patrolman leaned into it.

"Did you realize you were traveling too slow? That's against the law."

"No, I didn't," said my father. "I'm trying to get to the Santa Monica Freeway. We've been driving for the last week, I'm moving my family to L.A., and this is all, uh, confusing."

"Can I see your license?"

He headed back to his motorcycle, and my parents spoke quickly and quietly to each other. I didn't catch what they were saying from the back seat. The patrolman reappeared.

"Okay, sir, I'm going to let you go this time. But you need to pick it up—follow the speed of traffic. Welcome to L.A."

My father thanked him. Did I see him shake the cop's hand? I can't remember. As the patrolman walked to his bike behind us, my father turned to give my mother a look and slipped his Ray-Bans on. Then, glancing back over his shoulder once, twice, three times, he hit the accelerator and pulled into the heavy, fast stream of cars going west.

CHAPTER 3

The Storefront (*place*)

"Get in the other lane," Jack says from the passenger seat. "You don't want to be in this lane going downtown."

I continue driving the middle-left lane eastbound on the Santa Monica Freeway, keeping a steady 65 mph in my father's immaculate, leather-fragrant BMW compact sedan and scanning the surrounding landscape for familiar landmarks from my youth. It's December 2016 and I don't live here anymore, I remind myself. I'm on a research trip. But not my father.

"Don't let that car get in! Don't . . . Why'd you let him in? Laurence, look: Why does he leave so much room ahead of him? He doesn't know how to drive. Okay, don't listen to me."

We're passing the Vermont Avenue off-ramp just south of the Pico-Union neighborhood, and I quickly recognize a distraction. This is where we used to get off to visit Michael Harelick, the man who founded the bookstore my father bought. He lived up near the Jewish Federation when it was still at 590 North Vermont, where Jack would sometimes make special deliveries in the evenings or on Sundays.

"Dad, didn't we used to go visit Mr. Harelick around here when I was a kid?"

"That's right. I brought him the payments for the store."

"How much did you pay for it?"

"He sold it to me for $33,000, and I paid it out monthly to him over three years. But I also gave him $5,000 at the end of each year, so what was that, $500 a month I think?"

I can't do the math in my head to double-check him, and payments I don't remember. Just a small, dark apartment in a bungalow court complex and Harelick, with a walker, slowly getting a box of Van Houten chocolates from his fluorescent-lit kitchen to offer my brothers and me. He was in his late eighties by then and suffering from what I now know was bladder cancer. I always thought my father must have spoken to Harelick about his past, how he came to own a Jewish bookstore, but here's all he knew: Harelick immigrated to the United States from Russia as a boy or young man, but only arrived in Los Angeles in the mid- to late 1940s. He didn't know how Harelick started out in the book business, only that by the mid-'50s he was a recognized Jewish bookseller with his own storefront on Melrose Avenue, just around the corner from Los Angeles City College. Jack said Harelick had no wife or children and assumed he'd been a lifelong bachelor.

They first met in person in 1960, while my father was in L.A. repping for Behrman House Publishers at the National Association of Temple Educators. An older brother, Rabbi Michael Roth, who had moved there with his family in 1957, introduced him to Harelick, and Jack invited his prospective account out for coffee. By then, Harelick was selling and delivering books to the University of Judaism up on Sunset Boulevard and to Hebrew Union College when it was still located in the Jewish Federation building. He was a distributor for KTAV Publishing's reprint of *The Jewish Encyclopedia*, a pathbreaking work of scholarship originally published by Funk & Wagnalls in twelve volumes between 1901 and 1906, and for Judaica Press's reprint of the Blackman *Mishnayoth*, a celebrated edition of the oral Torah and its compendium of Jewish legal reasoning that was popular for study and reference. He was also a sales representative for Soncino Press, a premier Jewish publisher in the United Kingdom, which was founded in the 1920s and specialized in English translations of the Bible and the Talmud that included interpretations by academic scholars and Christian commentators.

Above all, though, Harelick was a Yiddishist, secular in outlook and, according to Jack, intellectual rather than political in his tastes. He was so devoted to the literature of the *mameloshn*, the mother tongue, that he once told a pesky customer looking for the latest novel by Leon Uris, author of the smash best seller *Exodus*, to go find such trash somewhere else. Still, he carried a large selection of English- and

Hebrew-language books, because, after all, he had to make a living. But there were no tchotchkes for sale in his store, no ritual goods or giftware, and when he met my father, he was impressed more than anything else by the fact that the young man in front of him spoke Yiddish. They hit it off immediately.

Was there more to Harelick than just that? Like much of L.A.'s Jewish history, Harelick was a fact I so took for granted that I don't recall asking anyone about him. Growing up, I never questioned whether Jews had lived anywhere else except the flats of Beverly Hills, around the Pico-Robertson neighborhood, or in the Fairfax District—a geographic area that, in my young mind, not only stretched east along Beverly Boulevard, past the old Pan-Pacific Auditorium, but also south past Wilshire all the way to Pico and Hauser Boulevards. Throughout the late 1960s and most of the '70s, all the Jews I met seemed settled and comfortable, European in descent or in fact, and well assimilated to the fashions and possessions of middle-class American life. Sure, I knew the Federation building lay somewhere on the long drive to downtown in a predominantly Latino section of the city, and my father knew a few friends and customers who lived in East Hollywood, but that was all far away, like a lot of things in L.A.

So during my winter break I'm driving the freeways with my father, running a tutorial for myself on where exactly Jewish bookstores first appeared here and in search of the retail origins of M. Harelick Books—and thus also of its heir, J. Roth Bookseller—during those flush years after the war. What was Harelick's story? When he showed up, was he as enchanted as I was on our arrival in 1966 that homes here were so unlike those in New York? In Queens we lived on the third floor of a red-brick, six-story apartment building facing the Long Island Expressway. In Los Angeles, our world suddenly opened up. The new apartment at 6450 West Olympic Boulevard was an airy ground-floor unit with two bedrooms, one large enough to fit three twin beds. It had a yellow-tiled kitchen with its own door for milk deliveries, a separate dining room, and a sunny living room, where we parked the Steinway baby grand piano. The front windows looked out onto a common courtyard and garden, around which the other apartments were arranged. When you opened the front door, you could hear birds chirping and the light traffic on Olympic washing by.

We had moved to South Carthay Circle, just southeast of Beverly Hills, because it was where Harelick's bookstore was located. Our neighborhood was beguiling, too, in its difference from the nondescript Jewish neighborhoods I remembered in Queens. Our six-unit complex was designed in one of the eclectic revival styles popular in Los Angeles from the 1920s through the 1940s. Up and down the streets were Spanish, Colonial, and Mediterranean Revival houses and apartment buildings. Ours was French Chateauesque, complete with two turrets capped by black spires that guarded each side of the courtyard's front entrance. Everything around us seemed whimsically old, but that was the idea. The folks pouring in during the 1910s and '20s were lured in part by the sly mirage of L.A. as home to romantic California rancheros and orange groves, and then came a frenetic burst of construction in the 1930s, '40s, and '50s that liberally adapted architectural styles from Spain, Italy, England, and France, as well as from ancient Egypt, Mesopotamia, and China. To me, Los Angeles wasn't just a city, it was a historical adventure.

As I lower the temperature in Jack's car, trying to keep us comfortable under the bright December sun, I recall yet another quirk of the bookstore's neighborhood that I discovered a few years after we moved in, when I was around nine years old. At the base of a wall behind the birds-of-paradise in the front courtyard of our apartment complex was an access panel that could be jimmied aside, allowing me and my brothers to squeeze into the crawl space underneath the building. In New York, we had basements for storage and heating, which we weren't allowed anywhere near, but in California, look, no basements! Except now we discovered that California had a different kind of place beneath, built just the right size for children to shimmy around between the foundation and the first floor, where we could hear when a kitchen sink drained or a toilet flushed. Even better, in the hot, dry summer a little chill leaked through the earth, and lying flat on it we cooled off, the dirt powdering our skin.

"Alan! Laurence! Benjamin! Get out of there right now!" My mother was exasperated.

"What are you doing? You can get stuck underneath there and I don't know what, you'll hurt yourselves. Get out now! Look at you, you're filthy." We slid out one by one and pretended to dust ourselves off.

"Go over to the store and see if your father needs any help."

To get there we headed out to the alley behind our apartment complex and then over to La Jolla Street. Down La Jolla we passed our family doctor's house and then turned right on Whitworth Drive. We walked another three blocks until we reached a short driveway that made a dogleg between the two halves of a large corner property on La Cienega Boulevard. There we cut through to the front of the bookstore. The large show window had a clear yellowish sunshade behind it to protect the stock, and lettered on the plate glass was "M. Harelick Books."

This is my earliest image of his storefront. It's reproduced in a triptych of black-and-white photos of Harelick that hang in my study, one of which shows him standing beneath that window sign. His bald, kippah-free, round head and the few wisps of white hair left on it obscure the bottom right quadrant of the first "O" in "Books," inadvertently suggesting a chain link between business and owner. He's a short man with black plastic mid-century glasses, his dark shirt buttoned up to his neck, no tie, a light-colored sweater peeking out from under a rumpled and boxy old suit jacket, gripping in his right hand a plain wooden cane tipped with a rubber foot and angled away from his dark pant legs.

Harelick looks straight at the camera, projecting a friendly if noncommittal demeanor. He's on show as much as the merchandise framed in the window behind him: books arranged mostly spine out on three ledges in the bottom third of the window, a few volumes perched on four narrow shelves that line each side, two small decorative vases and a couple of framed prints artfully anchoring the lower corners. The only titles I can make out among the faced-out books are *6000 Years of the Bible* by G. S. Wegener, *A Treasury of Jewish Folksong* by Ruth Rubin, and *Abraham Lincoln: The Prairie Years and the War Years* by Carl Sandburg.

This is the storefront as both the entrance and public face of a retail business. It's a street-sized picture of a store's goods and character, and whether a storefront has a custom-built design or is simply crude signage tacked onto a private home, it signals to potential customers the cost, quality, class, and brand of the product or service being sold. Put a few together on a block and, in the time it takes for the eye to scan it, a neighborhood or commercial strip takes on a recognizable identity, sometimes intended, sometimes not. The items for sale in the show windows are not just consumer goods, they're also tokens of belonging; by appealing to certain tastes, every storefront advertises those things most prized by the clique of people who shop there. Patronizing these stores and purchasing the right items signals an insider's knowledge and confers privilege. That's why storefronts are often comforting, even enjoyable. They tell you where you are in time and place and lend that locale a certain reputation and value: M. Harelick Books, another Jewish-owned and -oriented business along a key artery through the quiet residential blocks of South Carthay Circle, mid- to late 1960s.

Such cultural capital is never at rest, though. It's always in motion, just like the neighborhood and the various consumers in it. Leon Uris may have seemed a poor choice to Harelick, testifying to his customer's dubious understanding of Jewish literacy and want of cultural distinction. But clearly the community of Jews surrounding the store was changing. The storefront at 1070 South La Cienega Boulevard was one of three or four clustered in that corner property, a little retail complex that included a beauty salon, a printer's shop, and a couple of apartments in the back. It was another of the many quickly built, mixed-use developments that made up the small commercial strips thrown up just before and after the Second World War that accompanied the White flight to—and population boom on—L.A.'s Westside. The biggest neighbor on that stretch of La Cienega was Temple Beth Am, founded in 1934, whose steadily expanded campus across the street from the bookstore housed one of the larger Conservative congregations in the city.

As Jack tells it, Harelick knew what he was doing when he moved from Melrose Avenue to a storefront next door to Beth Am sometime in the late '50s and then, when the temple bought that building to make way for a new Hebrew school, to the east side of the boulevard in '64. Beth Am was one of a number of synagogues in the Fairfax, Carthay Circle, Beverly Hills, and Pico-Robertson neighborhoods that served the Jewish professionals, mass media employees, aerospace workers, and small shopkeepers who were rapidly gravitating toward the ocean and into the San Fernando Valley. Perhaps tellingly, Harelick's storefront at 1070 had no Hebrew or Yiddish on any of its signage. Like the book on Abraham Lincoln so prominently featured in its show window, his shop catered to a generation of increasingly affluent Jewish Angelenos with diverse literary interests and tastes, still fascinated by great emancipations and making a quick exodus themselves from urban Jewish enclaves in the Midwest and Northeast or from older neighborhoods in L.A., such as Boyle Heights, the Central Avenue corridor around East Adams Boulevard, and Wilshire Center.

As I pass all the store signage lining the I-10 on my way downtown, I reflect on that old black-and-white photo and think: Isn't Los Angeles just one large storefront? This occurs to me not just because I'm immediately reminded of the city's infatuation with businesses whose storefronts look like giant hot dogs, tamales, coffee pots, ice cream buckets, and doughnuts. Or even because an artist like Ed Ruscha thought that photographing every building on the Sunset Strip and documenting the quirky architectural styles of the city's gas stations and apartment buildings revealed both the ingenuity and banality of L.A.'s ephemeral mass culture.

No, it occurs to me because Harelick's bookstore, and my father's purchase of it, molded my thinking about the complicated relation between the city's shape-shifting commercial landscape and its fugitive consumers. Harelick's storefront was like so many others in the city: another attempt to stake a claim on transient grounds, to fix one's being and business into the fast-moving scheme of things and say, "I'm here," or "We're here," though always under the shadow of being taken over or turned out. Location, so crucial to retail success, was important as well to my education about this, even though it didn't sink in until much later. La Cienega wasn't Fairfax, and would never become what Pico Boulevard is today, and so I appreciate only now how that snapshot, in addition to the nostalgic comfort it still summons for me, also captured a moment and a locale in Los Angeles Jewish history that was not just in-between—in property use, demographics, and time—but also in-process. Our arrival and Jack's choice of Harelick & Roth Booksellers as the new name for the store evidenced just as much, as did the store's customers, with their multiple affiliations, senses of Jewish self, and ways of talking about both of these. For many, this went entirely without saying, because the contemporary flux and flow of their social lives appeared entirely stable and natural to them.

I see in Harelick's storefront a reflection of that complexity, multiplicity, and naïve self-regard. And, consequently, how his and my father's trained me to read for contradictions. Their storefronts were my primers for how to grasp, whether in books or in built environments, the interpretive clutter of a text and its confusion of meanings. They taught me how to attend to the various stories I heard told about my space and my place, as I thought of it, and how these landed tales of our Jewish life continually bumped up against other stories and geographies that I stumbled into in dependably unpredictable ways. Think of the eclectic revival styles of my childhood neighborhood, where the exteriors looked like one thing, the mostly Jewish people inside sounded like something else, and only paid handymen, curious kids, and insects explored the crawl spaces underneath.

Storefronts come and go, expand and contract, toggle back and forth between expressions of their owners' tastes and those of their clientele. They're how I imagine that Jewishness and memory continually relocate in this city, moving sideways and close to the ground but not subterranean, always next to or among—a history in rebuilds and add-ons, like the Los Angeles described by various writers as a tale in concrete of its residents' dreams, or as Mike Davis says in *City of Quartz*, a "utopia *and* dystopia for advanced capitalism," a place where people and things define, distort, and then redefine each other again in ways as protean as the architecture.

I check the speedometer and then glance at Jack. Was Harelick even there that day in '67 or '68 when I arrived to help? Standing in front of the store with my brothers, the Ships Coffee Shop sign up the street caught my attention. Maybe Dad will get us tuna sandwiches to eat in the back room for lunch. We looked in through the show window to see if he was alone or taking care of a customer, but the glare bouncing off the glass was too strong. All we could see were ourselves hovering ghostlike over the books on display.

"Why didn't you ever take us to Boyle Heights when we were kids?" The downtown skyline expands on the horizon, free of the smog I remember when I was younger, and so crystal clear I'm shocked at the view.

"What are you talking about? I took you boys there a few times. I showed you the Breed Street Shul, don't you remember?"

Not really. That's why we're headed there now. If I'm going to figure out where and when Harelick enters the longer history of the city's Jewish book retailers, I'll have to reconstruct their story both in my mind and on the street. Begin here: The dry goods, clothing, and general merchandise stores near the old Plaza downtown in the decade after California was admitted to the Union in 1850. This is where Isaiah M. Hellman and Samuel Hellman opened a store in Bell's Row (a large commercial building on the corner of Aliso and Los Angeles Streets), and an 1857 sketch of their storefront and shop sign makes plain their specialty, the first of its kind in town: "Books Stationery and Cigars."

The brothers Hellman arrived from Bavaria in 1855, right before the cattle boom went bust and unfurled a host of opportunities for ambitious newcomers like them and their cousins, Isaias Wolf Hellman and Herman Wolf Hellman, who joined them in 1859. Isaias opened his own store in 1865, there beginning his career as the city's first banker. He went on to found the influential Farmers and Merchants Bank in 1871 and, firmly ensconced among the California political and social elite, began purchasing large tracts of land and cementing his legacy as one of the most important California financiers of the nineteenth century.

Herman Hellman, in the meantime, started his own general store on Main Street, selling it in 1870 to Leopold Harris and Nathan Jacoby, who sold books and stationery too, for a time, before deciding that clothing was a better retail bet. Harris and Jacoby split up in 1875, and Jacoby kept the shop and brought in his brothers to found the Jacoby Bros. Clothing Store, while Harris eventually founded the Harris & Frank Department Store. Herman dumped both books and clothing for the wholesale grocery business and made a fortune with Hellman, Haas & Co. That enabled him to buy land too, which provided the financial and social heft that made him cofounder of the Los Angeles Chamber of Commerce and president of Congregation B'nai Brith, the first synagogue in L.A.

As for Samuel and Isaiah Hellman, they went their separate ways in 1862, after which Isaiah disappears from the historical record. Samuel, however, went all in with books and stationery. By the 1870s he was the largest wholesale and retail bookseller and stationer in Los Angeles, though you could also get sheet music, musical instruments, fancy goods, and of course cigars at his store. In 1883 he added a partner and became Hellman, Stassforth & Co.

There were about a dozen other booksellers, stationers, and news dealers listed in the city directory during the late 1870s and early 1880s, but Samuel Hellman faced only two other serious competitors, Stoll & Thayer, founded by Swiss immigrant Simon Stoll, and Louis Lewin & Co. Lewin was a printer who dabbled in land development, and his partner, Pincus Lazarus, had come from Germany to L.A. via New York and Tucson, where he'd also run a book and stationery store, and he soon bought out Lewin and ran the operation under his own name. When in 1882 Lazarus married the daughter of Maurice Kremer, another successful Jewish merchant who'd arrived in the 1850s from Alsace, the *Los Angeles Daily Times* described him as "owner of one of the finer large book stores."

Like Kremer, Lewin, and all the Hellmans, Lazarus was a member of Congregation B'nai Brith, housed downtown first on Broadway and then on Hope Street, and eventually relocating as the Wilshire Boulevard Temple when its upwardly mobile Reform congregants drifted westward in the late 1920s. There's no record that any of these first immigrant entrepreneurs carried Jewish books or ritual items. But it's hard to imagine that, like their eighteenth-century forerunners back East, they wouldn't have acted from time to time as agents for the synagogue in obtaining prayer books and educational materials. General stores with a bookish twist like theirs were an important distribution arm for all types of publishing during the western expansion of the mid- to late nineteenth century.

"Ah, now we're going to get stuck," my father says as we slow down approaching the four-level interchange where the Santa Monica Freeway meets the Hollywood Freeway and Interstate 5. "I could have told you this would happen. This is a bad time to go through downtown. Do you want to get off?"

"I thought you wanted to see Boyle Heights."

"Sure, of course. But if it's going to be like this, do you really want to sit in traffic all day? I mean, if you do, it's okay with me."

"Dad, it's a beautiful day, relax. Look, there's the Los Angeles River. I hear they're trying to restore parts to how it used to be before it became concrete."

"Uh-huh." He turns his head away to stare at the car inching forward next to us.

Color photos of the 1070 storefront show a blue-and-white light box sign for "Books / M. Harelick / Books" above the show window and store entrance, which remained there for a number of years after my father bought the bookstore. He said he kept the sign up out of respect, and though their business partnership was legally dissolved in 1968, he also kept "Harelick & Roth Booksellers"—with all signage, merchandise bags, and stationery in English only—as the store's official name for another eleven years. From the start, however, everyone recognized that Jack was the main proprietor. In July 1966, a month before he arrived in L.A., a letter from M. Harelick Books went out to publishers, rabbis, and potential customers "announcing the association of Mr. Jack Roth as a general partner": "[He] brings to our firm a vast knowledge of Judaica, and a gracious manner that has earned him an enviable reputation in Jewish book circles across the land." Anyone who knew my father well knew that "vast," "gracious," "enviable," and "across the land" were straight out of his lexicon, and that the subtext of his self-penned announcement was that Jack was taking charge.

Letters came back from Abingdon Press, the Jewish Publication Society, the Jewish Education Committee of New York, Hebrew Union College–Jewish Institute of Religion, Rabbi Eugene Borowitz, and rabbis from congregations in Chicago, Houston, Memphis, Nashville, Phoenix, and Portland, and in California from Beverly Hills, Burlingame, Sacramento, and Ventura. Each variously congratulated Jack on his "new launching" and his "new business venture." The short announcement of his new position in *Publishers Weekly* only underlined that the store was entirely his.

So did the reorganized sales floor. Harelick had never bothered to organize his stock systematically, believing that browsing would be more interesting for his customers if it was also a treasure hunt. I heard from Larry Scher, a former shipping clerk of his, that if Harelick learned a particular title was becoming popular, he'd shelve it in six different places where he figured someone might stumble across it. Jack immediately set to work cleaning up the chaos, arraying the stock in clearly marked sections, refreshing the show window with seasonal titles, and regularly sending out catalogs, which my mother helped him put together, "for the temple, religious school, library, home." He paid greater attention to customer service, put in a billing computer, and sent a letter to Paul Nathan—who wrote the Rights column in *Publishers Weekly* that tracked and reported on rights acquisitions in the industry—asking how much he could legitimately claim as pilferage for a tax write-off (4 or 5 percent). Up went sales.

At first, Jack followed the general pattern of Jewish bookselling at the time, as he'd known it in New York. He expanded his textbook line, essentially becoming the West Coast distributor for a number of Jewish publishers. He also developed a brisk seasonal mail-order business, wholesaling dreidels, Simchat Torah flags, and gragers, which he maintained for many years.

Yet he also began responding to specific customer requests and focusing on his retail business. Just after Hanukkah he'd fly back to New York to visit the Jewish publishers and the Jewish Book Council, but also Bookazine, a Jewish-owned book wholesaler that published *Judaica Book News*, from which he bought titles and took notes for his expanding Jewish American list. Building on Harelick's already strong and diverse backlist in English, Yiddish, and Hebrew books, he purchased even more books from non-Jewish publishers and regional distribution companies. He started ordering one or two copies of a title that he thought a particular customer might buy or, increasingly, that seemed interesting or important to him. He stocked books from a variety of genres and covering a range of subject matter, applying the lessons in publishing and bookselling that he learned at Behrman House and through his contacts among Jewish educational and communal organizations across the country. Familiar with the leading Jewish studies scholars of the day, he also began ordering all the new titles that seemed to be pouring out of university and education presses.

He was also in the right business at the right time; 1967 was a turning point for Israel and American Jews. That year the television was standard background noise at our dinner table, a sure sign that it was the end of the day and a chance to see my mother in concentrated form—cooking, interrogating us about school, talking about her shift at the store, letting us know exactly what she thought of Mrs. G. or that stinker Mr. S. Our Zenith color TV sat on a rolling cart at the head of the table, where my father would have been if he came home from work, but he rarely did, so there was usually a clear view for everyone of Walter Cronkite's receding hairline and graying moustache as he somberly informed us about the latest anti–Vietnam War demonstrations.

A few weeks after Passover, Cronkite reported that the Egyptian president, Gamal Abdel Nasser, had closed the Straits of Tiran. Fourteen anxious days later, on June 5, Cronkite opened his newscast with the first images of Israel's preemptive attack on Egypt, and then my parents were glued to both the television set and the phone, trying to get word from relatives in Israel. Saturday at Beth Jacob Congregation there was more than the usual talking among the men as the cantor plowed through the morning service and the rabbi had to ask for silence. That evening, after *havdalah*, the ceremony marking the end of the Sabbath and the beginning of the workweek, my parents turned the Zenith back on, and soon the phone was ringing. I heard my mother ask, "Is it over?" I went to bed, and when I woke up the next morning the front-page headline of the *Los Angeles Times* read, "Israel in Control from Suez to Galilee as Fighting Stops." Did my mother, brothers, and I walk over to the store that Sunday afternoon? The way I remember it, we found my father in the middle of a knot of customers, talking, laughing, everyone saying "Jerusalem" again and again and again.

In the months afterward a wave of new books on Israel and the war showed up in the bookstore, and they sold quickly: Winston and Randolph Churchill's *The Six Day War*, Walter Lacquer's *The Road to Jerusalem*, Michael Bernet's *The Time of the Burning Sun*, the Associated Press's *Lightning out of Israel: The Six-Day War in the Middle East*, David Dayan's *Strike First!*, William Stevenson's similarly titled *Strike Zion!*, David Kimche and Dan Bawly's *The Sandstorm*, Refa'el Bashan's *The Victory*, Ephraim Kishon and Kariel Gardosh's *So Sorry We Won!*, and a slim volume of essays, *A Commentary Report: American Reactions to the Six Day War*. My favorite was *Israel Defense Forces: The Six Day War*, an album-sized book published by Israel's Ministry of Defense that was mostly maps and photographs, in black and white and in color, of soldiers, tanks, jets, and triumphant Israeli commanders.

I wasn't the only one high on victory. All these books expanded the Israel section in the store, and related titles soon occupied even more shelf and table space. Sales of Hebrew primers shot up, and the display window featured Hebrew dictionaries. The storefront was changing. No matter the name on the signage, the business's English facade and Yiddishist interior was being refigured not only by Jack but also by the neighborhood whose evolving identity the store had to serve. And maybe it was then that I noticed how often the families of certain friends traveled to Israel, or that I recognized there were actual Israelis living in Los Angeles. They, too, now came to the bookstore.

Five years after the war, Temple Beth Am across the street hosted Israel Expo West, a celebration of all things Israeli, with folk dancing, music, lectures, and, my mother said, "authentic Israeli food" available in the social hall. Despite the papier-mâché Jerusalem stone and Hebrew-language menus festooned about the serving stand, it looked to me like the usual synagogue potluck. Only here it was doled out by an excitable teenager who wore a *kova tembel*, the iconic Israeli "fool's hat" that was all the rage after '67 because it was associated with kibbutz workers and regular Israeliness, a kind of secular kippah.

My mother insisted I try the falafel and hummus, my first time. I can't recall what I made of the taste, but I do remember the happy noise in the hall as I ate. All the adults seemed, like those in my father's bookstore, to delight in the crowd, showing off their purchases, everyone buying into the illusion of this Jewish elsewhere that conjured for us a new sense of place, everyone feeling strangely yet proudly at home on our stretch of La Cienega Boulevard.

Crawling along the I-10 behind a tractor trailer, I'm at sea. Should I know this neighborhood, or was it always just warehouses and graffiti? I'm not listening to Jack, so he isn't in a talkative mood. In the retailer's story unfolding in my mind, I'm as adrift in time as I am in space. Is it the 1890s? Then the heart of the Los Angeles bookselling district was anchored northwest of here, where Second Street crosses Main, Spring, and Broadway. A decade earlier the Southern Pacific and Santa Fe lines had finally connected the city to the rest of the country, and a wave of migrants from across the United States descended on Los Angeles. The real estate craze this provoked soon collapsed, so Colonel Harrison Gray Otis, a former Civil War officer, anti-labor activist, and new publisher of the *Los Angeles Times*, decided that conservative, Bible-reading Midwesterners were what L.A. really needed. In his view, they were a better population investment than the fortune-hunting or tubercular sightseers brought in by the low cost of train tickets and the purported healing qualities of Southern California weather.

Quickly organizing the downtown landowners and bankers, Otis helped turn L.A. into what the writer Carey McWilliams judged, as quoted in *Los Angeles: Portrait of a City*, "the most priggish community in America." The effect on bookselling was equally dramatic. New booksellers arrived who brought with them the style and marketing tactics of the Midwestern and East Coast personal bookstores. Frederick Jones, J. W. Fowler and W. A. Colwell, Charles Parker, and James Smith all emphasized books (while still carrying stationery, pens, and novelties) and began dividing the market into sales niches, which at first were simply new and used books. Their newspaper advertisements hawked encyclopedias, fine-bound editions of James Fenimore Cooper or Wilkie Collins, school textbooks, and, naturally, Bibles.

By 1910, five years after Ernest Dawson opened his first bookstore on South Broadway and started the career that made him the dean of L.A. rare booksellers, there were forty-seven listings in the city directory under "Books & Stationery," the most yet. There was the Catholic Book Store, and book departments were added at the Broadway Department Store, Bullock's Department Store, and A. Hamburger & Sons Department Store, kingpin of the old German Jewish mercantile stores, later to become the May Company. But there were no overtly advertised Jewish bookstores.

Pincus Lazarus, who owned that large, refined bookstore in 1882, was by then out of the book business entirely, and Samuel Hellman had sold his share in Hellman, Stassforth & Co., now the Grimes-Stassforth Stationery Co. Yes, a few recognizably Jewish names appear as booksellers in all the directories. The majority are secondhand dealers in downtown locations unrelated to the main Jewish commercial neighborhood around Temple Street, although there's a listing for Hyman Tyre's bookshop, later to become Samuel Romm's bookshop, at 920 West Temple, a block east of the Orthodox Congregation Anshei Sfard. Still, I can't find any evidence that their stores catered to a specifically Jewish market. By the end of the first decade of the twentieth century that market was once again on the move, according to the historian Caroline Luce, shifting east across the river and down Brooklyn Avenue thanks to new bridges and streetcar lines that made the affordable lots and rentals in the subdivisions there attractive to downtown's ethnic and immigrant working and middle classes.

"When was the last time you came out to Boyle Heights?" I ask Jack. Hopefully one of us has a clear sense of what our destination looks like.

"Oh, a long time ago, maybe not since you were kids," he says, looking south out his passenger window. "The only time I go downtown is for concerts at the new Disney Concert Hall. But I haven't been there in a while. All the streets are a mess, they're tearing everything down. It's one new development after another."

A good description of L.A. bookselling in 1910 too. While the Midwesterners were transforming the English-language book market, a different and mostly forgotten one developed around East First and South San Pedro Streets. Gentaro Fukushima, J. I. Moriyama, H. Yamamoto, K. Okazaki, and the Kinko Do Book Co. were some of the first Japanese bookstores established in the years after another of Colonel Otis's development schemes paid off. The Port of Los Angeles in San Pedro was intended to loosen the Southern Pacific Railroad's stranglehold on commercial shipping to L.A., but, as other investors understood, it also opened the city to the Pacific basin and trade with Asia. Japanese immigrants had first settled south of the Plaza in the mid-1880s. It's only after 1910 and the completion of the harbor, however, that East First Street became the center of a thriving Japanese book culture that lasted until 1942, when President Franklin Roosevelt's infamous relocation order sent thousands of Japanese Angelenos to the Manzanar internment camp out in the Owens Valley.

Even less well remembered are the Spanish-language bookstores that dotted old San Fernando Road north of the Plaza, in the area that White folks derisively called Sonoratown. Cuauhtemoc Villagrana, Rafael DeLara, and Pilar Robledo never get listed in the bookstore directories published back East, only in the Los Angeles city directory. Yet one of the most important bookstores in L.A. history was among them, Rómulo Carmona's Librería Mexicana "La Aurora" (the Dawn) at 652 San Fernando Road. His was the first anarchist and revolutionary workers' bookstore in the city, an important storefront for the political networking and marketing that helped spawn the Mexican Revolution of 1910. Carmona had come to L.A. from El Paso, where he'd been part of the literary circle formed by expatriate members of the Mexican Liberal Party, the PLM. Their leader was Ricardo Flores Magón, one of the PLM founders and editor of the anarchist newspaper *Regeneración*, who was on the run from the dictatorial Porfirio Díaz government for publishing anti-Díaz articles and editorials. After a failed raid into Mexico, Magón fled in 1907 to L.A., where Carmona hid him in his home next door to the bookstore. But the police and private detectives—hired by Colonel Otis and his allies, who, besides opposing unions, not coincidentally owned large tracts of land in Mexico—discovered Magón and arrested him for violating U.S. neutrality laws. Carmona eventually fell out with the *magonistas*, but he continued to operate his bookstore. He was last listed as a bookseller in the 1932 city directory as doing business at 611 North Spring Street, the new Anglo name given to San Fernando Road around 1917.

These types of socially conscious bookstores didn't disappear, though. In 1941 Alfred Ligon opened the Aquarian Library and Bookshop, which became the Aquarian Book Shop, at 802 East Jefferson in South Central Los Angeles. It may or may not have been the first Black-owned bookstore in L.A., but it eventually became the longest-running one in the country and a hub for Black writers and cultural activists. Adele Young opened the Hugh Gordon Bookshop five years later at 4310 South Central Avenue thanks to a bequest from the eponymous donor, a business leader, writer, and Black nationalist intent on seeding community activism. New storefronts were quickly entering the book business.

"Laurence, what are you doing, get over, you're going to miss the exit. This guy will let you in. Go on."

I cut across a lane and head up the ramp toward a red light at East Cesar Chavez Avenue.

"You've got to pay attention when you drive. Do you drive like that at home?"

"Dad, relax."

"Relax, he says. I'm relaxed, are you?"

No, not at all. I switch subjects in my head: Did the emergence of Jewish bookselling in Boyle Heights owe anything to local labor and cultural activism too? If not, how did Harelick's store suddenly show up in the '40s like a weed among a forest of Jewish bookstores mainly peddling religious titles and Judaica?

"When is this light going to change?" Jack is staring straight ahead.

"Soon," I say, but not soon enough, I think, my eyes fixed on the rearview mirror and all the traffic fast lining up behind me.

"Laurence, do you know where you are?" Jack is swiveling around trying to take in the surroundings.

"Why are you asking me? I think we're headed in the right direction . . ."

I imagined Cesar Chavez Avenue, formerly Brooklyn Avenue, as a typically wide and flat L.A. street with mini-malls and gas stations, more like Lincoln Boulevard, Pico, or even Sixth Street. But here I see that the 2000 block, the heart of the old Jewish neighborhood, is a leafy Main Street–style thoroughfare whose gentle slope follows an old ridgeline because, hello, this is Boyle *Heights*. Caught in late-morning traffic, I slowly cruise the dense strip of mom-and-pop businesses: tax services, party supplies, tailoring, discount clothing, liquor, videos, car insurance, groceries, hair and nail salons, dentists, and check cashing services. The storefronts on these low-slung commercial buildings, some of which look to be from the 1920s, '30s, and '40s, have a hodgepodge of English and Spanish signage on their awnings and faded light box signs. Clustered on or near the corners are Mexican restaurants, bakeries, *tortillerias*, and fast-food joints. Later, when I double-check my notes with a quick stroll on Google's street view, I notice a few *botánicas*, an immigration consultant, and a number of money transfer stores too.

From the passenger seat my father finds his voice. "Let's see the Breed Street Shul," he says, because of course we're going to repeat that forgotten childhood experience. I turn right on Breed Street, and there it is out my passenger-side window, surrounded by a razor wire–topped chain link fence, apparently undergoing some sort of renovation. The concrete front steps look to be crumbling away, but the Byzantine Revival facade is still holding its own. High above the double-arched entry, fresh plywood backs the little empty frames surrounding the stained-glass Star of David, and the chiseled "Congregation Talmud Torah, Los Angeles" on the pediment beneath it is clean and clear.

Honestly, though, I have no interest in the building. To me, it's just another quaint historical synagogue that will inevitably launch some kind of mini-lecture from my father. I see the fence as far more significant. It's less a safety measure than an undisguised contact point showing everyone where the Jewish past and Latino present are elbowing each other, throwing off a little heat from their cultural friction, as the anthropologist Anna Tsing calls it, in a neighborhood where both land and money are fast being transferred.

I pull closer to the line of cars parked bumper to bumper along the curb, but a tired-looking Chevy of some sort is trying to pull out of a spot just behind me and I'm blocking it. I drive two blocks down, make a three-point turn, and roll up to the shul once more. Staring at the old synagogue, our pilgrimage to Boyle Heights is starting to feel more like a dutiful family visit to some distant relative. I ought to be fascinated, as so many of my professional colleagues are, by the multiethnic past of this neighborhood, by the sudden bloom during the first two decades of the twentieth century of a west coast Lower East Side amid the Armenians, Chicanos, Japanese, Russian Molokans, and African Americans who settled these blocks too.

But it's not my neighborhood. I have nothing invested in it. It's the most distant part of a Jewish geography whose center for me is my father's storefront. Double-parked on this street I'm just another tourist, and my tour guide is still the trusty Dr. Luce. "The demographic diversity of Boyle Heights, both in ethnicity and income, threatened the community cohesion and collective identity of the neighborhood's Jewish population," she writes in "Reexamining Los Angeles' 'Lower East Side.'" "To bolster them, local rabbis and religious leaders worked to increase the observance of Jewish law and ritual among the immigrants and to erect dozens of synagogues in the neighborhood." The Hellmans, Hamburgers, and other Jewish downtown elites organized charities to help support and Americanize these new arrivals, according to Luce, which included a significant cadre of socialist labor organizers and journalists who preferred establishing their own organizations. The Jewish Socialist Verband, Jewish Retail Grocers

Association, Jewish Mothers Alliance, and Jewish Art Institute of America were more concerned with creating a self-sufficient, politically progressive, and Yiddish-speaking Jewish public life, which set up a long-running tension between the city's liberal Jewish activists and the acculturated elites who feared L.A.'s Jews being labeled communists.

No such worries about the first-known dedicated Jewish book and religious goods retailer in Los Angeles. He looks to have been allied with the city's rabbis and religious leaders, not with the Yiddish socialists or culturalists. According to his granddaughter, when Chanoch Kapshut opened his bookstore, C. Kapshut Beyt Mis'char Ha'sefarim, House of the Book Trade, in Boyle Heights in 1913, he sold Hebrew books, prayer shawls, phylacteries, and other ritual items and was a distributor for Manischewitz Passover food products. Four years later, when Kapshut appears under "Books & Stationery" in the city directory, he's listed as doing business out of his home at 2111 Brooklyn Avenue, the address where the granddaughter, Fran Oberman, believed her grandparents landed after their long journey, starting in 1904, from Russia to New York to Chicago and then to L.A., arriving in 1912.

Kapshut brought with him the Eastern European model of the entrepreneurial *moykher sforim*, the Jewish version of a general store for books, getting his start by serving the domestic religious needs of the folks living up and down these side streets. Like the Jewish booksellers of my father's youth, Kapshut was a denizen of the Jewish bazaar, hawking a mixed inventory of books, Judaica, and food, using his storefront to give his family a leg up into Los Angeles's burgeoning middle class. Like the non-Jewish booksellers downtown similarly wedded to their own kinds of mixed inventory, he had successfully carved out a lucrative niche within the city's expanding book market. In that sense, his personal bookstore was very much of its time and place, which favored both traditionalism (of either the Midwestern or Jewish varieties) and specialization.

Still, when Kapshut moved his bookstore to 2205 Brooklyn Avenue sometime in the first half of the 1920s, and then eventually to 419 North Soto Street, Boyle Heights was where most of the Yiddishist editors, advertising managers, and bookkeepers for the *California Jewish Voice* (*Kalifornyer Idishe Shtime*), *California Jewish Times*, *California Jewish Review*, the L.A. editorial offices of *The Forward*, and the communist-affiliated *Morgen Freiheit* all lived. Did they shop at Kapshut's, or at Sol Mirsky's bookstore (at 246 and then later at 236 North Soto Street), or at Hyman Goldblum's (in the former *Freiheit* offices at 2429 Brooklyn Avenue)? Who catered to them?

All I know is that starting in the 1930s, a second, larger wave of Jewish bookstores appeared in Boyle Heights, a number of which my father knew as Fairfax Avenue transplants, and of course they primarily sold religious books and goods: Solomon Herskovitz Hebrew Book Store, Fox's Hebrew Book Store, Eastside Book Shop (owned and operated by Goldie Lasher), Gans Book Store, J. Sojcher Religious Book Store, and Solomon's Hebrew & English Book Store, which was the largest of these retail operations by the time my father arrived.

Jack had quickly understood that Chaya and Elimelech Solomon were his biggest competitors among these traditional religious bookshops. The Solomons had emigrated from Jerusalem, according to Sherrill Kushner's short history of their store, where the Solomon family had lived since the early nineteenth century. During the tensions leading up to the 1929 Palestine riots over Jewish access to the Western Wall, Elimelech decided to try his luck in America, and Chaya followed with their four children the year the Arab Revolt started, in 1936. It was Chaya who decided to use their contacts back in Jerusalem to make extra money as a Judaica dealer. She must have appreciated that the domestic rage for gifts and novelties from Palestine was a profitable consequence of Zionist fundraising and the increase in Jewish tourism to the Holy Land. The Solomons' advantageous religious, social, and commercial connections in Jerusalem helped stock their bookstore's local cultural capital and, along with their attentive service, ensured success. When they moved to Fairfax Avenue in 1945, so too did the dominant model in Los Angeles of the traditional *moykher sforim* store.

Their assets, however, left Boyle Heights a long time ago. Sitting in Jack's car and craning my neck to see a half-finished renovation, I register my own kind of friction between past and present in this neighborhood, though I'm only passing through it. That's because I feel at the moment like a contact point between two contradictory ideas about Jewish bookstores, one a memory of the kind that emerged here and the other embodied in the man sitting next to me. I don't see a connection between one and the other, or to Harelick, and I feel as if it's we who don't belong in this spot, that our double-parking and gawking are just adding more heat to that fence. To me, Boyle Heights is just another place, once Jewish and multicultural, now both Latino working-class and a hotbed of middle-class gentrification.

"Where do you want to go now?" my father asks.

"Let's do Fairfax for lunch. Maybe we can eat at Canter's." And then I ease the car onto Chavez Avenue and its heavy midday traffic, heading for the interstate, the neighborhood already tucked away in my mind like some souvenir postcard I'll forget to send.

"Well," Jack announces out of nowhere, "now we can say we saw Boyle Heights." He sounds relieved.

Not long after joining the parking lot of cars crawling along the Santa Monica Freeway, I can tell Jack is out of patience with our field trip. Allowing another BMW to cut in front of me sets him off.

"You don't want to go to Fairfax. There's nothing there anymore."

"I don't want to see where the Jews *are*, I want to see where they *were*."

My father shrugs.

"Why don't we go to Pico first. That's where the action is. You can go to Pico Kosher Deli."

Noticing the change of pronouns, I dig in.

"It's not that much longer to the exit. Let's just go in historical order and take it from there."

"I'm telling you, the traffic is terrible."

And of course, he's right. South Fairfax is locked up bumper to bumper. Jack keeps pointing out streets where I can turn off, and also there's the former synagogue, now a Korean church, where he knew the cantor, "that pompous jerk," and look, this has become an Ethiopian neighborhood, which I can see, but I also recall that this was where we went to the non-kosher deli where no one I knew ate, the place where I ordered a ham sandwich for the first time. And neither Jack nor Rochelle said a word as I politely gave the waiter my *treyf* order, pointedly letting me make an "adult" decision.

When we finally inch up the 300 block of North Fairfax, I see the old neighborhood isn't quite as Jew-free as Jack made out. Chabad is still here, and there's a Moroccan Jewish synagogue, the Babe Sale Congregation, across the street, both surrounded by hipster boutiques and restaurants, including the pizza joint that I hear is the most desired reservation in L.A. this year.

"You know Harelick had a nephew. I think he worked for the State Department. Or maybe some organization like RAND. Anyway, he was a specialist in Russian studies, Russian diplomacy I think."

"He had relatives here? How? Do you know where to find that guy? You've got a pen in your glove compartment—write that down for me."

"I must have gone to Harelick's funeral," my father says as he neatly jots a few lines on a notepad from the Los Angeles Jewish Home's Connections to Care. "Maybe that's how I know about him. But I can't remember it. I do remember when they unveiled the tombstone someone read Yehoash's *Tehillim*. There was no rabbi and very few people. Sad."

Yehoash sticks in my head, only because I know that he translated Longfellow's *The Song of Hiawatha* into Yiddish. But this final tidbit of information is all Jack has left, and as we turn left onto Melrose Avenue I think to myself, he's right again. The real Jewish commercial action is over on Pico. Why would Jack be interested in where Jewish bookstores were? He'd already lived that. Where they went was my old neighborhood, awash now in Jewish goods and services, and where the city dedicated the intersection of Pico and Wetherly Drive as Schneerson Square in honor of the late Lubavitcher Rebbe. There's a 47,000-square-foot building on the northwest corner built to look like the Chabad-Lubavitch headquarters at 770 Eastern Parkway in Brooklyn, a feat of cultural and religious importation that makes the Solomons' pre–World War II storefront display of Palestinian Judaica seem quaint by comparison. I suggest to Jack that we call it a day and head back to his house for a very late lunch. I don't recognize half the buildings I see on our way there.

Back home in Pennsylvania a few weeks later, with my photo triptych of Harelick and his storefront propped against a pile of books on my desk, I go hunting for his nephew on the Internet. I enter a string of search terms in academic and commercial search engines, even trying "Horelick," and "Gorelick," and still no luck. Out of ideas, I enter just

Harelick's name and date of death and, a few hits down the page, find a link I've never seen before to an archived photo of his grave. Opening it, I discover that Harelick is buried at Sholom Memorial Park in Sylmar, way out on the northeastern edge of the San Fernando Valley. Inscribed on the smallish stone laid flat on the ground is just his name, the years of his birth and death, 1883 and 1972, and a short Yiddish epitaph: "A zeltener mentsch."

A rare, exquisite man. There may have been few people at the unveiling, but whoever they were they certainly loved him. And then I remember Yehoash, the poet Solomon Blumgarten, and see in my *Encyclopaedia Judaica* that his Yiddish translation of the Hebrew Bible including *Tehillim*, or Psalms, was a blockbuster publication among Ashkenazi Jews, that he's considered an important modernizer who introduced world literature into the Yiddish language. For a moment I imagine Harelick as a kindred modernizer, a literary translator of sorts, and in thinking that, I begin to grasp something far less fanciful that I missed on my tour.

I check my notes again and, this time, take seriously the seemingly misremembered detail in one source that Harelick's first bookstore was at 228 West Fourth Street downtown. That's where *The Jewish Daily Forward* editorial office was located in the 1940s, in room 328. An office space couldn't have been a retail location, could it? I look up the L.A. city directories in the Library of Congress and realize it has Yellow Pages from the 1940s and '50s that the Los Angeles Public Library didn't archive digitally. And there in the 1949 edition I see Harelick listed for the very first time—at 228 West Fourth Street. So I rerun my directory searches again, and in a 1956 White Pages directory I find a familiar address, but also a little surprise: "4228 Melrose Ave., M. Harelick Books, Yiddish Scientific Institute."

Harelick, it turns out, began his retail business as a neighbor to *The Forward*, which makes sense given that its editors, staffers, advertisers, and visitors were a lucrative customer base. He was also, at the same time or perhaps a little later, an agent for the preeminent Eastern European Jewish research institute of the twentieth century, today known as YIVO, the acronym for its full name, Yidisher Visnshaftlekher Institut. Did he just sell their scholarly titles? Was he associated with them in other ways? No way to tell from the listing, but I realize that in my stubbornness about historical order and knowing where the brick-and-mortar Jewish bookshops stood, I forgot that storefronts are often semi-imaginary. Why wouldn't Harelick have initially run his little Jewish bookstore out of a room near the West Coast office of the country's largest Yiddish newspaper? With enough stock, my garage or even my living room can stand in for a store. Many of the small-time used and specialty book dealers in the city ran their businesses in the dingy little rooms of prewar office buildings too.

My discovery brings home another aspect of the complexity and multiplicity of Harelick's storefront, and of all storefronts; that I have only a tenuous grasp on how readers who were also salespeople or retail clerks in other jobs operated a sideline or briefly made their living in selling Jewish books in L.A. Or acted for a time as representatives for cultural organizations and publishers back East and in Europe because there was money to be made in that as L.A.'s Jewish population rapidly expanded. How many of these "storefronts" did I miss? How many do the directories and histories leave out?

And if I wanted to know how agents of Yiddish culturalism had contributed to the growth of Jewish bookstores in Los Angeles, wouldn't Harelick's westward-moving storefront, devoid of Hebrew on its shop sign, be evidence? Inside, the telltale proof is the absence of ritual goods, Israeli giftware, or other tchotchkes. Harelick does stock a large selection of religious books, especially scholarly editions and hard-to-find classical texts, because of course they're literature and they sell well too. But bar mitzvah supplies, records, kosher wine—no.

Harelick wasn't so much a modernizer as he was a Yiddish *bricoleur*, a cultural improviser, exquisite indeed, his store another kind of L.A. rebuild and add-on. Adapting his personal bookstore to a specialty niche within the Jewish bookselling establishment, and likely familiar with nineteenth- and early twentieth-century Jewish bookstore-publishers in Warsaw, Odessa, or New York who had also curated their stock to reflect their cultural sensibilities, Harelick carried only those sections of the *moykher sforim* store that appealed to his particular aesthetic tastes. That also allowed him to add English-language titles, even about non-Jewish subjects, as long as they were of Jewish *cultural* interest, as determined by Harelick and his understanding of the store's market. Unlike the bookshops on Fairfax that catered to a loyal but limited clientele interested mostly in religious goods, Harelick's *Yiddisher Angeleno* version proved a more adaptable, attractive, and prescient retail model for the time. It was uniquely suited to serving the city's increasingly diversified and literate Jewish customers.

In a way, doesn't this make Jack's store an inheritor of L.A.'s secular Yiddish-speaking world, first established in Boyle Heights over a century ago? After all, it's the combination of Jack's business vision, his Judaic knowledge, and his penchant for order with Harelick's retail innovations and Yiddishist values that cemented the bookstore's significance. A literary outlier among the other Jewish storefronts, Harelick & Roth was a historically and geographically contingent partnership that relocated and remodeled a particular type of modern Jewishness from the Eastside to the Westside of the city. It made possible in Southern California yet another version of the Jewish bookstore.

Excited, I call Jack to share my discoveries.

"Yeah, Harelick probably sold the YIVO journals and books to professors at the University of Judaism," he says. "But Boyle Heights was almost gone by then. There was a Workmen's Circle on Robertson, I remember. Didn't you go to your friend's bar mitzvah there?"

"I'm not saying you yourself are a connection to Boyle Heights," I start arguing. "I'm saying that it's like six degrees of separation, right? Harelick's generation of booksellers, which is what, from the teens and twenties really, Yiddishists with no interest in kiddush cups or Leon Uris, *they* develop new and different types of Jewish bookstores, in Europe and over here, because they're committed to Jewish enlightenment, or radical politics, or literature, or just by chance. You take it to the next level in L.A."

"Uh-huh, maybe. You still have my signed letter from Uris? It's framed very nicely with a sketch of him below the letter."

I feel a familiar heat rise in my stomach.

"Yes, of course. I hung it right below my photos of Harelick. They look good together."

"Very funny. Look, let me ask you something serious. Has Mary cleaned out your basement yet? You know you have to get rid of all that junk. You can't let it collect like that."

And immediately I'm back in the car with him. I want to tell him that it's none of his business, and why is he making this about my wife, Mary? It's a woman's job to clean the damn basement? When will he stop with his mania for throwing away old things?

But I don't say any of this. I'm at the wheel here. It's my basement.

"Dad," I reply in my politest voice, "trust me. I'm working on it." Then we both hang up, and I turn back to my computer.

Greystone Park, New Jersey, 1935, 1940

There are no origins, I learn again, only beginnings, beginnings that have nothing to do with myth or the making of something out of nothing. Beginnings are more prosaic. They're a process, the effort to start over and imagine a different present out of futures past, so in this case you could say that M. Harelick Books began out of need for asylum.

Michael Harelick wasn't a bachelor, it turns out, but he never did have children. He married Flora Sawburg on March 16, 1916, in Chicago. How he met her, what he was doing in Chicago, I haven't a clue. He could have been a traveling salesman by then, though according to the 1910 census he started out in the clothing trade in New York, his occupation listed as "operator" in a "coat shop," just like his older brother Aaron. His younger brother, David, worked in a "pants shop." Michael's father, Gamlice, was a teacher, "private family," so a *melamed* of sorts, either a tutor or what today is called a homeschool teacher, but there's no way to know the specific subjects he taught or the age of his students. Michael, Gamlice, David, and Aaron and Aaron's wife, Rachel, and their three daughters, Hannah, Ida, and Mary, all lived together at 478 Bushwick Avenue in Brooklyn. They'd arrived four years earlier, in 1906, on the RMS *Caronia* of the Cunard Line, just a few of the one and a half million Jews from the Russian Empire, including Michael's wife, Flora, and her parents, who came to America between 1881 and 1914. There's no entry in the census for Gamlice's wife or for Michael's three other older siblings, Max, Abraham, and their only sister, Gutta.

On his World War I draft registration card, filed in September 1918, Michael named Flora as his closest living relative. They lived at 208 Rochester Avenue in Brooklyn, and there he was a salesman for "K & C Popoff Bros." This was a famous Russian tea trading company, its teas distributed throughout Europe and, following the path of Russian Jewish immigrants, in North America, until the war ravaged the tea fields of the Caucasus and the Soviets nationalized all the tea companies.

In 1925, Michael and Flora were listed in the New York state census as still residing in Brooklyn, at 664 Lafayette Avenue, which they shared with one other family, the Municks, also from Russia. The address was, and still is, a handsome brownstone in the Bedford-Stuyvesant (Bed-Stuy) neighborhood across the street from Tompkins Park, with its shady canopy of maples and oaks. Today it's Herbert Von King Park, originally designed by Calvert Vaux and Frederick Law Olmsted, the architects of Central Park. Michael's occupation was recorded as "book salesman," hers as "housework."

I'm getting a picture of his start in the business, even if his employer isn't recorded. He's obviously a good salesman and drawn by disposition (perhaps inculcated by his father) to New York's book trade at the height of its postwar expansion. He and Flora were settled in an all-White block in Bed-Stuy populated with carpenters, plumbers, bookkeepers, cooks, barbers, shoe makers, and even a bank president and physician. When Michael signs his formal oath of allegiance to the United States on July 5, 1927, at the age of forty-three, I'm hard-pressed not to see him by the standards of his time as an immigrant success story, one whose middle-class literary intellectual flavor has a familiar taste.

Then I discover Flora's death certificate. She died suddenly on February 6, 1931, at Kings Park State Hospital, and when I read that I do a double take: How did she end up at a psychiatric hospital out on the north shore of Long Island? Kings Park was built in 1885 to handle the overflow of indigent patients in New York City, and Flora had been a patient there for only one month and nine days. Her primary cause of death was listed as bronchial pneumonia, which took her in four days, but the secondary cause was listed as "dementia praecox." A quick search and I find the translation: it's the late nineteenth-, early twentieth-century term for what today is called schizophrenia.

According to the certificate, she'd been ill with the disorder for two years and one month.

I backtrack and check the 1930 U.S. census. I can't find Michael, but Flora comes right up as a patient at the McFarland Sanitarium in Westport, Connecticut. Unlike Kings Park, this was a private psychiatric hospital founded in 1898 by the physician David W. McFarland for a more well-to-do clientele and, later, for those who could afford better care than what the state system offered. Had Michael run out of money to keep her there as the Great Depression got worse?

There's no telling from these documents, so I move on and check the 1940 census, where I find an "M. Harelick" listed as an inmate at the New Jersey State Hospital in Greystone Park.

What?

I can't find any other Michael Harelick in the census, and he's not recorded as living with his brothers Aaron, Max, or David. Despite the questions I have about the listing (Who is "E. Harelick" on the line above him? Is gender listed correctly for these patients?), the age and birthplace are right, so I assume this must be Michael. Scanning the page, I see under "residence, April 1, 1935" again the word "Greystone," shorthand in the census and across New Jersey for the state's largest public psychiatric hospital at the time. How long, I wonder, had Flora really been ill? In women, schizophrenia usually appears in the late twenties to early thirties. By the end of her life, she was already in her forties. Did Michael have a breakdown after years of trying to take care of her? Or did the decision to move her into Kings Park, where she died so quickly, perhaps undo him?

Whatever the reason, and if I'm correct, Michael spent at least five years, if not more, in Greystone Park. So much for my imagining for him such a pleasant immigrant story. I should have known better. If the tenements, boroughs, business districts, hospitals, and cemeteries were overcrowded, so were the asylums, and not for nothing. The steep personal cost of immigrant life was the essential plot point for two generations of Jewish writers in America: Abraham Cahan, Anzia Yezierska, Henry Roth, and others. Their stories propelled the growth of a Jewish book business, which created both profits and an American Jewish collective memory from all that recollected pain. Which, I realize, was likely the most personal part of Michael's bookstore, for his own trauma must have also shaped his literary tastes. The store really was his safe house and refuge, just as the personal bookstores on the Lower East Side were for the Jewish booksellers at the turn of the twentieth century. Maybe that's another reason why he so disliked Leon Uris's overboiled tales of Jewish woe and triumph. It was his form of activism against what wasn't true to life.

I admit I'm relieved when I find out that by April 1942, when Michael registered for the next war's draft, he was then living at 213 Sip Avenue in Jersey City, the home of his younger brother, David, and his family. Michael's employer was *The Forward*, at its office on 175 East Broadway; David was listed as the "Person who will always know your address."

Family led Michael west for a new start. He had a nephew, his older brother Max's son, who had moved to Los Angeles in 1942. In fact, Abraham (Abe) Horelick, as he spelled the family name, was married there on June 9, 1948, so if Michael hadn't already come out to work at *The Forward*, maybe he timed his arrival for this family occasion. Later, Abe's cousin Shirley Klein would direct me to a photo of Michael and Max on Ancestry.com, where they're posed together on a sidewalk, their backs to the street, across from which is a house with a Spanish tile roof. Was it taken at the wedding? Michael turned sixty-five that October, and by November he was writing to the Dial Press on M. Harelick business stationery (where the word "Books" is printed in both English and Yiddish), asking the publisher to send him "one copy of Dr. Oscar Janowsky's 'Jewish Welfare Board Survey'" and to bill him or send it cash on delivery to room 330 at the West Fourth Street office building, where *The Forward* was next door, in room 328. Did the money to start his business come from savings? From family? No telling.

What's clear is that the beginning of Michael's bookstore, a year earlier than I thought and in a different room, was the second act in his life. It's not an unusual story for his generation, neither the misfortune nor the time in an asylum. Nor the imperative to keep figuring out how to make a living when retirement isn't an option. Beginnings can happen both early and late. It's the mystery of his relationship with Flora that still haunts me, though. What brought them together? What life plans did they share? What secrets did they keep to themselves as they tried to salvage their own welfare? The bookstore owes its existence, I think, not just to Michael but to Flora as well, and to the fifteen years of their unrecoverable intimacy. She had a voice too, although trying to imagine it is like trying to imagine the sound of reading in other people's minds.

"I know what happened," my mother confides to me a few weeks later on one of our Zoom calls during the COVID-19 pandemic. "But I won't tell you, because he leaned over me and made me promise not to tell."

"Are you kidding? Why not?"

"When I make a promise, I don't talk. It stays with me. All I can say is that he knew what he was doing, and he knew how to pull himself up. I liked him very much. He was a wonderful person."

I cradle my head in my hands, my temples pounding like fists on a locked door. Okay, I think, then let's talk about another marriage.

CHAPTER 4

The Second Store (*gender*)

The way Rochelle explains it, her launch of a Harelick & Roth branch location in the San Fernando Valley was an opportunity to grow the store. By the start of the 1970s, it was arguably the leading Jewish bookstore in Los Angeles and fast gaining a regional reputation as a quick and reliable distributor of textbooks and as a nonsectarian retailer for Jewish books of all kinds. Jack was poised to expand our family business because of his increasing revenue, even if there wasn't a lot of spare cash. So was my mother. It was she who lobbied for us to move out of the apartment we rented and into a house of our own, and with Jack's consent she started looking at homes in Beverly Hills and Hancock Park. But word was also spreading that the Valley was the place to go, that you could get a better deal there and that the streets were light on traffic and heavy on open spaces. Soon my brothers and I were spending hours in the car as we went from one open house to another, motoring up and down the hills of North Hollywood, Sherman Oaks, Tarzana, and Encino.

Rochelle found our new home on a quiet block just off Ventura Boulevard. Located about a mile away from Rancho Los Encinos State Historic Park, it was down the street from the Encino Theatre, a one-thousand-seat venue built in 1949 that by the time we showed up in late summer 1970 showed second-run movies and, as my brothers and I soon discovered, soft-porn films. Our home sat on a flag lot, which meant easing our car up a long narrow driveway to reach our $72,000 yellow stucco rancher with brick accents and a green-and-white garage door. Our pool, the developer said, was all that was left of the musician Billy Eckstein's place, torn down to make way for the homes that surrounded us. Rochelle's mother, my Oma, took care of the down payment.

I was excited by our move and of having that pool to myself; no more locker room and crowds at the La Cienega Municipal Swimming Pool, no need to make that long drive to the beach. What else might change, I wondered, or would our new home be more of this: Each year around Easter, one of the television stations in Los Angeles would broadcast *The Wizard of Oz* as a special event, and Rochelle would excitedly gather us around the Zenith in the living room of our apartment on Olympic to watch it as a family. I thought it was my mother's favorite movie. I hated it. More specifically, I hated the Wicked Witch of the West and her loathsome flying monkeys, both of whom reappeared in the nightmares I had for days afterward. Rochelle loved the songs, though, and she happily goaded Al, Ben, and me into full-throated renditions of the chorus from "We're Off to See the Wizard." We'd sing and play-act clicking our heels three times saying, "There's no place like home, there's no place like home, there's no place like home," until it was time to go to sleep. And then, once my brothers and I were tucked into the three twin beds stuffed into our shared bedroom, Rochelle would close the door, and I'd wait for the first slow crescendos of my parents' voices as they rose into that night's argument.

Most of the time their disagreement was about some aspect of the store or with money as it related to the store or something that bothered my mother, whose source originated in my father's always being at the store. It was hard for me to tell, however, since their preferred tongue for argumentation was Yiddish, and like so many American Jews of my generation I was never taught it for fear that I would crack the code of my parents' secret language. Nevertheless, I gleaned a few words and phrases—*fuftsik, tsvey hundert, toyznt, hak mir nit in kop, di kinder, takeh, gey avek, fartik!*—whose disclosure of numbers and heartache hinted at the context and direction of their animus, but not its content.

"Your father didn't want to listen to me," I recall Rochelle explaining on one of our Zoom calls. "He claims he started the business himself, but my mother, your Oma, gave him money for it, and he never paid her back. I was there helping right from the beginning." She tells me that Oma used her only daughter's inheritance, which had already been set aside for Rochelle, for this capital infusion. My grandmother's meticulous budgeting made it evident why Jack trusted her in the beginning to do the store's bookkeeping too.

I already knew about my Oma's "gift," because I have two financial statements from the bookstore, one from December 31, 1974 and another from April 30, 1975. Each shows under "fixed liabilities" a note that Jack owed to Ida Theilheimer, my Oma, for $33,000, the exact amount for which Michael Harelick sold the store, but that Jack told me he paid out in monthly installments to him between 1967 and 1969. I also knew about it because it was repeated early and often in our family. Which is why most of my memories of Jack and Rochelle in the store still vibrate with the metallic, cold anxiety I felt in my stomach whenever my parents were alone together on the sales floor. What are they going to argue about now? Why do they make each other so angry? When will they stop?

As it turned out, living on Noeline Avenue, or Christmas Street as I thought of it, didn't seem to bring any cheer to my parents' marriage or stop them from bickering. And I saw my father even less since he spent more evening hours at the store given his longer commute—and perhaps his desire to avoid yet another high-volume argument about who owed whom what in the business and at home. By the time Rochelle suggested to Jack that she could help grow their operation out of a separate storefront in the Valley, the distance between them emotionally and physically was plainly expanding too.

Nevertheless, Rochelle had the right idea. In the early 1970s close to 30 percent of Los Angeles's Jews lived in the San Fernando Valley, up from only 9 percent in 1950. A number of places like North Hollywood and the strip of Ventura Boulevard between Encino and Tarzana were clearly Jewish neighborhoods with numerous synagogues and Jewish-owned businesses. They may not have looked like Fairfax and Pico-Robertson because of their overwhelmingly Reform and Conservative cast, but according to the sociologist Bruce A. Phillips, they were less outposts of assimilation than "Jewish beachheads in Anglo territory." The only Jewish book retail operation on our side of the Santa Monica Mountains was the House of David in North Hollywood, a modest Judaica shop opened in 1956 by David Goldin to serve Jews living around Coldwater Canyon and Victory Boulevard.

That left our new neighborhood, with its slightly higher income level, wide open for a Jewish bookstore like my father's, and perhaps Rochelle thought that volunteering to lead its expansion into a promising market in the fall of 1973 might be a way to show Jack that despite the continual conflict between them, they were still in the family business together and that she cared about the same things he did.

"You know what?" Rochelle mimics her conversation for me. "I'll open a second store in the Valley and people will come!"

I'm both impressed and skeptical at the large-heartedness my mother is conveying for my edification, as if I were still that quiet and self-absorbed little boy who listened to everything she said and who seemed the least worrisome of her three sons. It's not that she's trying to prove something about her side of the story that nags at me. It's that I hear her claiming the bookstore could have kept our family together, that it was the source of our common purpose as opposed to a font of tension whose constant pressure creaked and pinged throughout our family like an ill-tempered cast-iron radiator.

Go easy, I say to myself, Rochelle's interpretation is what I called her for, so why wouldn't she tell her own tale about the past? She met Jack in 1956 at the Queens Jewish Center, an Orthodox synagogue in Forest Hills, New York, when she was seventeen, he was twenty-three, and everyone said she looked just like Audrey Hepburn. She'd graduated high school in three and a half years and in the spring went to the recently opened Stern College for Women, part of Yeshiva University, but it was too religious for her taste, so she didn't continue. Instead, she married Jack in October 1957 at the Roosevelt Hotel in Manhattan. While Jack was getting his start in Jewish publishing, she worked at a home audio equipment store and then as a secretary for the Jewish National Fund, where she quit rather than join a union she believed was mafia-run. She took a business course at one of the many small for-profit business schools in the city, and after Al was born she did a short stint as a telephone switchboard operator for ABC. Once in L.A., though, Rochelle pitched in at the store. She helped put together the sales catalog, learned from Jack how to check in stock and take care of customers, and because of that business course she'd taken, which included a little computer training, helped program the billing computer that Jack bought from the Friden

Company. She did so well at it that the company offered her a job. She turned it down.

"But I always wanted to go to Israel," Rochelle says. My mother had gone there when she was fifteen to visit her stepbrother and thrilled at seeing the historic sights, meeting its prickly and self-confident Jews, and learning how to strip a Sten gun.

"Even before Jack met Harelick I said we should go, and he told your Opa that I just wanted to travel and waste money. And Papi told me not to go. Still, your father promised me we'd try and live in Israel for a while."

That proved an empty promise after the business took off and profits swelled, tethering Jack to Los Angeles. Also, and for the purposes of my own tale, I think his paternalism and need for control over his collection of both books and family predisposed him to dismiss Rochelle's schemes and assign her a subordinate role in their partnership at home and in the store. This was a major corrosive in their marriage, which was especially brittle by 1973 and would end shortly after the second store closed a year later. I see that subordination, too, as a telling expression of Jack's mid-century understanding of gender and the book business, his perspective on what it meant to be the man in charge, which, in my view, also accounts for his and Rochelle's corporate and domestic schism. My mother had a different take on what it meant to be a partner, which she had learned from her parents and, especially, from the women on my Oma's side of the family. For her it was a promise of mutual support. My father, however, seemed to define partnership in terms derived from a very particular view of gentlemanly bookselling that was integral to his sense of self, his pursuit of success, and his treatment of women in the business. It's a view epitomized by his competition with another bookshop that he was nervous about other than Solomon's Hebrew & English Book Store, which I should tell you about first if I'm going to explain with any persuasiveness my belief that the bookstore may not have been the primary catalyst of their breakup, but it was certainly the accelerant driving them apart.

The Jewish American Book Shop was founded in the late 1930s by Bertha Blatt and was originally known as the Jewish American Library and Palestine Gift Shop, located at 4209 West Third Street in the

Wilshire Center neighborhood. It began operating under the new name starting in 1940, when it moved to 450 South Western Avenue. It was the first Jewish bookstore on Fairfax Avenue, setting up shop at 317 North Fairfax around 1943, two years before Chaya and Elimelech Solomon relocated their bookshop there and five years before another retail émigré from Boyle Heights showed up, Canter's Delicatessen. By 1948 Bertha and her daughter Lucille, who had by then joined the business, moved to 332 North Fairfax, and their boxed boldface listing in the Yellow Pages touted "Texts–Classics–Juveniles–Etc.–Music–Records–Ritual Supplies–Pictures." Their 1953 listing was the first to include "moykher sforim" in Hebrew letters.

Unlike the Solomons and their imitators, whose retail and educational sales focused on a more traditionalist market, the Blatts built a strong trade in textbooks, religious books, and supplies for schools, libraries, and synagogues affiliated with the fast-growing Conservative and Reform movements in Los Angeles. Jack noticed their success even before he moved to L.A. He'd met Lucille (who eventually took over the store after her mother fell ill) at the National Association of Temple Educators and the Western Association of Temple Educators conferences while he was still working for Behrman House in the early sixties, and he knew he would have to push her store out.

"I felt guilty about taking away her business," Jack says to me during one of our interviews, as he wipes down his already immaculate kitchen sink. He sees me uncap a pen and flip open my notebook. "I went to see her in '66 or '67, and I said, 'I don't really want to take your business away.' But she wasn't much of a talker."

"What did you think she'd say? You just told her you were going after her customers."

"She didn't close the Jewish American Book Shop until around 1980, I think. And then I offered her a job. I don't remember how I broached it. I said, 'Why don't you come to work for me, and I'll pay you a salary, more than what you made at your bookstore.' I think it was $40,000 or $50,000 a year."

Elana, who helped manage Jack's finances after their marriage in 1980, verifies that magnanimous offer, equal to around $180,000 a year today. My father folds the morning's newspaper, returning each section to its proper place and order.

"She did the bookkeeping and the banking, did it all by hand. She was honest, diligent, always dependable. Old-fashioned. She didn't like it when customers took advantage of me."

I try to connect the protective woman my father was describing with my own memories. These aren't any more accurate; they're how I saw Lucille when I was young, which is to say they, too, were formed through Jack's eyes. When he first introduced her to me it wasn't as his new employee, but as the owner of the recently closed Jewish American Book Shop, a short, rectangular-shaped middle-aged woman whose mussed-up, bottle-blond hair was anchored by stubborn gray roots. The impression Jack tried to convey at the time was that she was his new business associate. Given Jack's opinion about the "shlock shops" on Fairfax, I was dubious. My most enduring image of her is hunched over a desk in the business alcove of the store on Pico Boulevard, her beige cardigan draped over a white-and-emerald-checked dress. Her square-framed glasses were focused on a mass of papers that she was laboriously working through, and she tapped at a mechanical calculator whose rhythmic shuffle-chunk echoed off the walls. My only recollection of her sales technique is one that could just as well have applied to every salesclerk who worked at the store, which was calling out to my father or coming back to the water cooler while he was hurriedly eating a bag of Fritos and asking him for answers to customer queries.

But my father can't answer a number of questions I still have about Lucille and her bookstore, so instead I scan the Internet and my library's databases in search of a less judgmental portrait. It soon becomes clear that she and her mother were also innovating a Los Angeles style of Jewish bookselling. Fairfax became the Jewish commercial center in the 1940s and 1950s for the same reasons that had fueled the rise of Boyle Heights. Affordable housing attracted young families with growing incomes looking for modern amenities and better opportunities for their children, and then the synagogues, schools, political organizations, cultural and community centers, and Jewish press followed. Like a number of postwar Jewish book retailers on the West Coast, the Blatts realized there was a need for local wholesalers who could provide the products that Jewish educators and religious professionals required without the hassle of dealing with publishers three thousand miles away. While the discounts may not have been as generous, what these customers saved in mailing costs and lack of worry over unexpected returns and slow or frustrating correspondence more than made up for it.

This solution for quickly getting books to customers was yet another instance of what book historians see as a distinctive quirk in the book industry's historical development: figuring out how to distribute books published in the East—and particularly in New York once it became the center of American publishing—to a market that stretched farther and farther west. Only when railway shipping costs became more affordable in the 1920s were booksellers in the country's distant regions better able to compete with wholesale distributors and publishers in the East and Midwest for a larger share of the new book, schoolbook, and school supply markets. After the lean years of the Depression and the Second World War, entrepreneurs like the Blatts, hearing the early rumbles of the baby boom, turned their customers' increasing desire for convenience and speed to their advantage. By the late 1950s, they, the Solomons, and Harelick ran the three most successful Jewish bookstores in Los Angeles.

In other words, the Blatts were considerable competition for Jack, especially since his business starting out was, by his own reckoning, 75 percent textbooks and 25 percent retail. Yet why should the Blatts' bookstore be the only one my father felt guilty about putting out of business? No doubt the Jewish American Book Shop was going to feel the pressure when he started pursuing the same customers and market share. If he succeeded, they'd be in danger of going under. Still, he never talked about any of the other Jewish bookstores that way, and he certainly had no problems competing against the Solomons and the Herskovitz Hebrew Book Store when it came to selling books published for the Orthodox market.

Perhaps, I think now, my father's comment reflected something deeper, something related to his reflexive understanding of the nature and role of a bookman. "He's a real bookman," Jack would say to me after talking with a dealer browsing his rare books, or "Rosenbach was a famous antiquarian bookseller in Philadelphia, a dealer and a real scholar. You don't see bookmen like that anymore." This was the laudatory term he used for those in the business who he believed exemplified the attitudes and attributes of a successful bookseller—and who was, naturally, always a man. It mostly popped up in the course of his comments about the various characters he met through the store, and while it was never the subject of his many lectures to me, I assumed I was supposed to learn something from his use of "bookman."

And I did. I paid attention, for example, when that honorific was attached to the Orthodox publisher Philipp Feldheim, who founded Feldheim Books in 1939 after fleeing Austria for New York, running it out of the bookshop he opened on the Lower East Side, first on Hester Street and then later on East Broadway. My father thought him not only a sharp businessman but also a debonair bibliophile, a survivor from the decimated world of Austrian and German Jewish modern Orthodoxy who effortlessly balanced Torah Judaism with secular knowledge. "He brought a certain kind of elegance to his Orthodoxy," Jack remembered.

On the buying trips to New York that my father made each year after Hanukkah, he always noted the publisher's smart jackets and rich ties, and he was gratified to see his own tastes validated by Feldheim's attire. Invariably, Jack wore one of his suits from Bullocks Wilshire or Saks Fifth Avenue when he visited. One year my father walked in sporting a luxurious blue-gray silk scarf, and Feldheim immediately reached out and fingered it.

"Jack, I'm older than you, I'm in business longer than you, and I never treated myself to a scarf like that."

"Mr. Feldheim," my father replied, thinking quickly and strategically, "I'm happy to give you the scarf!"

Feldheim refused, of course, but Jack was also happy to be complimented in such a backhanded way, feeling at the time that Feldheim wasn't envious, but simply voicing a kind of respect, bookman to bookman, for Jack's ambitious personal style.

My father equally relished Feldheim's ritual of ordering kosher pastries and coffee so they could confer over business in proper Central European style. And then Feldheim would take Jack down to the basement, crowded with books, where he kept the rare used Judaica. These he bought from the aging immigrants who'd arrived earlier in the century, or from their heirs, or through the sale of personal and institutional libraries.

"See this, Jack?" Feldheim said, nodding at the valuable inventory he'd amassed. "You can't just buy. You have to sell!"

Feldheim was a "real" bookman in that he seemed to appear to my father as the very model of the modern, male Jewish book lover, part aesthete and part speculator. He was, altogether, well-balanced in a number of senses—European and American, Orthodox and secular, bookish and worldly. I see him as a pattern, quite appealing to Jack, for how to *do* Jewish bookselling, which is to say a pattern for the performance of a type of Jewish male identity attractive to a young, middle-class American Jewish man like my father, with his yeshiva education and weakness for carriage trade bookstores like Rizzoli. Don't we all look for examples of how to perform our identity? Doing so helps us express who we think we are, or who we want to become.

Judith Butler would call Feldheim's manner a type of "corporeal style," the way we physically present our gender, not just through clothing but also in the way we walk and move. It's a style we learn through observation, one we construct and embody through a myriad of conscious and unconscious behavioral choices that are modeled on what's available or socially acceptable in our time and place. Feldheim's is a male style of mid-century, white-collar Jewish sophistication, and in remembering it so vividly, it's clear my father took their visits to heart. What Feldheim offered my father was not just professional mentoring, but also a kind of gender mentoring. Not that Jack was conscious of that, or Feldheim either. For both, such corporeal training went unseen since it appeared to them as part and parcel of their working life, dispensed and absorbed without a second thought.

Am I overreading "bookman" here? Maybe. Yet take a look at *The Bookman*, a conservative literary journal published in New York between 1895 and 1933. It was founded by the publisher Frank Dodd, of Dodd, Mead and Company, and it's the journal that invented the U.S. best sellers list (the idea for both the journal's title and the list itself were lifted from *The Bookman* in London, launched in 1891). James Montgomery Flagg, the famous illustrator and poster designer, drew the April 1896 cover. It depicts a bearded man who appears to be a newsstand vendor, or perhaps a bookstore clerk, reaching over to a stack of *The Bookman* in order to hand one to the genteel woman standing with her back to the reader. Clearly, she has good taste, which is to say that her taste is legitimized and validated by this bookman and by the bookmen for whom the publication speaks. To be a bookman in this sense is to be a cultural and social broker, a fellow who puts the right things into the right people's hands by sorting both into their respective social standings and commercial categories. Someone who knows exactly what the men and women he caters to supposedly need.

I think my father felt guilty about putting the Jewish American Book Shop out of business because he didn't see Bertha and Lucille Blatt as bookmen in either the American or European-Jewish molds to which he aspired. Yes, they were the sole owners of their store, unlike the women my father knew in the Jewish book trade at the time, all of whom he identified to me as Mrs. Scharfstein, Mrs. Rabinowitz, or Mrs. Solomon, women he regarded as junior partners in their husbands' businesses despite their seeming to run things. The nervous Rose Scharfstein, wife of Zevi Scharfstein, founder of the Shilo Publishing House, was always the only one there whenever Jack made a pickup, and she made him feel nervous too. Remembering the Solomon Rabinowitz Hebrew Bookstore on Canal Street in the Lower East Side, he couldn't recall Mrs. Rabinowitz's first name, "but she was a little dynamo who ran the show twenty-four hours a day." And Chaya Solomon really was the primary operator of Solomon's Hebrew & English Book Store, but by the time my father started to compete with them he thought of her son Philip as the main force and owner.

Jack admired the Blatts' work ethic and their success, no question about it, and he never called Bertha "Mrs. Blatt." But I believe he saw her and Lucille as merchandisers and bookkeepers, not as bibliophiles and taste makers. Because of his background and mentoring, because he was a self-styled bookman who valued professional sophistication and who was meticulous about putting all his things into their correct places, perhaps the Blatts, whose store was no less cluttered than all the other Jewish bookshops on Fairfax, appeared more like innocent bystanders to him rather than real players in the book trade—just two women trying to make a living as best they could in a tough business. From that gendered perspective, they were simply out of place. Subjecting them to the rough-and-tumble of competition was, well, ungentlemanly. Hence his sense of guilt.

Once that was out of the way, however, my father deemed Lucille perfectly suited to the role of support staff. She even brought her own desk from the Jewish American Book Shop. Combing through the books one year, she discovered that Jack was entitled to an alimony deduction on his personal return that his accountant didn't catch, which resulted in a $30,000 refund from the Internal Revenue Service. Jack gave her 10 percent of the refund as a bonus. But the 1980s were his flush years, and it was only a matter of time until he hired a better accountant, incorporated the business, and contracted a payroll service. By 1990 Lucille felt there was nothing for her to do, so she quit. Her brother came and took her desk home.

Lucille and the Jewish American Book Shop swiftly became a footnote in the grand narrative of J. Roth Bookseller—the narrative, that is, that my father established through newspaper interviews and in family legend. My mother refused to go that easily or quietly. Rochelle saw herself as more than just support staff, even if she didn't aim to be a bookman like Jack, and let me tell you, credit will be given, as she's reminding me over the phone, using her patiently aggrieved voice to ask me for the umpteenth time, "So, is this going to be your father's story or are you going to tell the truth?"

When we were still living in the apartment on Olympic and I wanted to escape the din of Jack and Rochelle's squabbling, I would find a book or a magazine or the back of a cereal box and drift off, sometimes into the text in front of me and sometimes into my own thoughts, perfecting a there-but-not-there presence that my parents called "reading," and that as I got older drove my friends crazy.

Had I also absorbed my father's example of such emotional deafness, especially his not listening to the women in his business—my mother, Oma, Lucille Blatt? That would be ironic, because as I'm on the phone with Rochelle and she falls once again into her well-practiced litany of complaints about Jack—his self-centeredness, his dismissal of her, his dependence on Oma's money—an old relay switches on in my brain. I hear myself remark to no one in particular, and in a self-soothingly neutral way, how women have always been part of the Jewish book business, going all the way back to the first printers in the fifteenth century, as Jennifer Breger explains in her entry for the Jewish Women's Archive.

There was Estellina Conat in Mantua, Italy, wife of the printer Abraham Conat, who contributed to the family business by setting and printing Jedaiah ben Abraham Bedersi's book *Behinat Olam* in 1477. The daughters of the converso printer Juan de Lucena were similar partners and helpers in their father's business in the 1470s and 1480s. All of them were eventually accused by the Spanish Inquisition of illegally printing Hebrew books, although it's unclear what happened to them as a result. Over in Constantinople in the late 1500s, there was Doña Reyna Mendes, unusual for both that time and place in that she owned her own Hebrew press, which was also the only printing press in the city according to Breger.

"Look, it was your father's store, I give him that. He made it a success. I'm just saying . . ."

. . . That in the seventeenth, eighteenth, and nineteenth centuries, when Jewish printers relocated to Amsterdam and then to Eastern Europe, more Jewish women became owners, either as heirs to a family heritage or through inheritance after their husbands' death, which I learned from Zeev Gries's *The Book in the Jewish World, 1700–1900*. Yehudit Rosanis was the granddaughter, wife, and cousin of printers. After her husband died, she moved in the 1780s to Lviv, now part of western Ukraine, and ran her family press there until her death in 1805. But in the 1830s and 1840s she had a notorious second life as the fictitious publisher of a number of Hasidic and Yiddish books. Their real printers used her name and press to help them evade the Austro-Hungarian and Russian censors and government duties charged on new books.

"It wasn't right what he did, it wasn't right, but I thought . . ."

. . . The most famous widow was Devorah Romm, who took over her family's celebrated press in Vilna, Lithuania, after her husband's death in 1860. Founded in 1799, the Romm press, as Gries documents, reached its peak under her guidance when in 1867 she hired Samuel Shraga Feigensohn as managing director to modernize the firm's operations and printing technology. Between 1880 and 1886 they published the scrupulously edited Vilna Shas, the Vilna edition of the Babylonian Talmud, which established the model for most subsequent modern editions of the Talmud.

And then, as my mother dives into the details of her own family history (if I'm going to write all this down, she figures, I might as well know that truth too), I remember Hagit Cohen's story in *At the*

Bookseller's Shop about the less well-known widow of Avraham Zuckerman, owner of a small bookstore in Warsaw. Predictably, her first name is lost; Cohen says she signed it with just the letter aleph, perhaps for *almanah*, "widow." She survives now in Jewish book history for waging, along with her sons, a bitter fight at the beginning of the twentieth century against a major Jewish publishing house that opened a competing retail outlet right in their neighborhood. I then wonder what these snippets I've gathered from history books and online articles say about the role of Jewish women in publishing and bookselling, or in modern commerce altogether. Are they just a reflection of the growing number of entrepreneurial Jewish women claiming a place in Europe's fitful march toward liberalization? How do they complicate the popular but also problematic stereotype about Ashkenazi men and women that I grew up with, that husbands were expected to study Torah and wives to support the family through various mercantile or retail ventures?

Maybe the bigger picture here, one that encompasses both of those questions, is best framed by an insight about Ashkenazi Jews and European commerce that Hasia R. Diner offers in *Doing Business in America: A Jewish History*. She explains that Jewish involvement in trade from the Middle Ages through the nineteenth century wasn't only about discrimination—about Jews being shut out of some businesses and shunted into others such as moneylending. It was also liberating, freeing Jews from the unpredictability of agriculture and "from a commitment to any land," and despite regular cycles of oppression and expulsion, trade was a steadying economic and social force that European rulers often protected, and so offered Jews "some modicum of security to an otherwise insecure existence." Trade, in other words, was a way to achieve agency and power, so why wouldn't Jewish women also appreciate commerce as liberatory. It was a means by which they could achieve a measure of control over their own destiny, whether because as widows they had that opportunity or because trade was the only available route to any kind of independence, no matter how cramped, within cultures and political systems inimical to women's equality. Through the book business, then, Jewish women could aspire to be partners or managing directors, not just in commerce but also in the development of Jewish literary activity and intellectual life.

Yet as Diner also points out, trade promoted intra-Jewish competition and rivalry within the limited types of business in which Jews were allowed to engage, leading to class conflict and professional jealousies. Couldn't this sort of stress also account for my parents' disharmony at work and at home? Being in business together as a consequence of marriage is always a complex dance between husband and wife especially given the "consensual subordination" of women in liberal Western marriage, evidence of the continuing sway of traditional gender roles, says Laura Levitt in *Jews and Feminism*, and of the "asymmetries of power that continue to define liberal marriage" even today. And that stereotype of Ashkenazi family roles? It may be a vexed ideal, but it does acknowledge a long history of Jewish women's need and desire to work (marginalized and impoverished women don't really have a choice), but what happens if partnership stokes competition and conflict instead of cooperation? Which is why I'm talking with Rochelle, sort of. I want to know not just her side of things, but also how she learned about the social and cultural power of working a business and what being a good Jewish partner means.

My great-grandmother's family, the Tydors, lived in Bochnia, western Galicia, in what is today southern Poland, just southeast of Krakow. Galicia was a province of the Austro-Hungarian Empire and generally encompassed the region between Krakow in the west and Lviv in the east, the city where Yehudit Rosanis had her press. A cousin's book on the Tydors and her father's experiences during the Holocaust helps me flesh out the family's history. Like many Galician Jews, the Tydors were religiously Orthodox and followed Hasidic customs and liturgy, in their case maintaining a connection with the Sanzer and Bobover sects. My great-great-grandfather, Menachem-Mendel Tydor, really did devote himself to study, but here's the lucky twist for him: his wife, my great-great-grandmother Mecha Scharf Tydor, won a lottery shortly before her wedding (in those days lotteries were a convenient way for local, provincial, and state governments to raise money). Now a relatively wealthy bride, Mecha retained control over the winnings and became a sharp young businesswoman, using the money to set up a grocery and purchase a large house in the center of Bochnia. It also enabled her to matchmake her children into a higher social class, and so my great-grandmother Chaya was married to Aaron Tennenbaum, the scion of a wealthy merchant and landowning family from Tyczyn in eastern Galicia.

The First World War, which turned Galicia into a battlefield, upended Aaron's fortunes, and at some point—either during the war while escaping the Russians or after it as refugees—he and his new family, a son and three daughters, moved to Munich. Both my mother and cousin proudly relate that Chaya inherited her mother's entrepreneurialism and that it was she who'd gone to Munich first, peddling sewing notions and supplies to the women in Munich's surrounding countryside and using the money to bring her family over. She opened a store specializing in bedding and textiles. Thus, once again, a maternal forebear's economic successes helped steer the family into different and better social circles. In 1920 my grandmother Ida—Chaya and Aaron's youngest child, a petite brunette described by all as vivacious and beautiful—married her first husband, a diamond merchant named Herman Erteschek.

"He was an SOB," Rochelle says, lowering her voice on the phone. "She wanted a divorce, but he wouldn't give her the papers for ten years. He was in Switzerland during the war. Oma got money from him afterward. He asked to meet her in a synagogue on the Lower East Side, and he gave her $500,000. Half went to your Uncle Bernie"—that's Ida and Herman's son, my mother's half brother—"and the other half she invested in Manhattan real estate, and whatever profits she made went into CDs that provided for her and your Opa until they died."

It strikes me that Rochelle is telling a story about how my Oma divorced a controlling husband, but I let that slide. We're both more impressed by Ida's smart investments, which she made as a legal partner in the Theileast investment company that she started with her second husband, Paul Theilheimer, and her strategizing for their shared economic benefit just as her mother and grandmother had done for their husbands and families. That must have been a powerful example for my mother of a wife's role and how partnership was supposed to work.

I note as well how that $500,000 payment, equivalent to around $6 million currently, conveys the class difference that existed between my mother's family and my father's. Whereas Jack's memories of shopping for books on the Lower East Side evoked for him a Jewish bazaar that he wanted to leave behind, Rochelle's memories bring back an example of Jewish resiliency that we both want to hold on to. Her hushed delivery recalls for me the inviting old black-and-white photographs of my always impeccably dressed grandparents seated together on a European park bench, or posing with friends around an anonymous restaurant table, my grandfather a stocky man with closely cropped gray hair and tortoiseshell glasses and partial to light-colored three-piece wool suits and my grandmother in black satin or dark wool cocktail dresses. They complement each other in both dress and demeanor, and like Mr. Feldheim, they too exude a bygone Central European Jewish elegance. As I puzzle over that connection and its import for Jack's attraction to Rochelle, I suddenly recollect sitting next to Oma in synagogue on the High Holidays, the balsamic smell of her perfume mixing with my prayer book's papery scent; of dancing with her like a proper little gentleman, captured in one of the few photos of me at Al's bar mitzvah; of the heartbreaking disappointment on her face when she caught me sneaking back into the house late one Friday night after I'd gone AWOL on the Sabbath to photograph a high school football game for the school newspaper. "Ach, this is not like a Jewish boy," which is to say a boy who puts religion and family first.

"Are you listening?"

I am now because my mother is finally on to my Opa, Paul Theilheimer, Ida's second husband, who was born in Hamburg and plied the exotic wood trade for the Woerman shipping company in pre-1914 German East Africa, where he also fought during the First World War and was captured by the French, who screwed his thumb flat to squeeze information out of him, but he somehow managed to steal documents and escape the POW camp. Here I begin to sense the onrushing and inevitable impact that the Holocaust will have on Rochelle's understanding of partnership. When Paul's first wife died sometime in the early thirties, he presciently packed his teenage son and daughter off to live with family in Palestine, not exactly willing participants in the Fifth Aliyah, that mass immigration of middle-class European Jews exiting before the storm. He left Germany himself in 1935, later meeting my grandmother in Antwerp, where she had stopped to visit relatives as she made her own way out of Germany. They married in October 1937, and a few months after their wedding they sailed to

Tel Aviv, but he hated the weather, so after my mother's birth in 1938 he scrambled to get the three of them into the United States, and in 1939 they ended up in York, Pennsylvania, where this former technical director of a plywood factory and engineering consultant for the German timber industry labored in a warehouse during the Second World War.

"We left York after the war and went to Europe," my mother continues. In England they reunited with Aaron, Chaya, and Ida's two sisters and their families, who got out just in time too, thanks to their business and social connections. "I remember the destruction in London and Holland. Your Opa and Oma left me in Switzerland while they went into Germany to see if anyone survived. There was no one—Opa's older sister was killed in a concentration camp, and you already know Oma's brother, Dovid, and all his family, three little girls, were gone, finished, we never found out how. Oma and me and your Uncle Bernie went to New York afterward and stayed in a hotel in Jamaica, Queens, but Opa stayed for a little longer. Then Oma bought our house in Forest Hills, paying cash, but when Opa came home he changed it to a mortgage."

I wonder what Oma thought of that. Did they argue about money like my parents did? Listening to my mother's narrative, I wonder too at my grandmother's forbearance and find myself speculating that perhaps Rochelle's offer to open a second store reflected a similar tolerance and restraint, a willingness to keep the family business going despite the increasing emotional cost. It seems to me that my grandparents' Holocaust experience deepened Rochelle's belief in the importance and efficacy of mutual support between spouses. When their family's stability or safety was threatened, the Tydor-Tennenbaum women went to work; it was a sign of their love and care.

"But we weren't Holocaust refugees or survivors," Rochelle insists. "My parents were immigrants."

"What? You don't think having to leave Germany because of Hitler makes them refugees? That it didn't have an effect on them?"

"No, Laurence, you don't understand. They left before anything happened, and to claim to be a survivor? What kind of thinking is that?"

Rochelle can't see her mother as a victim, doesn't dwell on Ida's loss and anger, scrimping and searching. For her the heroic story is Ida and Paul's struggle to recover their wealth and to raise a new daughter amid it all, a reprise of Chaya and Aaron's story. She won't acknowledge the abject parts of their tale or consider the conflicts that their working together might have generated, won't give up on her optimism that if a husband and wife pull together with enough force—whether in Galicia, Germany, Palestine, Pennsylvania, or Encino—they can make their business, their relationship, and their family whole again. Later, Rochelle emails me two photos of Paul and Ida from sometime in the 1950s, showing my grandfather as he first reaches toward and then kisses my grandmother on the cheek. Although Ida is smiling in the second picture, in both photos her right leg is crossed away from him and she has her arms folded like a shield in front of her chest.

"They loved each other very much," Rochelle writes. "How beautiful."

That was my mother's education about the meaning of partnership. My father's took an entirely different tack, one markedly more individualistic in both ethos and practice. Harelick, after all, was really a partner in signage only, a kind of fiction necessary to make the most of the old Yiddishist's retail reputation and existing customer base. A partner in that sense is a means to an end. And despite the two names, the business was still a personal bookstore, Jack's bookstore, so he was the only partner that counted in Harelick & Roth. A partner, but not a partner. I find that a resonant formulation for Jack's domestic arrangements too, but of course I'm biased. And then there was his continuing mentorship by other bookmen that fostered a metaphoric partnership of men, colleagues all, who recognized each other as professional equals and who looked out for each other because it was both enjoyable and lucrative. Jack considered Louis Epstein and Jake Zeitlin, two famous L.A. booksellers, as such partners. They were his West Coast mentors, yet I don't remember meeting either of them, maybe because I was only a boy when Jack learned the ins and outs of L.A. book retailing from them in the late sixties and on through the seventies. They, too, straddled the secular and Jewish book worlds, though each in his own way, and they offered Jack two additional models of how to be a true bookman.

Zeitlin was at first the more familiar name to me, since on our way home from a visit to Hollywood or from a drive on Sunset Boulevard we'd occasionally pass his three-story Pennsylvania Dutch barn, covered in red board-and-batten siding with white-trimmed windows, at La Cienega Boulevard just north of Melrose Avenue. As another of the geographically misplaced buildings that fascinated me, I wondered as we drove by how a farmyard barn could also be a bookstore and how to pronounce the name on its outside, Zeitlin & Ver Brugge. Jack says Zeitlin heard about him from other booksellers, heard that the new Jewish bookseller from New York spoke Yiddish and knew his way around old Jewish books, a real asset for L.A.'s premier used and rare bookseller, who made his reputation by combing through the city looking for choice finds whose value the other dealers couldn't recognize.

By the time my father showed up, this sort of hunting and gathering was second nature to Zeitlin. He'd arrived back in 1925, a twenty-three-year-old aspiring poet from Fort Worth, Texas, where his father, an observant Jew, owned a vinegar company. Zeitlin started out as a retail clerk at Robert Holmes's bookstore and in the book departments at Bullocks and the May Company, and he was briefly a traveling salesman for Ernest Dawson's rare book business. The historian Kevin Starr says he was a natural literary entrepreneur who helped bring together a burgeoning art and literary scene in the twenties and thirties, a group of journalists, printers, architects, professors, and artists who contributed to or supported the short-lived literary magazine *Opinion* and Zeitlin's first bookstore and art gallery, which customers called "At the Sign of the Grasshopper" because of its distinctive shop sign. He founded the Primavera Press in 1933, imported fine press books, and did very well supplying the film studios with books for their considerable reference libraries. In 1942 he incorporated his business with his third wife, Josephine Ver Brugge, as Zeitlin & Ver Brugge, moving into the red barn in 1948.

"Always check the file cabinets," he advised Jack on one of their sweeps through an estate sale. If Zeitlin came across a Yiddish book, he'd call Jack, who'd help him determine its worth. What did my father get in return? I think it was the same as with Mr. Feldheim: validation of his taste for and knowledge of the right sorts of books, and a feeling of having been accepted into a fraternity of the similarly gifted. Also, the chance to hobnob with literary royalty.

Louis Epstein, on the other hand, Jack thought of as both a mentor and a friend. Founder of the legendary Pickwick Bookshop, Epstein emigrated with his family to the United States from Russia in 1909 when he was eight. They relocated to L.A. in 1923, hoping that the climate would help cure Epstein's tubercular brother and sister, while he studied law. But he quickly saw that the city's book trade revolved around used books, driven by the ebb and flow of its peripatetic inhabitants, so in 1924 he opened a bookstore in Long Beach and shrewdly snapped up books from unclaimed storage. Epstein soon moved his business to Booksellers Row in downtown L.A., which in the twenties was on Sixth Street.

Like Zeitlin, he stayed afloat during the Depression by serving the film studios. He did so well that in 1938 he bought a building out on Hollywood Boulevard and opened Pickwick. There one might bump into F. Scott Fitzgerald, Orson Welles, Raymond Chandler, Marlene Dietrich, William Faulkner, Charlie Chaplin, Lauren Bacall, or Aldous Huxley. Epstein not only understood the importance of attracting a glamorous clientele, but after the war he also realized that many of his customers now had the income to afford new hardcover books, while those on a budget would see paperback books as a convenient bargain. In Starr's opinion, Epstein was especially gifted at identifying his customers' needs and intuiting exactly how to move particular kinds of books. He became a kingpin of postwar bookselling in Los Angeles and eventually president of the American Booksellers Association. By 1970, when Dayton Hudson bought him out in order to add Pickwick to its B. Dalton chain, Epstein had sixteen branch stores across Southern California.

Epstein was a garrulous fellow, another nattily dressed bookseller that Jack couldn't resist, whose pompadoured gray hair was complemented by fashionable horn-rimmed glasses framing his mustachioed, square-jawed face. He took a shine to Jack, inviting him to lunch at Musso & Frank Grill for regular get-togethers, where they'd talk books and gossip. Epstein gave him crucial background about both general and Jewish bookselling in L.A., since he had also helped supply Temple Israel of Hollywood's religious school as well as a few other synagogues in the area. If Jack had a Ben Shahn Haggadah, he'd call Epstein and ask what he thought it was worth.

"I was the only sophisticated Jewish bookseller," Jack says to me, explaining his friendship with Epstein as a kind of proof text for his own right placement at the top of the L.A. Jewish book scene. And it's true, there he was on page 17 of the April 6, 1981, issue of the *Los Angeles Jewish Journal*, his photo lined up alongside those of Epstein, Zeitlin, the *Los Angeles Times* columnist Jack Smith, and writer/historian John Weaver, all five men perched above an article publicizing a bookseller's retrospective at the Jewish Community Building celebrating the bicentennial of L.A.'s founding in 1781. Only in the fourth paragraph do we learn that the panel will also feature "representatives from the Solomon's Hebrew and English Bookstore and the now-closed Jewish American Bookshop [*sic*]."

Yet Epstein's approval was a more complex affair. Reading the transcript of Epstein's 1977 interview for the UCLA Oral History Program, I see that he also praises the Solomons' store—his family was friends with their family when they all lived in Boyle Heights—and that he especially admired Bertha Blatt's store. What might have set my father apart from those two in Epstein's mind was that Jack had bought Harelick's shop, one that Epstein believed was on "a much different plane" than any of the other Jewish bookstores. Harelick "had a broader knowledge of Jewish books, of Jewish content, rather than strictly as Solomon's were [*sic*] textbooks for Jewish schools," Epstein says. "Solomon was the expert on the Hebrew. Harelick became quite expert, and quite a fine bookman for Jewish religious books. And he was a very fine person."

There's the operative word again. I can almost predict the kind of language that will follow when Epstein recalls advising Harelick to resist giving discounts to every customer who asked for one, telling him, "You've got to teach the people to respect you, because you are providing a service that they can't get anywhere else in the city." Like the Blatts, Harelick was saving them from paying postage and from the inconvenience of dealing with the New York publishers, which in turn gave him real leverage over his retail pricing. Noting that my father had taken over Harelick's business, Epstein commends Jack for "doing an excellent job." In his calculus, Jack qualified as a real bookman not just for his commercial sophistication, but also because he commanded the right kind of commercial respect. He was a tough guy, but fair, just like Epstein.

Zeitlin and Epstein thus taught my father a type of collegiality that valued male partnership in its social sense as a professional resource and support system. It was predicated on men consulting, approving, mentoring, and befriending other men who shared the same urbane, bookish values and astute business skills, and who recognized in each other a similar corporeal style. It appealed to Jack's individualism because by helping other men he helped himself, and without the messy emotional and financial side effects that went hand in hand with officially pledged partnerships. How could my mother compete with that? Their rivalry over the store wasn't for ownership but rather for recognition, and the hurt each endured in not being acclaimed for what they believed was their due must have exacted a cost on the sales floor and in the bedroom.

"You know, things between a man and a woman . . . ," my mother tries to explain. She's hinted a few times over the course of our conversation that they had issues with intimacy. I don't ask for details, but I begin to see a pattern where intimacy is both a problem and a potential solution. "To try and fix the marriage I said, again, we should go to Israel, just me and him, but he backed out and I went with Aunt Geula instead."

So they tried opening a second store. Jack and Rochelle found a modest retail space at 4847 Paso Robles Avenue, a little side street north of Ventura and just west of Balboa Boulevard. The rent was low and, consequently, so were the stakes of their experiment. Rochelle remembers that the store did pretty well. Customers started coming in to browse and shop or would order books from her that Jack would deliver, usually during the day, but sometimes he'd bring them home in the evenings, where she'd prepare them for pickup at her store in the morning. Occasionally on a Sunday I'd keep her company, wandering around the small sales floor and thinking that the few dark wood tables and wire bookracks made the place seem like a mini version of the store in the city. Rochelle seemed happy to have a shop of her own.

Jack remembers that the store only did okay, and even if it made their working together more feasible, it was still an extra expense he wasn't sure would pan out. He placed two ads in the *Los Angeles Times* in November 1973, both the same, informing the public: "Our Valley store will be open on Sunday Dec. 2, 9, & 16 from 12 P.M. to 5 P.M. for your Chanukah shopping." Maybe he could maximize his holiday business.

And then sometime in December the box appeared in front of the shop door. It must have been a weekday and just another mild, sunny L.A. morning as Rochelle pulled up to the curb in her black four-door Lincoln Continental. It was the Wednesday Continental, the one she'd specially ordered from the dealer, insisting that it had to have come off the assembly line on a Wednesday, when the workers would, according to her labor calculations, be at the peak of their attention to quality and safety.

Rochelle slid out from behind the wheel and approached the storefront. Since Jack took care of delivering and picking up books, a square, book-sized cardboard box addressed to her but without a publisher's name on it immediately struck her as highly suspicious. When she picked it up, she thought she heard a metal-like rattle, so she quickly but gently put it down again. It was, after all, only a month and a half since the end of the Yom Kippur War, that disastrous surprise, when my mother had anxiously waited by the phone hoping to hear from her stepbrother and his family, and all the while watching television news reports about the mounting Israeli losses. Sure, we were nine thousand miles away, but Los Angeles had seen its share of antisemitic incidents in the past, enough that Rochelle felt justified in regularly advising my brothers and me on what to do should the Nazis come looking for us in Encino, which may have been a Jewish beachhead, but that didn't stop her from warily noting to us that there were still a lot of WASP-like locals she didn't trust who'd come out to the Valley in the 1940s and '50s to enjoy the horse farms and their distance from all those unwelcome newcomers flooding into the city.

And so in an instant her highly calibrated danger radar—a product of her upbringing and of her childhood in southern Pennsylvania, where one of her first vivid memories was of a neighbor boy smacking her head against a picket fence and calling her a dirty Jew—flicked on and sent a screeching warning signal down her spine. The box could only be one thing: a bomb.

The story gets a little muddled here because, knowing my mother, wouldn't she call the police first and stay out of the store? In the version that's stuck in my mind, though, she calls the fire department and waits inside. An engine arrives and the firefighters gather around the box, some already removing their jackets and helmets under the warming L.A. winter sun.

Rochelle can't see the box now, only hear the firefighters' voices through the plate glass of the door, but it's clear that someone's already carefully opening it, and soon she hears a smatter of laughs that gets louder and louder as the men seem to pass something around. Finally, one looks in through the door and, pulling himself together, comes in and shows Rochelle the source of that ominous clinking in the box. At first she thinks it's a baby's sock with a Santa Claus head where someone's tiny toes should go, a little metal bell sewed to the top of Santa's hat. But the extra ball of material attached to it makes no sense until the smiling firefighter explains that, ma'am, it's a penis warmer. It's a Santa penis warmer. For Christmas.

How did I hear the story this way? Was it the heated subject of another too-loud argument that evening whose details drifted through the walls of our rancher, or did Al explain it to me later? No matter. Here's the pattern in bold relief, my mother trying to fix their lack of intimacy through a second store that would reunify her and Jack in business and in bed, my father trying to address their problem with a problematically erotic solution. How could he have thought that his gift, not of lingerie or even perfume but of a phallic costume that just begs to be interpreted as a gift of his virility and dominance, would produce any kind of desire in my mother. And why Santa Claus? What kind of Jewish man sends that?

The kind, I suppose, that finally relents and goes to Israel with my mother in the summer of 1974, taking my younger brother, Ben, and me along with them because, they said, this was also my official post bar mitzvah pilgrimage there. Al stayed at home with Oma, since he and she had gone to Switzerland and Israel after his bar mitzvah two years before. We stayed for two weeks in an apartment in Bat Yam, a hardscrabble neighborhood of Middle Eastern Jewish immigrants south of Tel Aviv, where between tours to Jerusalem and Masada, Haifa and the just-cooled battlefields of the Golan Heights, my mother would regularly urge Ben and me to go downstairs for a couple of hours and play with the Israeli kids hanging out in a crowd on the street. Now I know why.

Whatever their hopes were, it didn't work. Before the Jewish High Holidays my father closed the second store, claiming that it was losing money, and in the December 31, 1974 financial statement he reported that the year's expenses for the Encino store were $5,200.56, which amounts to around $33,000 dollars in 2025. In any event, not long after, Rochelle had divorce papers delivered to him. By the beginning of 1975, my first and most influential example of Jewish male corporeal style was living back in the city along with his meticulously arranged closet full of suits and his secret stash of *Cheri* men's magazines.

That's how I came to understand what it meant to be a real bookman. It's how I learned to recognize and imitate a type of gendered cultural authority, which was never as universally respected as my father believed. Even now, knowing better, I realize that I still dress with just as much attention to self-control and projecting clout as Jack did, that I perform the same little rituals of admiration and approval when I encounter like-minded men. That I still expect from these men the same sort of honorable agreements about our professional and social relations that my father banked on with Mr. Feldheim. Like my father, I always expect too much.

Yet the price of my father's idea of a bookman was the loss of that second store. It was the loss not just of my mother's partnership, but also of a historical kind of partnership that helped define Jewish family business in the twentieth century. And what's a family business if the family falls apart? By closing the store, my father had also closed the book on our edition of the Tydor-Tennenbaum business model, a powerful engine of family success for nearly a hundred years. It's not that such husband-and-wife partnerships disappeared in America. Rather, my father at the time saw that type of partnership as unnecessary and himself as an independent modern bookseller, a true bookman disdainful of the cheap merchandising and domestic squabbling of those mom-and-pop stores on the Lower East Side and over on Fairfax.

What my father didn't see was that the second store was modern too, but in another sense. It brought my parents' loss of intimacy into the open in a way that reflected the gender conflicts of their time and place. For about a year in the 1970s, they were together yet apart in shops, both under the Harelick & Roth Booksellers sign, where each seemed to struggle with the emotional distance generated by their attempts to be partners, as they understood that term, and to conduct a normal marriage. Which for their generation of acculturated suburban Jews meant a straight, White, middle-class American marriage. The very notion of a "branch" or "satellite" store, in fact, materialized a common problem with that kind of marriage. My mother's attempt to be a visible partner in my father's life and business instead made painfully obvious her junior status as a wife as well as the sort of pleasure my father expected to collect as his dividend for being such a profitable husband.

In other words, my parents' relationship was shaped by the dominant heterosexual values and attitudes of mid-century America, which proved dissatisfying to both, although for different reasons. My mother yearned for the sort of mutual support and respect that defined her view of a traditional Jewish family and reflected the mood of the contemporary women's movement; my father yearned for something a bit more kinky. His Christmas gift to my mother dressed up a myth about modern secular love that he'd learned through the erotica section of his bookman's world: that pornography expresses and eroticizes the kind of courtship women ought to want.

And all that sticky family business, it's never really private anyway. It seeps into the public eye through the sorts of goods that get delivered to bookstores and, as queer theorists Lauren Berlant and Michael Warner observe, through society's continuing arguments about the meaning of "partnership." That the heterosexual family is asserted in the United States to be the fundamental unit of social, political, and economic activity, they argue, makes some forms of partnering seem righter than others, makes the very idea of "couple" appear natural and beyond remark. It trained me to see only in twos: father or mother, husband or wife, owner or clerk, modern or outdated, controlling or controlled, right or wrong, man or mouse.

These were my choices in the winter of 1975. The divorce proceedings stretched over weeks and then months as my parents continued to argue even over their arguing. Lines were drawn and allies enlisted. I remember my father telling me that Louis Epstein was a witness during a later phase, when the judge was trying to determine alimony and what Jack could afford to pay.

"He was good at being on my side," he recalled.

Having to be on a side was something my brothers and I were quickly learning. Yet what if I didn't want to be on anyone's side? What if I didn't want to be a bookman, or what if I couldn't be the Jewish boy my Oma wanted me to be, her little well-dressed dance partner with an embroidered Swiss kippah and a look of worried concentration on his face? What if I didn't want to make a choice?

And yet I did.

Jack posing in front of the Pico Boulevard store just before the celebration began for its grand opening in June 1979. Factor's Deli is visible in the show window's reflection.

Jack, in the center of the photo, surrounded by the grand opening crowd at its height. The man wearing a kippah and vest is Avrum Schwartz, cantor at Congregation Beth Kodesh in Canoga Park and Jack's longtime employee and resident intellectual. My cousin Lynn Roth is on the phone, and standing next to her with his hands on Jack's desk is our uncle Cantor Jacob Konigsberg.

Michael Harelick standing in front of his show window.

The storefront of the La Cienega Boulevard store in August 1969. The M. Harelick Books light box sign is still up, but Jack has expanded Harelick & Roth, as he renamed the store, into the renovated space of the old beauty shop next door. Boxes of books are visible through that shop window and its entrance. To the right is the short driveway that made a dogleg between the two halves of the corner property.

Rochelle Roth and her three sons (from left to right), Benjamin, Laurence, and Alan, circa late 1970s.

Dancing with my Oma, Ida Theilheimer, at Al's bar mitzvah, August 1971.

Jack and Ben helping customers at the sales counter during the grand opening. Behind them are the sections for Hebrew grammar, dictionaries, and miscellaneous Hebraica, one of the passages back to the shipping area, the staircase to the small loft where Jack kept a limited selection of collectible paintings and silver items, and Jack's desk, behind which is the rare and fine bookcase.

Looking down at the sales floor from the small loft. To the left is the northern end of the long eastern wall, the gift, cookbook, and new book tables, and the paperback displays. In the center are the paperback wire racks, the sales counter, and Jack's desk. To the right are the children's books and the Hebrew grammar and dictionaries section.

A photo of my great-great grandfather Dovid Roth hung on the support column at the far end of the new book table in the Pico store. He functioned as a kind of store greeter, wielding a Jewish gaze that welcomed but also sized up everyone who came in. A double pile of Robert Slater's *Great Jews in Sports* is neatly stacked at the near side of the table, facing the entrance.

The main store sign, made by Josef Pelzig, fastened onto the red brick of the new Olympic Boulevard location. Its background had been switched to blue gray and its gold letters repainted silver. The yellow caution tape in front of the entrance was to keep customers from stepping onto broken Spanish roof tiles that had fallen off the facade during the Northridge earthquake on January 17, 1994.

Jack standing in front of the blue-gray plastic laminate sales counter at the Olympic store. Above him are Yehuda Lavi's decorative wooden beams. Just visible at the left rear is the very end of the long white greeting card display rack, next to which is the glass window of the fine art room, and straight back is the passageway to the shipping room, where the back door to the alley behind the building is open. At the right rear the refinished wood bookcases from the Pico store line the long wall on that side of the store.

Jack, wearing his black polyester velvet yarmulke, packing boxes in the shipping room of the Olympic store in the winter of 1994. Note the Ingram boxes and how empty the top shelf looks.

CHAPTER 5

The Sales Floor (*collection*)

My brother Ben talks to me over Zoom and tells me I'm Jack's favorite, so of course I'm going to defend our father rather than holding him to account. Time to air this out. Ben was right when he accused me of never calling him, that I didn't keep in touch. I heard the anger in his voice, and I didn't blame him. Even if he did live nine thousand miles away, that's no reason for treating him like an afterthought, like some distant relative that I have to shame myself into calling on the holidays simply because it's the right thing to do. But Jack's starting to forget a lot these days; it's the natural course of his dementia, although he's lucid enough to realize that it's important to make peace with each of us before it's too late. I know Ben thinks I'm just making excuses for him, that once again I'm on his side. That he treated me better than Ben and Al because I was the one who did what he said, the one who was most like him. Yet I know what it's like to be angry at him too, feeling trapped in his collection like the miniature books he later kept in their own miniature bookcase and hung on a wall in his foyer, an artful exhibit. I didn't know how to get out, or if I even wanted to. Ben said Jack kicked him out when he needed him the most.

Was I his favorite? Am I really like him? I keep going over those two questions, worrying my own memories and puzzling over my place in the family story. When I asked Ben to forgive our father for not taking care of his youngest son when he got ill and was hearing voices, I knew well enough to admit that I needed to ask for Ben's forgiveness too. If he thinks that I'm Jack's enabler, then I need to be honest about why I didn't do more to speak up for him and why I didn't want to upend my father's order of things, even though it was clearly unraveling in front of us. I need to explain myself.

It's difficult to do that without sounding defensive or smug, yet it ought to be easier than this to write about my brother. We shared a bedroom for sixteen years, me with my model airplanes, track-and-field awards, transistor radio, and poster of an Israeli tank on the wall, Ben with his . . . what *did* he have in his half of the room? It's funny, I can't remember any of his things. It shouldn't be that way. We had some real adventures together, like that time back on Olympic when Ben and I walked over to his friend's house on Whitworth Avenue. He had a pool, and while he and Ben played at one edge I walked around to the other side, where a long metal pole, the handle for the skimmer, beckoned to be converted into a long oar for the boat I rowed into the South Pacific on a maritime adventure into the unknown. Until I suddenly saw Ben fall into the pool and begin thrashing around. At six or seven he didn't know how to swim yet, and without even realizing how the thought popped into my head, I calmly stretched the pole out to him, which he grabbed wildly, and I pulled him over and up into my concrete schooner. Coughing and sputtering, Ben said he wanted to go home. I still recall the squish of his sneakers as we walked and my feeling vaguely embarrassed that I had saved his life because I was so caught up in a silly daydream.

For years it felt to me as if we were a two-volume boxed set on Jack's bookcase, shoulder to shoulder on the shelf and both spectators of the same family show, "Father Knows Best," not quite as funny as the *goyishe* version with Robert Young and Jane Wyatt that we watched together during late afternoons. We ought to have the same memories about our place in Jack's library of Jewish stuff.

I want to ask Ben if he remembers how Jack filled the new house in Encino with all those books and the art we couldn't touch or move out of place. Oils, lithographs, and pen-and-ink drawings went up on every wall, limited and signed first editions crowded the oak-paneled library. And mind the delicate ritual and decorative objects made of filigreed silver or hammered brass lovingly arranged on top of the two-tier living room bookshelves, on the dining room sideboard, and behind the glass doors of the china cabinet. No touching!

We shared Jack's attention with these things, but it was always a contest. His greatest treasure, the piece our father adored, was the bronze sculpture by Perli Pelzig in the living room. It represented that gruesome story in the Talmud about Hananiah ben Teradion, the second-century rabbi sentenced to death by the Romans for teaching the Torah. They wrapped him in the scroll, placing wet wool on his chest to prolong the pain, and then set it on fire. "Woe is me that I should see you under such terrible circumstances!" says his daughter in S. Mendelsohn's rendering that I read each year on Yom Kippur in Media Judaica's *Mahzor Hadash*. "I should indeed despair were I alone burned," replies the martyr, "but since the scroll of the Torah is burning with me, the Power that will avenge the offense against the Torah will also avenge the offense against me." As the flames consumed his body, his students, horrified, asked him what he saw. "I see the parchment burning while the letters of the Torah soar upward."

Jack would always look up when he said that, his eyes following that phantom trail. I wasn't sure if I believed in that kind of sacrificial magic, but I was sufficiently awed. The sculpture was about two feet high and sat on a slender but heavy three-and-a-half-foot-high mahogany pedestal, with a long narrow door built into it that opened onto storage space within. No human body was represented in the sculpture, but thin sheets of bronze mimicked a rising helix of parchment in jagged flames, with little bronze Hebrew letters rising off them, culminating at the top in a single floating *shin*, the first letter of the word "Shaddai," one of God's ineffable names.

Fast-forward to the Sylmar earthquake, Tuesday, February 9, 1971. I woke up thinking, hey, Dad must be in a bad mood. Why would he come into our bedroom and wake me by shaking the bed so hard? I opened my eyes and realized the entire house was shaking. A coiled rumble slowly unwrapped itself beneath us, and Jack yelled out that it was an earthquake and that we should all stay put. I could hear things in other parts of the house jittering and clinking and thudding.

Then it stopped. I heard the quick slap of my father's slippers coming down the hall, saw the blur of him rush past our bedroom on the way to the living room, where he groaned loudly. Pelzig's sculpture had fallen from its mahogany pedestal, snapping God's name off its tip and sending it flying across the red-and-blue Oriental rug. Did it seem as natural to Ben as it did to me that Jack checked on his most valuable art first?

Our mother, of course, made up for that by racing into our room to place her hands on each of us, promptly followed by her fluttering about the house, yelling at Jack to mind the broken glass, and getting increasingly panicked by each aftershock. Those little tremors actually seemed fun to me, once I realized we were going to be safe, as if our house were suddenly part of a new ride at Disneyland. Rochelle turned on the radio, and eventually we heard that bridges were out and some buildings had collapsed at the Veterans' Administration hospital in Sylmar, on the north end of the Valley, up by the foothills of the San Gabriel Mountains. All schools were closed, even Hillel Hebrew Academy, so Al, Ben, and I stayed home, while Jack drove over the hill to the store, where a few books had fallen off the shelves. The place was more or less unscathed. Still, Rochelle was taking no chances. She kept us at home for the rest of the week, despite getting a phone call from Hillel that classes were resuming and she could send us back without any worry.

When I finally returned on Monday, my Hebrew-language teacher, one of those Orthodox Israeli expats, looked at me with disdain.

"Roth," he said, "if God wanted you dead, you'd be dead by now."

Not if my mother could help it, I said silently to myself, which was immediately followed by a more confusing thought: Did God want Pelzig's sculpture to fall? Was that a message to my father? To us? Why would He be so concerned with our personal possessions?

No good answer to that one. But look at how expert I became at thinking about my brothers and me and God all in relation to Jack's collection.

Where did Jack's mania for collecting books and art come from? When I first started thinking about it, I tried to connect it to bigger issues, larger forces. I told people that my father was a product of his time and place, that as he began expanding his inventory of books from both Jewish and non-Jewish publishers and regional distribution companies, he sensed the commercial possibilities of a Jewish bookstore that seemed more like a library. He had the foundation of Michael Harelick's eclectic stock when he bought the store, and he added to it, enlarging the number and range of titles the store carried in English, Yiddish, and Hebrew that were published in the United States and abroad by both trade and university presses. Expanding his stock also seemed like a form of gambling to him, and maybe that was part of the attraction. He once wrote to me explaining, when Hanukkah came "I gambled and ordered as many children's Chanukah books that I could find," and when "Pesach came I gambled and ordered as many different kinds of haggadot that were in print." What was the worst that could happen? He'd just put them away for the next year. But people loved the wide range of choices, and eventually he was the king of Haggadahs in L.A., selling annually during his peak years over 1,000 copies of the Central Conference of American Rabbis' *A Passover Haggadah*, illustrated by Leonard Baskin; over 1,000 copies of Media Judaica's Silverman Haggadah; 750 copies of the Rabbinical Assembly's *The Feast of Freedom* Haggadah; 3,000 copies of Rabbi Nathan Goldberg's little red-and-yellow *Passover Haggadah*; and Haggadahs from every walk of Jewish life in the United States, including a vegetarian one, *Haggadah for the Liberated Lamb*; a feminist one, *The San Diego Women's Haggadah*; and a secular one, *The Humanist Haggadah*.

Finding the good stuff, the collectibles and hard-to-find books, must have seemed like an exciting gamble too. Even though he was friends with Louis Epstein, who often helped him out, he'd still slip into the Pickwick Book Shop on Hollywood Boulevard to rummage through the remainder section and see what he could find. On his buying trips to New York, he started visiting the Heritage Club in search of limited-edition Jewish books. He haunted rare bookstores in the cities he visited in the United States and abroad, picking up a few items if they weren't too expensive. Jack told me once about a Jewish bookseller in London that he'd heard about from other book hunters and dealers. After he knocked on the door of a three-story house in Golders Green, a Hasid in a black hat let him in to what seemed like an *otzar*, a treasury, of used and rare Hebrew and English books. "It was a *balagan*," Jack said, three floors of complete chaos, and of the thousands of books there, not a single one had a price on it. He tagged along behind the Hasid, and if he saw something he was interested in, he had to show it to the man and ask in Yiddish, "How much?" While he was there, a non-Jewish book dealer came in to look around. He picked up a book and in English asked for the price. The Hasid feigned not to understand what he was saying, so the dealer left. My father thought that was a dishonorable way to do business, and he never went back.

Jack also developed the habit of buying a personal copy of signed first editions and particularly beautiful or collectible books that he was purchasing for the store. Influenced by the decor of upscale bookstores he admired, he trolled New York galleries for a few select paintings and lithographs of Jewish interest to display in the store and dropped in on Lower East Side silver dealers who might show him their secret trove of rare and unique ritual objects in the back. He intended to sell all these, but just as often he brought them home for himself.

These habits and traits are how I recognized Jack in Solomon Freehof's *On the Collecting of Jewish Books*. A true collector, Freehof says, is someone who aspires to creativity in collecting and to contributing to the making of a culture, who begins with a desire for "*exclusive* possession," that is, "there is something that no one else has and *you* have it." It wasn't just that my father wanted to have books that were sought after, rare, or out of print. He wanted to have *the* largest selection of Jewish books—that was Jack's exclusive possession and the measure of his creativity as a collector. It was something no other Jewish bookstore could claim, and I remember him bragging about it as we ate at the oak dining table at our house in Encino.

Did having the largest selection also mean that he aspired to help make a culture? Let's say that it did, even if he wouldn't have put it that way. When he started all these habits and tried to make good on his collecting ambitions it was the 1970s, and why or how to remake everything was all the boomers seemed to be arguing about, or at least that's how it appeared to me when Hillel Hebrew Academy gave me *The Jewish Catalog: A Do-It-Yourself Kit* in eighth grade as part of the school's senior class present. It seems weird now that our Orthodox day school gifted us a Jewish counterculture handbook from the havurah movement, the Jewish variant of the *Whole Earth Catalog*. But it was a good example of just how many different kinds of Jewish books and readers there were at the time—and the intense ferment and crossover that was happening between them all.

Whether he meant to or not, Jack contributed to the making not just of *a* culture but to many kinds of Jewish cultures in L.A. What he sold to customers was access to the widest possible variety of books that helped them to validate or construct their own traditional or entirely eccentric understanding of Jewishness. Say you were a customer interested in Bible study, you had your choice of the Jewish Publication Society's *Tanakh: The Holy Scriptures*, Koren Publisher's *The Jerusalem Bible*, Moznaim Publishing's *The Living Torah*, Soncino Press's *The Hertz Chumash*, the Union of American Hebrew Congregations' *The Torah: A Modern Commentary*, S. S. & R. Publishing's *The Pentateuch and Rashi's Commentary*, Judaica Press's *Hirsch Chumash*, Shilo Publishing's *Ramban: Commentary on the Torah*, the World Zionist Organization's *Studies in the Weekly Sidra*, and the B'nai B'rith's *Torah Today* (which was all in Hebrew, and when the author, Pinchas Peli, saw it on the shelf during a visit he called Jack an angel). And this doesn't even include the non-Jewish Bibles that my father would gladly order for a customer, like Oxford University Press's *The New English Bible with the Apocrypha* ("Apocrypha," he lectured me once as I was looking one over, "are stories that didn't make it into the Tanakh"). Whichever you might choose to collect would inevitably formulate and reflect your own take on the Jewish Bible, your own sense of what constitutes Jewish study.

Collecting in this way is and has always been how people assemble a Jewish culture and identity that they can literally own. This is why the store always felt to me like a kinder expression of the more complex obsession I saw at home. Academic that I am, I agree with James Clifford's explanation in *The Predicament of Culture* that in our modern, consumer-oriented West, collecting things is an extension of "the idea that identity is a kind of wealth (of objects, knowledge, memories, experience)" and that analyzing the way Westerners collect objects may help remind us "of the artifices we employ to gather a world around us." Having stuff doesn't just validate who and how impressive we are—the books, sculptures, clothes, furniture, musical instruments, photographs, toys, cheap mementos, and family heirlooms that testify to what we talk about when we talk about "us"—but also, through all the personal stories this stuff banks on our behalf, helps purchase the social, cultural, and emotional capital that makes us feel authentic to ourselves and real to others. In other words, collecting is a form of cultural construction and control, as Freehof understood, and a way to gather authority and power within family, business, social, intellectual, and political circles.

There's a sort of magic, too, implicit in Clifford's definition of collecting, in the way that material things connect mind to bodies, scarcity to value, and identity to size. Did you ever drop something that meant a lot to you—a cherished keepsake, a cell phone, or perhaps one of your oldest and most fragile books—and as it hit the floor let loose some choice four-letter words as if *you* had hit the floor and hurt yourself too? That's what I mean. Things express us, make us more certain about who we are, and extend our identities into the spaces we inhabit, which for me was my family's home in Encino and the Pico-Robertson neighborhood of my youth. Walter Benjamin captured this perfectly when he claimed in "Unpacking my Library" that the "most profound enchantment for the collector is the locking of individual items within a magic circle in which they are fixed as the final thrill, the thrill of acquisition, passes over them."

I keep coming back to this insight about ownership because it's like Biblical commentary for me, a side gloss in the book of Roth that keeps prompting arguments about our arguments over the store's spell on our lives. Walter Benjamin thinks that circle is magical because through these individual items the collector can hold and see into the past, and yet by adding them to the collection, the collector makes the old new again, giving them a kind of rebirth. It's also, as he explains later, a zone of freedom where the objects in the collection can live in peace, protected and cared for by the enlightened owner who freed the collected thing from captivity in someone else's cruel possession. Benjamin even uses the language of battle to describe the tactical stratagems he uses against book dealers and auctioneers to liberate a book into his own library.

But I've been troubled recently by another comparison he makes, "how the collector rescued a book to which he might never have given a thought, much less a wishful look, because he found it lonely and abandoned on the market place and bought it to give it its freedom—the way the prince bought a beautiful slave girl in *The Arabian Nights*."

I know he means to romanticize the act of collecting through this reference to a classic children's book and to place himself in the position of the good liberator. Still, people and things are mixed up in pretty disturbing ways here, right? Possession isn't just a way to capture and reshape time by connecting old age with childhood; it also satisfies this utopian urge to liberate things that reproduces a contradictory-seeming exodus from slavery to freedom, a freedom whose character in fact resembles a higher-order bondage to . . . what? A more refined collection? A truly loving collector? How could you be sure?

That's dark magic, and I see why some scholars interpret Benjamin's work as a strange amalgam of critical theory and Jewish mysticism. And also why Clifford insists that these romantic ideas about collecting help explain the colonialism of Western museums, because buying and speaking for other peoples' cultures was how a supposedly more enlightened civilization safeguarded them for the future.

But the point for my brothers and me here is this: If we were living in Jack's magic circle—if family were just another a category in his collection—then, like all the other books and collectibles, our becoming a "Roth" meant fitting into Jack's collection. And *he* decided that, not our mother, because we were all J. Roth Bookseller, all of us representative in one way or another, willingly or unwillingly, of a personal bookstore curated by the owner to reflect his taste and sensibility. Maybe he thought he was liberating us from ever having to experience the squalor of the Jewish "bazaar," as he called the low-rent booksellers of the Lower East Side, but which also described an uncultured Jewishness that he associated with the lower-middle-class Orthodox Jews who ran those shops. It still felt stifling. My brothers and I lived in Jack's zone of bound freedom, a zone that wasn't just an expression of his identity and wealth—it was also a compulsively clean and tidy space that promoted his idea of right living and exhibited the correct organization of his stock and his Jewish world.

Is that fair for me to say? Because while I can see *how* my father invented himself and then used collecting to control that invention and his reality, I can't really say *why* he needed that particular kind of control and reality. Was it because in drifting away from the strict Orthodoxy of his childhood, he traded one kind of all-encompassing rule-bound system for another? Or does it have something to do with his upbringing, as in the story he told us of his father, Isaac, publicly slapping him in the pew for coming late to shul on Rosh Hashanah and so missing the first benediction of the new year? Is it related to his being the youngest of six children, or his mother, Pepi, and her strict supervision of their immaculately neat and shiny home, or a first-generation American's internalization of the majority culture's disdain for "dirty" immigrants who lack self-control?

All I know for certain is that he was a lot like other Jews born here in the late 1920s and early '30s who were also trying to figure out how to be their own kind of modern American Jew. Whether moving to the suburbs and the Sunbelt or looking to Zionism, the civil rights movement, or the spiritual and sexual countercultures for inspiration, they wanted something new and better. They wanted respect and self-validation. Jack was just more visible, both to me and to the L.A. Jewish community

Beyond this, what else can I say except what my brothers and I well know: that for Jack there was always a right way and a wrong way to do anything, that he endlessly instructed us at home on how to clean our rooms, make our beds, polish the furniture, hang a picture, shine and properly maintain a pair of shoes, dress for work. That he constantly corrected us in front of the customers, expecting that we ought to know as if by telepathy or osmosis how to remove a book from the shelf, how to stack a display, how to check in new inventory, how to gift wrap, how to use Bowker's *Books in Print*, how to read a copyright page in English, Hebrew, or Yiddish, how to count out change, how to pack a box of books, how to unpack a box of books, how to arrange an office desk, how to shake hands, how to answer the phone, how to tell a customer that Mr. Roth was unavailable. How to be Jewish as he saw fit.

When Jack told me in January 1983 that he was sending me to Boston to check on Ben, I figured it would be a fun outing on Jack's dime. I'd been working at the store since graduating from the University of California, Berkeley, the year before and I was glad to get a quick break to see my kid brother and catch up on his career dreams. I had always been impressed that Ben was the news anchor for the Beverly Hills High School TV station. To me, that fit him perfectly, because he was the popular one, the student body president of Hillel for whom I drew election posters and who could talk to anybody, totally unlike me that way. And in '79 when Rochelle took me and my brothers to dinner at Monty's in Westwood to ask if we wanted to move with her to Israel, Ben, who at that time was finishing up his junior year of high school back in the Valley and still living with her, said no, he couldn't go because all his friends were here, and besides, Jack had already offered to move Ben into his Beverly Hills apartment and said he'd take care of him. Of course he would. Ben was going to be a celebrity, and I was sure of it when he chose to go to Emerson College for broadcasting. I couldn't imagine him not ending up a star. I couldn't imagine him not being, as always, the most charming of Jack's three sons, everyone's favorite.

Had he already been accepted to Emerson when Jack married Elana in 1980? Ben must have been living with Jack when my father was introduced to her by mutual friends, she an attractive Jewish widow with blond hair, two small children, and an accountancy practice, he the most eligible bachelor in the Westside Jewish community. To prep me for my trip back East, Jack had me over to the house where he lived with Elana and her family, the one in Beverlywood perched on a shallow rise with a small pool in backyard. Jack told me that he'd asked Ben in the fall if he wanted to go back to Emerson or transfer to UCLA, and Ben chose Emerson, but now my brother had called to say that he wanted to come home. Ben told me later that Jack said no, he couldn't come home, that he'd made his bed and had to sleep in it. My father didn't mention any of that when he explained why I needed to fly back East. I simply got the impression from his version of events that Ben had said something to make Jack think Ben wasn't himself, as if suddenly his photo of Ben had mysteriously gone out of focus. I was sent to double-check the subject.

Boston was snowy, and it was colder than any winter I'd ever experienced. Ben had a studio apartment in the Back Bay—this was just before it started to gentrify—and I thought the building was a dump. The "studio" was just a room in an old brownstone with a lock on the door and a bathroom down the hall. The heat went on only intermittently. I saw that Ben had Arthur Hertzberg's *The Zionist Idea* on his dresser, and my brother said that Jack had sent it to him because he was reading it for a class, but I didn't see any other books or school supplies around.

I suggested we check out the Charles River and get some air, so we took a walk along the river path.

"They're looking at us," Ben said.

"Who is?"

"Don't look. *They* are. They're in the windows."

"No, Ben, there's no one there." I was looking right at the buildings. "I'm telling you, there's nothing going on. See?" I spread my arms and twirled around.

"Yeah, yeah, okay. Let's just keep walking."

The next day I shaved the nape of his neck to give him a cleaner hairline and sharper look as we neatened up before driving my rental car to go see our uncle Rabbi Harry Roth, out near Andover. That was part of the plan. Ben seemed okay that night and the following day, though quieter than he used to be.

When I got back to L.A., I told Jack about the river episode and that I believed Ben was in bad shape and we should do something. But he was noncommittal, and I didn't insist he bring Ben home. Why? It was Jack's responsibility, I remember thinking, but maybe I was also relieved that my father would find a way to take care of it and that I wouldn't have to do anything. Maybe I wanted to stay on his good side and show that I could listen, unlike Al. Or maybe I just wanted to be left alone.

So I went back to thinking about myself and how to get out of the high rent that Jack stuck me in when he gave me a rental agreement for an apartment in West L.A. as my graduation present. He paid the first and last month's rent and the security deposit, but after that I had to come up with $625 a month on my book-clerk salary, which was around $4 an hour, leaving me little left over for a social life. Luckily, my friend Jeffrey, who had lived across the street from us in Encino, helped me out. His mother owned a rental house on Fourth Street near the newly built Beverly Center. When my lease was up, I quickly moved in with him, our buddy Richard, and my college roommate Harry, who'd also moved back to town.

But that March Ben suddenly hopped a cheap flight home in the middle of the night and turned up at Fourth Street with a large suitcase and an entirely different personality. He was nervous and furtive, talked fast, and paced around the house with his head down, sometimes muttering to himself. He didn't eat much. He stored his stuff with me as he bounced around the city, staying over a few nights at Al's place in Venice and then at the apartment of Jeffrey's mom, Sharon, where he went to visit Jeffrey's brother Charlie. Sharon was a nurse, and when she saw Ben, she told him she had some pills that would help, something for his anxiety, I think. Ben was surprised, he said later, when Sharon told him to take a couple and not to worry; she wasn't trying to poison him, which was exactly what he was thinking. That night Sharon called me to say that Ben was exhibiting symptoms of paranoid schizophrenia and I needed to get him to a doctor right away. I didn't really grasp what that meant or augured, and maybe Jack didn't either, although he'd already called our family physician and a few psychiatrists. He said to keep Ben at my place until he had a plan, and of course I did what he wanted. I told Ben that he had to stay with me. I told myself that was all I could do.

A couple of days went by, and Ben, holed up alone in the house during the day while everyone else went to work, got worse. He skittered away from my roommates if they approached him, and he didn't look anyone in the eye. When I came home, I'd corner him and try to talk him down, but he'd go blank and tune out my lectures, I could tell. Then one night he grabbed his suitcase and said he had to go, he had to go right then.

"Ben, what are you doing? No, you have to stay here." I tried to block his way, but he rushed past me out of the house. I followed him down Fourth Street and toward La Cienega, trying to reason with him and talking a mile a minute.

"Ben, stop! Come on, just stop and let's talk. Where you gonna go? I know you're feeling bad, but it's dark, come on, let's figure this out. Listen to me!"

"I got to go, I have to go."

"Where?" He kept pushing me away. I didn't want to grab him, I didn't want to wrestle with him, I thought I could talk him down, reason with him because I could out-reason anyone.

He'd hustled out to La Cienega by then, the streetlights making me blink, the traffic humming by, a whole world going about its business as if the two of us were just a normal part of the streetscape, as if I wasn't about to lose this argument.

"You have to come back," I was yelling. "You have to come back to the house right now!"

Ben was already raising his arm to hail a cab, and I didn't imagine any would be driving by—who takes cabs in L.A.?—until there it was, and he yanked his arm out of my grasp, opened the back door, and slid in with his suitcase. I pulled my wallet out of my back pocket and took out a five-dollar bill.

"Here," I screamed at the driver, as I threw the bill onto the front seat, "I'll give you this not to take him!" He scooped it up as Ben shoved me back hard, slammed the door shut, and the cab peeled out.

I watched its taillights speed north up La Cienega.

I stood there hollowed out, my throat raw, and cried. Then I walked back to the house and called Jack.

Listening to Ben upbraid me on Zoom, I knew he wanted me to understand what it felt like to have that kind of breakdown, to be that confused and scared and then in the end tossed out for something he had no control over. Yet I wanted Ben to understand how hard it was for me to call our father to account and risk leaving the safety of his magic circle. I enjoy order. I liked it when Jack would show me a beautiful miniature Bible or how to spread the leaves of a leather-bound nineteenth-century book in order to see whether they hid a fore-edge painting. For me the attraction was easy because that's what books always meant in my mind: little gems of wonder and beauty you could hold in your hand, a place to go for some well-plotted peace and quiet away from the family.

And I understood Jack's order. Even if I disliked being made to feel like I was just another part of his fine and scholarly Judaica, that I was a matching piece along with Ben and Al in the section cataloged under "family" (Rochelle's preference for dressing us alike—inadvertently, perhaps unconsciously—rhymed well with Jack's overpowering impulse to gather, arrange, and exhibit), I still aspired to create my own category within the collection. That was the only way Jack would pay attention to me in the same way that he paid attention to his store. I understood that because I learned to read his cataloging system early on, walking the tile pattern of the sales floor in Harelick & Roth on La Cienega. It was like the store's own highway connecting all these different pages in the atlas of Jack's world. It led me to the children's section, which I knew best, to the dull rows of "serious books," to the chumashim (Pentateuchs) and siddurim that you had to kiss if you dropped them, to the back room and lunch, or to the computer room and Mom. The sales floor told a story. I wanted to be its hero.

But when Ben took off in that cab and disappeared for three days, it was as if he'd escaped the collection entirely, as if he'd stepped off into a void where no categories or collections existed. That petrified me, and when I told Jack what happened on La Cienega I think it was beyond his comprehension. Not that he didn't realize what was happening to his son, but that conceptually he couldn't grasp the full import of a situation so alien to him in its nature and presentation that there was no category for it in his mind.

I know that sounds overwrought, yet how different was our home from the store? Didn't the sales floor and its subject categories help bring into focus exactly how things became visible and meaningful to Jack? It was a guide for how to take possession not just of Judaism and Jewish literatures but of Jewish experience itself. It's what attracted customers to shop there. It offered an opportunity for self-investment and self-possession, a place to find words and objects that made scrutable for those customers an identity and view of the world that they often didn't even know they were searching for. I think it did the same for my father.

Let me explain what I mean. I'm looking at the photographs of the Pico store that ran in *Judaica Book News* and the *Jewish Journal*, the location that Jack moved to in '79 and that I thought was the best version of his bookstore. There's a picture of Ben behind the checkout counter helping customers at the grand opening in June; his job was to help ring up and bag the books. That's where we boys made the most sense to him on the sales floor, there and in the shipping room clerking for him and taking some of the pressure off his day-to-day responsibilities. The store resembled an old-fashioned oak-paneled library, exactly like the one he had built in the large guestroom in the east wing of the Encino house. Knowing how to read its sales floor meant knowing what he believed was worth his, his customer's, and his family's attention.

Entering the store, you faced that checkout counter directly ahead. Behind it was Jack's desk, and behind him was his rare and fine bookcase set against the lower landing of the T-shaped central staircase. If customers had a question or request, or were in search of something hard to find, they could seek the answer here in the heart of the store. No surprise that my father put himself at the center, though when he wanted to hide from customers he escaped to the back office, where the computer and business files were located.

Depending on which way you wanted to browse, you could read the sales floor in one of two ways. If you turned left at the entrance, facing west according to a compass, you were at the children's section, placed there because it was one of the most profitable sections in the store. Children did matter to Jack, but like most of the books in that section and his outlook on youth, the subject category was mostly educational in content. It signified a starting point for the purchase of Jewishness—for investment in the mind of a Jewish child—and it emphasized teaching and learning rather than mere entertainment and play. This was serious stuff, even if some of the material was lighthearted, so it was most important that I tidy up that section immediately after customers and their children had pawed through it, in order to restore the dignity of Jack's meticulous display of picture books and primers.

Next to and north of that section were the Hebrew grammar and dictionaries, miscellaneous Hebraica, and finally *sifrei kodesh*, holy books. Naturally, this would be the next stop on any educated person's self-guided journey through my father's interpretation of Jewish literature. At that point you'd be at the back wall, at the passage to the shipping area where the textbooks were stocked. Heading rightward along the back wall, and underneath the staircase to the small loft above the store where Jack kept a limited but well-curated selection of collectible paintings and silver items was the religious literature (Jack called it *frum* lit) in Hebrew and English—the Mishnah and the Talmud, later works of legal explanation and commentary, ethical and inspirational works, Kabbalah, and a section devoted strictly to the new and fast-growing ArtScroll publications, a powerhouse of Orthodox publishing today.

It made sense finding all these sections next to the high foot-traffic of the children's books and close to the checkout counter. For a Jewish bookstore this was the most traditional area of the sales floor, a power corner containing the sections that reverberated most with my father's childhood and upbringing. These were the books that I imagined surrounded him in the stories he told us about his education at Yeshiva Torah Vodaath, the ones that offered an easy conversation starter with him when we were shooting the breeze at the store. Their location near Jack's desk and deeper in the store also underscored their "insider" nature, that in taking possession of them—by showing the ability or willingness to read them in the original as well as in translation—a customer also took possession of a core meaning in Judaism and in Jack's scheme of things. They were tokens of religious belonging. I never felt entirely comfortable in that corner, but I forced myself to learn it.

Past the billing and office area you came to the English-language Bible section, which anchored the left side of the long eastern wall of the store. To the right of that section and going south along the wall was History/Holocaust/Zionism, next to which was Philosophy/Jewish Thought, next to Fiction/Poetry, next to Yiddish/Cookbooks. Here was the broad arc of modern Jewish experience spread out in a panoply of books that, unlike the prayer books and *sifrei kodesh*, resembled those you might find in any other bookstore. This is where the Jews looked most like everyone else, at least in the land of books. And that made sense because for my father this was the intellectual hub of the store, the place to find what the general bookstores failed to carry and the recognition that Jews belonged in every collection. Customers perusing the more traditional area of the sales floor often drifted over here, yet it seemed to me that many of the academics and liberal Jews who shopped at the store were drawn to this wall in particular. They were attracted, perhaps, not only by the largest selection of Jewish scholarship and literature they had ever seen in any Jewish or general bookstore but also by that overwhelming proof of Jewish intellectual and aesthetic equality. Standing before all that, you might even feel as if your purchase made you a participant in rather than just a witness to the mainstreaming of Jews and Jewishness in America's book business.

These were also the sections I spent the most time exploring, if only because they were in English and easy for me to read. This was where Jack would most often find the obscure title that I failed to locate for a customer. And it was in front of these shelves where I most remember obediently listening to one of his many lectures on how to help a customer, or on the intellectual accomplishments of a famous rabbi, or about the literary competitiveness between I. B. Singer and his brother I. J. Singer in service of helping me tell them apart. That wall helped me realize what I needed to know to find out who I wanted to be.

Arranged in front of the wall were three tables, miscellaneous Biblical scholarship in English, and two gift book tables, and continuing rightward from there would lead you to the cookbook table and the new-book table facing the first two store display windows. Turning right again and heading west past the three wire display racks of new and popular paperback books facing the third display window brought you full circle (really, full square) back to the store's entrance. From the gift books to the paperbacks, whose displays extended back toward the center of the store, this area was always busy because these were near the entrance and the sales counter, and because it's where customers looking for gifts, light reading, and new or reissued titles congregated. The up-front Jewishness framed by Jack's display windows was popular, practical, and affordable, just the combination to draw customers in, and it presented us—J. Roth Bookseller, the Jews—in naturally the best light. Purchases in these sections appealed to a mass market or to invitees to bar/bat mitzvahs and weddings, or to those for whom Jewish food satiated their hunger for identity. Jack seemed content to let me and the other salesclerks handle this part of the sales floor, maybe because in his mind these sections were, intellectually and sales-wise, the easiest to handle.

It's also where I remember helping him stack a pile of Isaac Babel's short story collection *You Must Know Everything*—the 1980 fifth printing with the striking purple cover—and listening to him go on about Benya Krik, Babel's fictional Jewish mob boss of Odessa. Yet it wasn't the quality of the stories or the book's table of contents that made Babel such an interesting writer to Jack, and it was this part of the sales floor that revealed to me how my father took possession of an author. The ones who caught his attention had to have written something that broke the usual expectations about Jews or Jewish writing, or about whom there was a juicy bit of gossip or special scholarly renown. He loved regaling and impressing customers with those kinds of stories. Jack was attracted to outsize personalities; those with more pedestrian credentials, not so much. I filed that insight under things I had to do if I wanted to be a writer myself. He showed me so many flap-jacket author bios and photos that I used to think it was one of the most important parts of a book. I tried to imagine myself on one.

Babel's title could have stood in, too, as the title for Jack's floor plan. The sales floor organized what was essentially an unachievable aim, carrying every book related to or in dialogue with the Jews. In my father's edition of Babel's book, the imperative to know was replaced by the imperative to have—you must *have* everything—and the reason for doing so wasn't just for wealth and fame, as it was for the bourgeois grandmother in Babel's tale of a writer's education. Thanks to the scaffolding of subject categories and Jack's will to order, he created his own fiction, an ever enlarging yet always organizable collection of Judaica. Walking its sales floor was for him, as its owner, a review of his knowledge, creativity, and power.

For customers, following the sales floor from the children's section to the paperbacks led them from the past to the present, from a Jew's foundational reading toward works that depended on previous knowledge to shape their understanding of their Jewishness. Walking the store in the opposite direction simply turned that teacherly narrative into an archaeology of Jewish writing. And each wall could also be read like a material commentary on the development of Jewish literatures, the most evocative but predictable one being my favorite wall, which reflected my father's and the publishers' thinking about the historical procession of Jewish writing: Bible, History/Holocaust/Zionism, Philosophy/Jewish Thought, Fiction/Poetry, and Yiddish/Cookbooks—it's the bookshelf version of "They tried to kill us, we survived, now let's eat!"

For me, being able to read the sales floor in both directions helped illuminate the contours and limits of Jack's ultimately impossible collection, the shape and physical presentation of its meanings, and the subjective value of its various sections. The subject categories in it were no less personal, even if my father borrowed them from publishers' catalogs and the conventional layout of sales floors in most bookstores during those years. Subject categories weren't even systematized until after World War II, and even then they were always a reflection of an owner's instinctive take on how books fit into their retail vision. They simply made clear how ownership conferred on

Jack the right to interpret what deserved to be in his stock and what belonged in his collection.

That right was evident, too, in another detail that both overlooked and was a part of Jack's sales floor. Rightward from the entrance, at the far end of the new-book table, was a large support column on which hung a sepia-tone photograph of a bearded old Jew in an old-fashioned, wide-brim beaver hat. He's leaning on a lectern in front of a Torah ark and looking straight into the camera. That was my great-great-grandfather Dovid Roth. Jack thought the picture might have been taken at a *shtiebel*, a small, informal synagogue, in the Batei Ungarin neighborhood of Mea She'arim. He certainly looks like he's straight from Jerusalem central casting. He was the *teudah*, the certificate, that privately advertised my father's ownership of the collection and publicly sanctioned its cultural and commercial purpose.

What I always liked most about it, though, was that the photo, placed just above eye level, surveilled each customer walking into the store. In other words, my *alter, alter zeyde* functioned as a kind of store greeter, wielding a Jewish gaze that welcomed but also sized up everyone who came in. It was a place to see and be seen with Jews. And in a store with a gold-leaf shop sign and a central staircase he assured customers, especially new ones in search of a title like Morris N. Kertzer's *What Is a Jew?*, that they were in the right place. When folks waiting at the bus stop out front wandered in to browse, Dovid Roth explained any confusion.

My *alter, alter zeyde* was also a kind of Jewish constable who provided a warrant for my father to police the sales floor as he saw fit. He was like the consciousness that Walter Benjamin attributes to a collection, one that reflects the owner's mind and tastes and that makes it a "living library." His looks spoke for Jack's ownership and surveillance of the sales floor and its metaphoric Jewish community—the Roths' little Jewish community, one that was dependent on me, my brothers, my mother, and the customers interacting with Jack's collection according to his design. Of course, not everyone followed that design to the letter, and my father was open to change; he had to be in order to expand the collection. He eventually added a Women's Studies section, and during the Orthodox resurgence in the 1980s he added one for Hashkafah, the Hebrew word for "outlook" that really means ideologically correct Orthodox literature.

Yet the real genius of Jack's collecting and of his living library was that his quest to have the largest selection of Jewish books made shopping and being seen there an act of self-definition and self-explanation, and it didn't even require that you identify *as* Jewish so much as *with* Jews. Or, to be more accurate, that you identify with the broad conception of Jewishness that one particular Jew, Jack Roth, had gathered around himself through his collection of books: a belief that you must have everything written by and about Jews if you wish to know anything at all about the varieties of Jewish identity and practice that helped construct modern Jewish experience.

That was certainly the appeal for customers of my father's personal bookstore. It was Jack's pleasantly ordered library of mid-century American Jewish possibilities, available in multiple editions and languages. Take your choice. That's why Jews of every denomination and ideological bent thought of the store, at least until the 1990s, as such a welcoming space. My father was especially proud about that. Rabbi Immanuel Jakobovitz, the Orthodox chief rabbi of England, was a customer, as was Rabbi Sue Levi Elwell, the Reform rabbi of Leo Baeck Temple up on Sepulveda Boulevard. Zev Yaroslavsky, Democratic city councilman for the Fifth District and later a member of the Los Angeles County Board of Supervisors, dropped by on occasion. So did Dennis Prager, the conservative writer and talk radio host and later a founder of the Prager University Foundation, or PragerU, a right-wing educational nonprofit. Irving Howe, Cynthia Ozick, Nahum Glatzer, David Hartman, Lucy Davidowitz, Herman Wouk, Shlomo Carlebach, Jerzy Kosinski, Barbra Streisand, Jon Voigt, Richard Dreyfuss, and Wolf Blitzer all shopped there. For a number of years, Abraham Joshua Heschel visited in the summer. Non-Jews came in too, especially the evangelical Christians, who suddenly arrived in the 1980s in search of the Jewish roots of Jesus. I'd lead them around the sales floor, happy to let them read everything for themselves.

For me and my brothers, though, the bookstore was Jack's command post, the sales floor a set of marching orders. Put these books here, those over there. Make sure you pile them correctly and double-check that this section is alphabetized by author and that one by title. The sales floor taught us how we were expected to act with and talk to people, for discovering how salesclerk small talk could connect us through books to other people and make *them* understandable: "Can I help you with anything? I think we have that in stock, but let me double-check. Everyone is asking for that. Yes, I read it too." Anything not found on the sales floor was either out of place, out of stock, or out of mind. "I'm sorry, but it's not in print, and Mr. Roth doesn't recognize the title. I don't think it exists."

Living inside and as a part of that collection was a continual exercise for us in trying to find *our* correct subject heading in Jack's world, our place in Jack's mind. I was pretty sure I knew where I fit in. By the spring of 1983, however, I don't think my father knew where to place Ben anymore. Of course, Ben put it much more plainly than that when I later asked him what happened after he left me standing there on La Cienega.

"Dad said he'd take care of me. And he didn't."

When I called Ben to get his version of events, we finally tried to fit it all together and get the timeline straight, but we couldn't do it. The only thing we both agreed on is that Ben stole the car in Venice. He saw the keys in the car's ignition and thought Al and I had left it there for him, and he drove until he ran out of gas up by Grapevine, where I-5 cuts through the Tehachapi Mountains, as far north as you can get in Los Angeles County. He ditched the car and started walking, and that's when the Highway Patrol picked him up. They held him at their station back down in Valencia.

I went with Jack to see him at the psychiatric ward in West L.A., and, honestly, I didn't recognize the person he'd become either. I noticed the dark circles under his eyes, his voice a monotone, his pleas emotionless. Ben wanted out. Jack replied that he either stayed there or had to go live with Rochelle in Israel. But at the court hearing the judge agreed with Ben, so thanks to a state law that forbid institutionalizing patients against their will, he was released, much to Jack's dismay.

Was it then that he brought Ben back to his house? Al claims that he took custody of him, but I could swear that was after the night that proved a breaking point for Jack. Ben, my father said, pulled a knife on him and Elana in their kitchen.

Ben always insisted that never happened, that Jack treated him like dirt. I knew when Ben told me this that he'd get angrier and angrier as he remembered it. He made sure I followed. That when Jack threw Ben out of the house simply for being too sick and too difficult, he didn't relent and go to him on the front doorstep, put his arm around his son and say, "We'll get this worked out, we'll get you some help," like my brother expected. Instead, he opened the little window in the door and said, "Ben, get out of here." Ben crashed with Al in Venice and then—was it a few days later, a week?—Jack came over to Al's place and told Ben to pack his bags. He was going to New York. From there my mother could take him back with her to Israel. Jack had done all he thought he could do, he was out of ideas, and he had a business to run, a reputation. It was Rochelle's turn now.

Here's something else I forgot as thoroughly as I did Ben's things in our room. I don't remember scrambling over to the Los Angeles Airport with Al and trying to catch him before he boarded the plane. I suppose that's how badly I wanted to wipe that story from my own collection. Because if it didn't exist, I wouldn't have to recollect it the way I do now, again and again, as I imagine it from Ben's words when he remembered it to me: Racing through the departure hall, seeing Jack turn around in surprise when we reached the gate, our brother just about to enter the jetway, and me and Al yelling, "You don't have to get on the plane, Ben! You don't have to get on the plane!"

But he boarded anyway.

Did I forget this because it was the second time he got away from me? Because I'd saved him once but couldn't again? Or is it that knowing he'd left for good, it was as if he disappeared entirely, not just from my father's magic circle but also from mine?

And who was I really talking about when in August 1983 I wrote this in my journal:

> Am trying to understand my father's brutality towards Ben. What drove him to it? This is the wrong tack. Let us say that he has reasons for wanting Ben out of his life. Are they valid? At what point can a man say he is no longer responsible for his son, that he cannot afford to care because it involves too much of his self. Jack is or used to be just and fair, always the equitable one and always the yes to my mother's no. He seems to have felt in the past few years that his reserve is unmanly and doesn't speak loudly enough to imprint himself as a force on those around him. He wants, so badly, to be seen and heard after

> so many years of feeling overlooked, and that is resurrecting his ego. His soul, the very best of the man, has left him, his *neshama* is gone. All that is really left, all that is known today as ego is merely *ruach ve'guf*, air and body. The corporeal demands to be fed and it is powered by nothing noble, just air. My father is dead. There is only a body called Jack Roth left.

I was so angry, I made Jack into an object, a body without spirit or feeling and as ownerless as air. I sentenced him to collector's hell. But in doing that, I also betrayed how terrified I was of becoming an object too and of recognizing myself in him as someone whose inordinate desire for possessions, order, control, and authority—no matter their contribution to his financial success—might end up the cause of a greater spiritual dispossession. I feared becoming all ego, a self that was just some breath in a body and certainly no hero.

That's why I asked Ben to forgive Jack. Because if he did, he could forgive me too for being more concerned with having stuff and being comfortable. For being lost in another, more powerful daydream while he struggled to stay afloat. For wanting a place in some larger collection, for knowing my place in Jack's, and for hoping to keep his together so we might have something to stop us from falling apart as a family. For not seeing my brother as his own subject category.

None of us wanted simply to be an object of Jack's affection. We wanted him to see us for who we were. Me especially. What child doesn't want that from their parents? I quit working at the store and didn't talk to Jack for a few years after Ben left. I refused all help from him. That's when I decided to go back to graduate school and do some more thinking about literature. I wanted to test what I'd learned: that collection may be a form of love, but it can also be a form of captivity. And for me, an ethics: If I am not for my father's collection, who will be? If I am for my father's collection alone, what am I?

Ben learned something different, of course. The hospitals, the medications, the hopeful treatments, the years passed in cigarettes and coffee, each offered plenty of time to think. "He wanted me out, well, I'm out now, leave me alone," he said. But Jack's collection is gone, there's no in or out anymore, and to imagine that's still the case is to grant him a power and authority he lost years ago.

And now my brothers and I have our own possessions, we've gathered our own worlds around us, we have our own power to remember not just what was done to us, but also how good it once felt to be fussed over and arranged, to be cared for and to know that we were protected. Forgiveness doesn't mean forgetting the past; it means trying to understand it so that we're no longer prisoners to it.

I'd like to believe that if we do that, we have another chance at redemption. Not just to free ourselves from Jack's magic circle, and not, as Walter Benjamin thought, because we think our love gives us the power to grant anyone or anything that communes with us a more enlightened freedom than they might have by living elsewhere. It's because what we love might one day free us to imagine ourselves as caretakers of our small collection of things rather than its owners.

U.S.S.R., 1976

And what did Jack's collection mean to him? What story did *he* think he was telling through his sales floor? To find an answer to these questions, I need to pause here and return to the mid-'70s just after my parents' divorce—before Ben's illness, before the store's move to Pico Boulevard—when Jack did something perhaps just as heroic as stopping a two-and-a-half-ton truck from crushing his fellow soldiers.

I'm backtracking to consider whether part of the answer has to do with my father's desire to advertise his personal bookstore's perfect independence. Newly single, not bound to any denomination or narrow clutch of subject categories, or to anything or anyone that fell outside the logic of his collection, he was at that time like a field agent for Jewishness, working alone on a mission to gather information about Jewish experience and distribute that knowledge to his customers. Which might explain why the Jewish Agency chose to send him to the Soviet Union during the Cold War.

In the early summer of 1976, Jack received a phone call from a mysterious stranger who asked if he'd be interested in taking "gifts" to Jewish refuseniks there. These men, women, and families, galvanized by a renewed sense of Jewish pride after Israel's victory in the Six-Day War, had applied for Soviet exit visas but were refused the right to emigrate, especially to Israel. Their plight sparked protest movements in both the United States and Israel. I remember attending a required assembly at Hillel where a refusenik spoke passionately about the ways the Soviet authorities had hounded him for his desire to leave simply because he wished to live freely as a Jew; I remember the rollicking choruses of "Am Yisrael chai!," "The people of Israel live!," that we sang at the top of our voices, over and over, after he spoke.

I didn't realize then that there was a larger argument among American Jews over how to pressure the Soviets (through American diplomacy, by taking to the streets?) and whether the campaign was about human rights or just Jewish rights. I also didn't realize then that, either way, the whole endeavor was suffused by American Jews' guilt over their previous inability to save European Jews from the Holocaust. Or that Israel was determined to pursue its own strategy advancing Zionism and stoking the embers of Jewish cultural consciousness among the refuseniks, so that once released they would go where the Jewish Agency believed they rightfully belonged.

Jack tells me during one of our long-distance conversations that the man who called him, an Israeli, knew that he was recently divorced and that he lived alone. He asked Jack to come up to his room at the Hilton in Beverly Hills for a meeting, and when the door opened Jack was struck by the oddness of the man's wearing a plaid work shirt in the summer. Was it Aryeh Kroll he was meeting? That's who first came up with the idea back in 1966 to send Jewish tourists with contraband Judaica into the Soviet Union. A member of the religious kibbutz movement, he then convinced the Israeli government, working through the Jewish Agency, to start funding the operation in 1968. It continued even after the dissolution of the U.S.S.R. in 1991; ultimately, about two million Soviet Jews emigrated, most to Israel, with the rest settling mainly in the United States and Germany.

Jack can't recall the name of the man he said acted like some movie spy—007 or George Smiley perhaps. He may have never even told my father his name. All Jack remembered was that the Israeli arranged for his plane ticket and for the tourist group he'd join and that he sent the books, records, pamphlets, and *luachim*, or Jewish calendars, that Jack carefully tucked into his large suitcase, which served as a bookseller's traveling collection and an extension of my father's operation under the Israeli flag. He told Jack not to bring any American magazines with him because that would bring unwanted attention from the Soviet customs agents, and anyway, if they discovered his cache, they'd just confiscate it; no worries about being hassled, since he was an American citizen. Finally, the Israeli handed him a list of names on a piece of paper—the refuseniks he was to make contact with—that Jack kept concealed in his pocket. My father's older brother Michael, renowned in L.A. himself as a freethinking rabbi, teacher, and scholar, was supposed to go with him. For some reason, though, he backed out, so Jack went with Michael's wife, my Aunt Geula, who seemed to be everyone's favorite traveling partner. It didn't hurt that they also made for a much more convincing middle-aged American tourist couple.

But I'll let Jack tell the rest of his story. Here's a draft of the report he wrote for the Jewish Agency:

> [A]rrived Moscow July 17. After waiting three hours for our baggage we proceeded thru customs. Both Mrs. Roth and myself were not asked to open our baggage. We were met by our [I]ntourist guide and taken by bus to the hotel Ukraine. If anyone suspected us of having come to the Soviet Union on a mission, or if we were under surveillance in Moscow we did not feel or observe it.
>
> On July 20, we flew with our tour group to a city South of Russia near the Caspian Sea called Baku. There we made our first contact. Michael Melnikov was his name and he was elated to see us. We gave him an assortment of books, pamphlets and Israeli records. He was overjoyed with the records but thought the books and pamphlets were too dangerous and risky to have brought in. Also did not think they were all that important. The luach [Jewish calendar] however he found essential and asked for another one which we brought with us the next evening as they insisted we must come back for dinner. While Mr. Melnikov is not a refusenik he is very involved with helping those who are. He expressed deep anger over those Russians who prefer to emigrate to the States and not Israel. Mr. Melnikov was born in Riga. Spent some years in Siberia in a coal mine and has been in Baku many years. He has retained an immense feeling for Jews and Jewish Culture tho he has not seen formal Jewish life since he was twelve. Future visitors, he asked, should call first before visiting.

From Baku we flew to Tibilisi. Here we met with Grigori Goldshtein and his mother. We had an extremely difficult time finding their address. It was late when we arrived but we were welcomed immediately and warmly. Grigori's brother, Isaj, and his family were away on a vacation so we could not meet with them. The Goldshtein brothers are known refuseniks and have been unemployed for over five years. They have not received their mail for over eight months now and despite this harassment and other deprivations, firmly believe that they will receive their exit visas one day. We left them with a few Israeli records, a "Luach," two "Facts about Israel," some Zionist pamphlets and a copy of "EXODUS" in Russian. Their apartment and economic predicament was a picture of sadness. The Goldshtein brothers are fifth generation Georgians yet Grigori did not complain—but looked with high hopes toward the future and emigrating to Israel soon.

From Tibilisi we were bussed to Erevan, a city in Armenia near the Turkish border. Here we had an address of an Iosif Goldman but could not find him. Since we had only a day and a half here we could not make a second attempt. Regretfully the cab we took could not find the street—when he did, the numbers did not correspond with the number we had. It was a futile search and after hours and rubles we had to return to our hotel. While all the addresses we had to contact were confusing and bewildering, I suggest that future visitors to this one be given some further information.

We arrived in Leningrad nursing a slight case of dissentary [*sic*] as did most of the group. Sick as I was we made it our business to meet with Solomon Rozin. For future visitors let it be known that as you enter the courtyard of his apartment dwelling one should make an immediate left and go up the stairs. There are four entrances in this apartment complex and were it not for the fact that he saw us from his window and waved us up we would still be looking for him. Rozin is a known refusenik and has not worked at his profession—engineer for almost five years. His wife is a doctor and has also been denied work. Rozin has been permitted to work as an elevator operator. He, his wife and their little daughter of six months live in two rooms with Mrs. Rozin's parents. Between his job as an elevator operator and his father-in-law's pension they seem to get by financially. We brought them the last of our records, books, cigarettes and all. They welcomed us with a "l'chayim" and a cup of tea. They had not been visited in almost a year and were extremely happy & grateful that we chose to visit them. Rozin was born in Leningrad and has served in the Russian Army. He walked us to the subway and rode with us back to our hotel. Again there was little complaint about their hardship. Life is miserable but the wait will be worth it. They look to a future in Israel that will permit them to start life fresh and clean. He did express the need for consumer goods—cassette, transistor, jeans and etc.

As difficult and risky as this trip may be for us the visitor, the conditions and frustrations for those whom we visited are doubly difficult and risky. By the measure of my standards they are heroes. Whatever we outside the Soviet Union are doing deserves to be commended—but more remains to be done.

Mrs. Geula Roth
Mr. Jack Roth

Aug. 12, 1976.

In reading this, it seems to me that Jewish bookselling was an adventure story for my father and his sales floor a repository of potentially life-altering goods, and not just for those living in the relative safety of America with the freedom and means to purchase the Jewishness of their choice. As his travels around the U.S.S.R. must have evidenced for him, what he had gathered in his collection were in other, less hospitable places crucial resources for Jewish heroes, for those who by accident of history or birth were compelled to risk careers, financial security, and prison in service of cultural resistance and resupply.

If being in the collection came with its own price for my brothers and me, having access to it appeared invaluable to those less privileged than we. The truth is that the bookstore's organization also exposed how complicated the collection's meanings could be and how dependent those were on the type of story you were looking for. My father's mission to the Soviet Union and his role in one of the major Jewish events of his time because he was both a successful bookseller and unencumbered by family reminds me that, as with all tales of espionage, every mission is more complicated than it seems. That includes his in the bookstore and mine in trying to spy out the store's design and break the code encrypting my and his customers' place in it.

More always remains to be done. So let's keep going and take a closer look at the store's book-lined walls and the mythology I absorbed through them and through two other bookstores in which I found refuge during the 1980s when I was estranged from J. Roth Bookseller.

CHAPTER 6

The Book-Lined Wall (*design*)

My colleague and close friend who teaches graphic design tells me of a new assignment for students in his web design course: creating a website for an independent bookstore. Pulling me into the computer lab, Mark proudly shows off his students' work. I nod in approval, genuinely impressed not only with the work but also with his cultural and commercial idealism. Mark's assignment is a crafty tribute to his favorite bookstore, Wonder Book in Frederick, Maryland, and to his faith that independent bookstores have a place in his students' professional future. Yet what really captures my attention is that every student uses a single image, over and over, as the arch-representation of "bookstore": the book-lined wall. It's a first-thought design element that taxes each student-designer's ingenuity only in that it presents the fairly straightforward problem of scaling, framing, or otherwise manipulating stock photographs of attractive shelves in rooms filled with books. Its visual popularity is so commonplace on the Internet and in films, newspapers, and magazines that it is, literally, unremarkable to my friend and his class; it's just another convenient shorthand for the self-evident. Or so it seems. Returning to my office, I find two examples from the books there:

The book-lined wall photographed in color. The brightly lit, pinewood shelving lends the print a golden glow. Snapped through a fish-eye lens, the composition resembles a child's snow globe view in close-up. Instead of snowflakes and a clichéd winter scene, the curved world before us is eight shelves of books, their varying spines arrayed in orange, black, white, and brown. The bottom shelf is a shallow, double-height display area with selected titles placed on a narrow gutter; a large, framed sketch artfully inhabits one gutter-shelf to the left. And directly in front, dominating the composition, is a wooden ladder whose rungs lead the eye up in receding perspective toward a heaven of books—a veritable Jacob's ladder of literary fantasy.

The book-lined wall photographed in black and white. Here it's two walls. Left and right, both are floor-to-ceiling jumbles of tired-looking volumes. A good number of oversize books are tucked in on their sides and stick out over the shelf lip, giving each wall a crenellated, three-dimensional feel. Against the back wall is a double-wide lawyer's bookcase of tightly packed volumes behind glass, the flashbulb's white explosion reflected in the upper right pane. The books frame a group of well-dressed literati, most sitting, some standing, and one perched on top of a stepladder. This is the celebrated 1948 Gotham Book Mart photo of the reception for Dame Edith and Sir Osbert Sitwell, often reproduced as the official club portrait of New York's mid-century modernist writers: W. H. Auden on the stepladder, Elizabeth Bishop, Marianne Moore, Tennessee Williams, Stephen Spender, Randall Jarrell, Delmore Schwartz, Richard Eberhart, and a very young Gore Vidal—writers in their native habitat, each a living book.

These photographs quickly take me deep into the mythology of the bookstore as I discovered it from the inside of my father's collection. If I think I understand why I couldn't leave Jack's magic circle, if I want my family to forgive him for too often treating us as mere objects in his order of things, then I need to unpack that mythology too and the sources of Jack's take on bookstore design.

Sitting in my university office, I glance at the book-lined wall behind me. Filled with scholarly volumes and fiction, poetry and reference works, journal issues and comic books, I think of it as a continually revised term paper about my course of design study at J. Roth Bookseller and, during the years I refused to work there after Ben's breakdown and exile, at the two most important graduate schools in my bookstore education, the Children's Book and Music Center in Santa Monica and Book Soup in West Hollywood. The moment I turn my gaze away and back to my computer screen is when I try my hardest to resist nostalgia and perfunctory states of mind—a too-easy reverence for self, books, or writers. Like my father and other bookish types,

I'm drawn to images of the book-lined wall as an aesthetic object that evokes emotions as well-worn as the book covers themselves. We're the perfect customers for the websites designed by my friend's students as well as for works like *At Home with Books* and Reid Byers's *The Private Library: The History of the Architecture and Furnishing of the Domestic Bookroom*. Byers prefers the term "book-wrapt" to Walter Benjamin's "magic circle," but both mystify just as much as they seemingly explain images of the book-lined wall.

Such images betray a mighty attractive mode of thinking and talking about the bookstore. As with those photographs in my office, to peer into their depths is to be primed by them into imagining bookstores as wood-warmed sanctuaries for learning, artistry, and celebrity. They present bookstores as selling a very special product, part consumer good and part fantasy. This mythology of the bookstore, especially as I learned it through my father's bookstore, is what I'm trying to understand in these photos, how it provides an explanation for my Jewishness in which, like my father, I clothe myself, for the designs through which I understand literature, and for the tastes that shape my preference for stories that tell, interpret, and judge—constantly judge.

Roland Barthes famously defined myth as a type of speech, the ways we talk about objects, actions, and emotions among ourselves and, today, through the press and mass media. These enable us to communicate socially shared assumptions about our everyday lives, so that they and the social conventions in which we see them reflected seem natural, inevitable, right. Einstein's brain, for example, which was removed, preserved, and dissected for examination under a microscope after his death, provoked discussions in the French public sphere about "genius," an elite quality, that gave rise to a social myth rendering genius as the ability to reduce the world's mysteries to a simple formula, $E = mc^2$, and to another asserting that the brain can be taken apart and understood as if it were a machine, some better built than others. The book-lined wall was long unremarkable to me because I walked by it just about every day of my life, at home, in the store, and at school. As with every modern myth, says Barthes, what it personally meant to me obscured or evaded all judgment about how it came to be and who made it so. My father only? Or also my teachers and the book industry? Like the fascination with Einstein's brain, or the spectacle of wrestling, or the nostalgia for wooden toys—all "meaningless" social phenomena that Barthes discusses—the visual ubiquity of the book-lined wall also reveals how and of what stuff modern, guileless beliefs are made. Because of the instrumental and metaphorical ways that we talk about books in public and in private, we use depictions of them, especially in the age of the computer, as a stable and comforting visual vocabulary that signifies "knowledge," "analysis," and "order," and the image of the book-lined wall as an illustration of its ever-changing grammar.

It's an image that articulates for me both a concept and a physical feeling about the bookstore that makes thinking about literature and Jewishness possible, but also makes my unraveling of that thinking inevitable. The wall of books imbues a well-lit and practical commercial space with a beguiling immanent spirit—call it knowledge or wisdom or language or culture or nothing at all but the reverberation of our idiosyncratic dreams about books. Or call it the ghost of every writer who lives on as both the subject and object of the bookstore. Whatever it is, this spirit is the heart of the mythology of the bookstore, the wonderment at the evidence of so many ideas, so much history, such a collection of *things* to read and think about. What was their beginning? What will be their end? What do they all mean? And integral to this wonderment, to this myth surrounding the book-lined wall, is a belief that ultimately the bookstore's allure will always escape the languages and technologies that give the store's products their shape.

Like Deists of the eighteenth century, those who subscribe to this mythology refuse to confine its spirit to any particular manifestation of the bookstore. A tiny, ramshackle used bookstore, a modest mall outpost, a warehouse-like corporate bookstore, even the humble flea market bookstall—all are equal in the sight of the true believer, though each serves the spirit in different ways.

So I learned. My first real job helping out in my father's bookstore was tidying up its book-lined walls. That was my father's idea of training his sons as apprentices. Along with hand selling, he taught me how important it was to keep the shelves neat and alphabetized. While he aspired to the same bookstore aesthetic as in the Gotham Book Mart photo—venerable, literate, clubby—he preferred his books orderly and spines straight. I remember my father brought me to the philosophy and literature wall in the La Cienega store, the one I'd later haunt for hours in the Pico store.

"They have to be alphabetized by author," he instructed me. "And then, see, you pull two or three books out a bit and then gently push them back in until the spine is flush with the edge of the shelf."

I gave it a try, inexpertly imitating my father's practiced hands.

"No, no. Make it neat. You have to stand them up like little soldiers."

This was my father's favorite description of his books. It was a simile, too, for the way he connected commerce, life, and art: a store neat and tidy and alphabetized and crisply arranged, its own universe—his universe—where everything was in its place.

It was the same when he finally built his dream library in the large and perfectly rectangular guest bedroom of our house in Encino. It was cherrywood-paneled throughout, with expensive crown molding running the entire room and with floor-to-ceiling bookshelves. A massive, lacquered wood desk and leather-upholstered caster chair were positioned at the far end of the room, as if an Oxbridge don or some captain of nineteenth-century industry claimed residence in our stucco-covered rancher. Here's where he kept his Bibles and siddurim, as well as the dictionaries, encyclopedias, Book of the Month Club selections, and a slew of trade and mass-market paperbacks—*Silas Marner*, *The Joy of Sex*, *I and Thou*, *Lord of the Flies*, *Exodus*.

I don't recall that the shelves were ever entirely filled before my father moved out of the house. Despite that, it still seemed to me that belief in the book-lined wall was for my father a belief not only in the disciplines of knowledge but also in the design of their refinement. Maybe that's why I felt a little out of place in his library yet also drawn in. It was a belief that the Pirkei Avot, the Sayings of the Fathers, was substance better than the crude, worn bookcases of Lower East Side book and gift shops, matter more long-lasting than the cheap acid paper of editions that would eventually burn themselves out, something heavier than the cardboard covers that bargain publishers favored.

Jack's was belief in a genteel Judaism of fine and scholarly Judaica arrayed in a capacious and stately personal library where Shakespeare,

Lion Feuchtwanger, and stories about the towering *iluim*, the geniuses of the European yeshivas, might sit side by side with *Erotic Art of the East*, each a little soldier of the human condition.

What was the source of that library's aesthetics and, ultimately, of my father's American Jewish book-lined walls? I consult Henry Petroski and Lydia Pyne, who make abundantly clear in their histories of bookshelves that how books fit into them has always invited interpretation and metaphor. Medieval chained books in churches and monasteries, they explain, determined the form and function of shelving for the codex, the initial form of the book as we know it, only larger and heavier. Where you put one of those had to accommodate its heft as well as its very necessary anti-theft device. They were worth the price of a small farm, after all. Yet since books on animal skin were quickly analogized as mortal bodies like ours, writers of the time saw chained books as object examples of chained people and ideas. To them, chains weren't only a way of housing books, they also symbolized a form of imprisonment. Knowledge wanted to be free, even back then.

The arrangement of private studies, forerunners of my father's home library, dates back to the Renaissance. These copied the lodging design for college students of the time, which, according to Petroski, was itself based on the design of reading spaces in monasteries. As shelving at universities, in bookstores, and among elites in Europe changed in response to the changing size, volume, and uses of books produced in the seventeenth, eighteenth, and nineteenth centuries, so did their interpretation. Petroski recounts that Samuel Pepys, the famous eighteenth-century diarist, treated his books and ornate bookcases as more personal art than library, paying for all his bindings to be made perfectly uniform and lining up his taller books on a slightly raised shelf behind the shorter ones on a main shelf in front so that both appeared through the carefully aligned glass doors like one seamless parade of books.

The beautiful woodwork of such shelves and cases—whether at Oxford and Cambridge, Milan and Paris, or J. Hofmeisterische Lees Bookstore in Zurich and Lackington, Allen & Co.'s Temple of the Muses in London, or Appleton's Book Store in New York—all helped establish over the course of around three hundred years a style that my father interpreted as "fine and scholarly." It's a design I can now trace back to those personal studies where a comfortable chair with practical tables in a cozy nook with good natural lighting invited enlightened readers to read. And to the churches and monasteries before them whose architectural DNA deeded to bookstores a sense that they're a private public space, one where reader-customers feel they can commune with themselves among others.

Obviously, I see at the root of the bookstore's mythology various permutations of religion. But this triggers an odd irony about my understanding of J. Roth Bookseller: What I thought was a Jewish aesthetic about its design and style, because it was my father's store, was in fact a Christian one. Not for Jack the jumbled display of *sifrei kodesh*, holy books, or dusty multivolume sets of the Talmud, either in the bookstore or at home. No whiff of the *beit midrash* or *cheder*, the synagogue study hall or religious school, in which the Jews' books, manuscripts, and scrolls were collected or of the small yeshivas in Eastern Europe with their *batlanim*, idlers and lazybones, who made a meager living off these libraries through their just passable scholarship. No awareness that *this* was the Ashkenazi Jewish version of book history, technology, and storage, still similar in many ways to the European Christian one to be sure, but less well funded, with different shelving constraints, and by necessity and practice more communal than esoteric in its purpose and function.

In the end, though, would that have really mattered to my father? Because the book-lined wall was ultimately his version of a Jewish religiosity, an object of veneration, his Western Wall. It was a totem of something larger that was only partly visible and mostly a matter of faith, the impressive trace of a reassuring cosmos reminding the faithful to go forth in dignity and be honorable. Wasn't that part of how his generation of mid-century American Jews understood Judaism?

Well, maybe not all of them.

"Laurence, look at that filthy station wagon. They're *frummies*, wow! Awful. Who drives around like that? They have no class—it makes us look bad."

"You know, Dad, I don't think the *frummies* are thinking about us when they think about Jews."

"Would *you* drive around in that car?"

"It's not mine, so no."

"I don't understand how they can live like that."

The assumption behind "they" was that, despite a few exceptions, the ultra-Orthodox were okay with dirt, disorder, and shabbiness, that all those *frum* Jews moving into Hancock Park and the Pico-Robertson neighborhood in the eighties—his new customers—were an incorrigible people who couldn't see how their presentation of Judaism came off as low-rent and light on esteem.

I used to wonder whether this explained our family's steady drift away from Orthodoxy and the Orthodox community. Jack's constant critiques of other people's households, especially the observant, didn't lend itself to thinking kindly about anyone else's practice of all the home rituals he still punctiliously observed, even if he did travel on the Sabbath and eat at non-kosher restaurants.

Or was it that these Orthodox Jews, like their synagogues popping up in private homes and in vacant retail locations, reminded him of those who ran the kitsch-filled bookstores on the Lower East Side, their congregations similarly short on sophistication and lacking the urbane rituals of the Central European modern Orthodoxy that Jack so admired. And then came the rise of what seemed to him a shaggy countercultural *ba'al teshuva* movement ("masters of repentance," returnees to and renewers of the faith) in the seventies and the eighties. Neither traditionalism nor counterculture was really Jack's style, but during the first blush of post-sixties cultural reappraisal he was genuinely sympathetic to all the young adventurers in the Jewish Renewal camp and all those "born again" Orthodox Jews who were turning up in his bookstore. He aspired, after all, to running his own more refined version of Jewish revival, so he liked the new kids with real passion who, along with their peers in Christian America, were seeking to refresh or reject their parents' uninspiring middle-class religiosity.

"In the early 70's I rebelled as teens are wont to do," wrote Tracy Salkowitz when she learned I was writing about my father's bookstore. "I wasn't into drugs or rock-n-roll, I started lighting Shabbat candles. My family just thought I was odd. In the fall of 1973 at 17, I was headed off to college and prior to leaving I visited J. Roth Booksellers[,] where I met your father. To say that he had a profound impact on my life is understating the fact," said this former CEO of the Jewish Community Foundation of Southern Arizona.

> I told your Dad that I hadn't any formal Jewish education, though I lived in a Jewish home, and that I wanted to learn more, I wanted to learn the Hebrew alphabet and learn more about Judaism.
>
> We then spent the next hour scouring the bookstore together picking out treasures that your father thought I would learn from and enjoy. He was amazing. When I went to pay, I asked him if he took credit cards and he replied—"I don't yet, but it is more important that you should learn about Judaism and your heritage than that I get paid." I was smacked in the face and heart at that moment by the power of our heritage and the amazing steward who was your father.
>
> I then pulled out my checkbook and said, "You are an amazing man, but that's no way to run a business!"

I can see Jack walking her across the black-and-white-tiled linoleum in the La Cienega store and over to the religious literature and Bible study bookcases near the front desk/sales counter. While the shelves where he finds just what Salkowitz needs aren't quite the right ambience for him yet, the feel of his store's design is abundantly clear. It's an honorable space where my father could do a mitzvah wrapped as a service offered up with the dignity befitting a heritage.

I actually like that last word, not because it suggests peoplehood, but because it's derived from "inheritance." It implies that his customers deserved to own a piece of Jewish property, whether they could afford it or not. That they deserved to take joy in it. No coincidence, I think, that my strongest memory of Jack chatting with the spiritual father of the Jewish Renewal movement, Rabbi Zalman Shachter-Shalomi, and his guest that afternoon, the Hasidic songwriter Rabbi Shlomo Carlebach, is of him laughing and laughing. And once again I find myself drawn to his empowering design, to his version of the mythology, to the bookstore as a place of commercial worship—a temple, whether of muses or of a monotheistic spirit—where anyone is welcome and where everyone is lifted up to find their path in life.

My father, of course, wasn't the only bookseller who treated bookselling as a religious calling and the book-lined wall as a sacred relic.

That first, color photograph I described earlier is the cover of Laura J. Miller's book *Reluctant Capitalists: Bookselling and the Culture of Consumption*. Miller well documents the tensions between mythology and commerce that characterize American bookselling in the twentieth century, but she traces a nearer beginning for it than I did, in the Gilded Age of the late nineteenth century. That's when New York and East Coast publishers and booksellers aligned themselves economically with the genteel culture of those wealthy upper-class Americans who were appalled by how the country's fast-expanding mass culture was threatening to dominate the marketplace. Books, finely bound and of approved intellectual and artistic merit, might appeal to upscale consumers not as merchandise but as cultural investments whose value lay in their symbolic representation of fine craftsmanship, deep learning, cultivated feeling, and sophisticated taste. Which is to say they could be marketed as the very opposite of the cheap entertainment—dime novels, vaudeville, sporting events, amusement parks, and motion pictures—of the working and middle classes.

If the ladder that so often accompanies the book-lined wall is an analogy for a type of intellectual and spiritual ascent, then bookstores were like a modern Bethel wherein customers, like Jacob, were amazed to find a gateway to Heaven, at least one that looked familiar to their kind of congregants.

Yet, as Miller points out, this sacred notion of the bookstore was and is hardly conducive to the profane work of day-to-day business. In the competitive world of best sellers and bottom lines, booksellers from the turn of the previous century to the present have been well aware of the contradictions inhabiting popular stereotypes about their social roles. Even if people think the product is different or special, booksellers can't be too reverent about books or too embarrassed to make a dollar if they want to stay in business. The rise of paperback bookstores in the 1950s, chain bookstores in the 1960s, and the book superstores in the 1980s spotlighted how merchandising—which recognizes books as ultimately consumer products—will always affect the look and contents of the book-lined wall. Although the bookstore may seem like an unrecognized place of worship, it's really and more appropriately another, modern version of Yeats's "rag and bone shop of the heart." It's a place where one can purchase the secondhand makings of belief.

This distinction between the bookstore as a quasi-religious space and as a commercial venture took time to perceive. I knew that my father's sales floor told a story, that his subject categories and collection could be read in terms of both their commercial and their personal meanings for Jack. What I didn't know, because I was so overwhelmed with my father's design, was that other bookstores could be read that way too. And not until I worked at a shop unlike Jack's that stocked a different model of the book-lined wall did I begin to appreciate the variety of beliefs capable of structuring a bookstore's look.

I couldn't stay on at my father's store, not after what happened with Ben. I was angry, though I could have easily played my part in the drama and pretended to get along with him. Instead, I quit with no blowup or accusations, simply as an act of avoidance. I didn't want to deal with Jack anymore or deliberate the latest emergency from Israel or help determine whether my mom or dad had f-cked Ben up, was guilty of neglect, or had worse genes. I just wanted out. But having few employable skills aside from bookstore clerking, I ended up working full-time at a fitting version of my primal scene, the Children's Book and Music Center in Santa Monica.

I remember that Laurie Sale, the owner, seemed confused that I was applying for a job with her rather than working for my father. But she accepted my vague explanations and happily hired someone who needed only cursory training in selling books to well-off Westside mothers. It was 1983 and her bookstore was at the height of its fame. The store itself was spacious and well organized, with new-book tables and musical instruments, primarily rhythmic ones, in the show space up front, where the floor-to-ceiling windows faced out onto Santa Monica Boulevard.

Walking past the checkout counter you descended a short ramp to the main floor, which was surrounded by three book-lined walls. In the center were bins of records that could be rolled out of the way for musical performances and readings. All the trestle tables, book racks, display cases, and storage units/tables were oiled and waxed dry knotty pine, designed and built by local furniture maker Stan Pike. The bins were varnished. In the middle of one of the walls there was a walk-through that opened on a passageway running behind the shelves on that side of the store. The passageway led to the shipping area and the back offices, but it was also a very narrow stock room, books on one side and records on the other, so that working there one was in a sort of mixed space—a book-lined wall to the right, a record-lined wall to the left. It also made a perfect hiding place for employees who wanted a respite from crying babies and demanding customers.

The mix of music and literature, the cheerful colors and sunny spaces, the female-centered ethos of the sales staff and customers were all a contrast to my father's darker, male-centered bookstore. At first this was liberating. Alphabetizing and restocking the shelves was no longer an anxiety-producing activity; no one expected the books to stand perfectly straight since they were destined to be grabbed by eager little hands anyway. And the books were primarily paperback, light to carry, and child friendly. I actually wanted to read them rather than venerate them.

Soon enough, however, I started to recognize the store's belief system through its plain bookcases stocked with classics and carefully selected examples of cultural diversity, its little wooden stools and banned book displays, its posters of Raffi and Pete Seeger. If the whimsical version of a children's bookstore is the Shop Around the Corner in the romantic comedy *You've Got Mail*, Children's Book and Music Center was the social activist version. While I felt a far greater affinity for the earnest liberalism of my employer than I did for the Upper West Side romanticism of Nora Ephron, both visualized attractive mythologies about children's bookstores. One promoted innocence and fantasy as the defining traits of such bookstores; the other promoted education and cultural uplift in the spirit of the reform-minded sixties and seventies. While I no longer worked in a religious bookstore, my co-workers and customers were still adherents, only of a different sort.

It wasn't just the public breast-feeding and the occasional anti–Ronald Reagan diatribes that gave the shop away. It was also the unstained, utilitarian bookcases, the open feel of the sales floor with low-height, movable furniture demarcating its center space, the way no individuals could hide out from the other customers to read in some protected cranny. That was on purpose, of course, to make it easier to keep an eye on the little ones. Yet given the sales floor's placement behind the show windows up front, its visual signification was "transparency." No secrets here; everyone inside agreed to be seen and heard as a collective, even as they were entitled as well to individual service.

There was in addition, and especially, the reverence and ceremony that accompanied book signings by Maurice Sendak, Tomie dePaola, and James Marshall; the impassioned first looks at new books by Steven Kellogg or Chris Van Allsburg or Richard Scarry. These were the saints and *zaddikim* of the shop, and its endorsement of them is what made it better than the big chains whose children's sections were promiscuous and unedifying and which were fast encroaching on the lucrative children's market, the one thing that *You've Got Mail* got right.

Do I seem disenchanted? It was hard to ignore my just-discovered aptitude for reading spaces and my smug satisfaction at having cracked Jack's code—at seeing how blunt the merchandising of a mythology could be. Yet I could make other connections now too. My mother's branch store, for instance, may have looked in design and color scheme like a smaller version of the main store, yet as with Laurie Sale's shop its shelves and book displays reflected a less fussy and owner-centered atmosphere. Also, I finally grasped that what all these stores generated in common was a palpable optimism that their book-lined walls would bring in the faithful, who might then turn such easy access to the objects of their literary, cultural, religious, or political passions into regular pilgrimages and customer loyalty. Hallelujah.

It's hard to invent a belief wholesale, much easier to buy a few ready-made truths. At least that's the view from bookstores I've worked in. Others will disagree with me about the way a belief is sent abroad, or at least about the source of its distribution, but working in bookstores helped me to understand one of the ways in which contemporary ideologies about culture and literature are marketed, browsed by consumers, and acquired. The main challenge to seeing this was simply getting past the pervasive mystification of the book-lined wall, as in glossy coffee table books like *At Home with Books* (personal libraries, but get it, they're about comfort) or titles such as *This Is My Bookstore: 100 Postcards of Beautiful Shops around the World* (I'll send you mine if you send me yours), *Unpacking My Library: Writers and Their Books*

(I'm in good company, right?), or *The Library: A World History* (remember, pervasive). And don't get me started on the cover designs for *The Bookshop of Yesterdays, The Bookshop of the Broken Hearted, The Bookshop of Second Chances, How to Find Love in a Bookshop*, and *Seven Kinds of People You Find in Bookshops* (only seven?).

The book-lined wall promises customers so much. And even if the actual books in the bookcases contradict that promise, the image of the book-lined wall insists on its own verity, because as an image it begs us to go see for ourselves: Spend enough time perusing the always replenished shelves and we're sure to discover exactly what we're looking for, even if it wasn't what we originally set out to find. The book-lined wall is revealed here as a prop, part of the stage machinery of bookselling that gives an illusion of plenitude to better promote a willing suspension of disbelief.

I saw this literalized in my father's bookstore when he moved it to the Pico Boulevard location in 1979. His computer billing operator at the time, Millie Brockway, was married to a carpenter/set dresser for one of the film studios. Brock, as I remember my father and everyone else calling him, was hired as the contractor for the renovation, and my father gave him a detailed vision for what he wanted the store to look like. It was modeled, predictably enough, on the two exemplars of my father's idea of refined bookselling whose shelving aesthetics were also derived, as Petroski helped me see, from Christian houses of worship: Scribner's Bookstore on Fifth Avenue in New York and Foyles bookshop on London's Charing Cross Road.

"Make it look old-world," Jack said to Brock, and he had the contractor create a loft and central staircase that echoed the one in Scribner's. That publisher's three-level bookstore anchored the building that Ernest Flagg designed for it in 1912, a Beaux Arts masterpiece that boasted a glass-and-iron frontage, a thirty-foot-high ceiling, and a grand stairway in the rear. It reflected the kind of elegance and social aspiration that described my father's notions of bookselling and interior design, and Brock masterfully fashioned the more modest but still impressive stairs in the Pico store as a testament to those convictions with what looked like hand-carved balustrades and newel posts that, with the application of the right wood stain, made it appear as if they had been there for years. He laid down brown linoleum tiles that to the eye mimicked a rough, wood floor; he painted the old, unvarnished bookcases ripped out of the previous store a dark chocolate and applied thin strips of wood along their edges to imitate molding.

As Brock set out each of these elements on the stage set of the sales floor, what took shape was a retail space unlike any other Jewish bookstore in America. It elicited reverence, as Jack intended, and the dignity, as he told me when I interviewed him for the *Judaica Book News* article, that he wanted to bring to the Jewish book. It also registered a contemporary sensibility among many Jews in Los Angeles and across the country that Jewishness should project a cosmopolitan design, one that was materialized, on the one hand, by synagogues built in a modernist, international style and, on the other, by the attraction that suburban Jews my father's age had for the clubby style of America's elite White Protestants, soon to reappear as a national obsession with "preppy" fashion.

When it was all done, the density and variety of books on the shelves also echoed Foyles, the bookstore Jack spoke about at home instructionally, reverently, endlessly. Before I understood that there was a mythology of the bookstore, I was well aware of the mythic nature of Foyles. Jack can't even remember when he first learned of that bookstore; as he recalls, it was already a part of his book knowledge when he worked as a teenager in Jewish publishing. Foyles, as he explained many times, was more than a bookstore—it was a book mart, the biggest bookstore in the world. On our way to Israel in the summer of 1974, we stopped in London for a few days so that my mother could visit her relatives in Golders Green, and naturally my father took us to the other Holy Land on his itinerary.

Foyles then still looked very much as it was described in a 1951 *Time* magazine feature article, "The Barnum of Books": "Jammed into a cluster of eleven shabby buildings on London's 'booksellers' row,' Foyle's has 40 miles of shelves, twelve acres of floor space, more than 4,000,000 volumes in stock." It also lacked air conditioning and seemed to me a dusty warren of narrow aisles, some blocked by piles of books, that threaded between heavy, dark wood bookcases whose shelves threatened to collapse beneath the weight of all the volumes heaped onto them. These canyons of book-lined walls described a succession of small rooms, and each room was one step up or two steps down from the previous one, so that after a while it was hard to say just what floor I was on. The shop also had an old-fashioned gated elevator that I, despite my supposed maturity at thirteen, and Ben could not get enough of. After two or three trips, we were shooed off by an unamused clerk.

Even now, though, I see it as my father had prepared us to see it: the epitome of the book-lined wall as living library. It was a mess to be sure, and it lacked the sort of gleaming presentation for which Scribner's was famous and to which Jack subscribed, but the tremendous breadth and depth of its stock testified to its remarkable power in collecting and selling. Jack wanted his own bookstore to have a similar impact when a customer entered. Look, they would say as their eyes slowly circumnavigated the sales floor, so many Jewish books, so much possibility, so little time to explore it all.

What I was unaware of then was that in England William Foyle's reputation wasn't as a fine and scholarly book dealer but as the circus barker of books, an inveterate publicity hound who was as willing to sell books by the pound as he was to sell them for their quality or rarity. The *Time* article relates one of his most famous stunts, cabling Hitler after Germany's public book burnings in 1933: "Can offer high price for all banned books. Do not burn them. Will you negotiate?" As Foyle asserts to the reporter, "A bookseller must never lose sight of the fact that he is a businessman, not a critic." To my father, Foyle's success and his sly, liberal valuing of all books, whatever their content, must have signaled to him that he could be both, and that, too, authorized the design style of J. Roth Bookseller, a cross of London with New York and of my father's ambition with the skills of a master prop maker.

In retrospect, that look wasn't rightly "old-world," but rather a new solution to Jack's contemporary design problem: how to combine his idea of Jewishness with his idea of a "real" bookstore given the available models and his limited resources. His version of the book-lined wall was no more timeless than the very subject categories he arranged around the store to help customers locate their needs and wants. Book categories as we know them are, in fact, relatively recent inventions. In the nineteenth century, bookstores categorized their stock by publisher; in the early twentieth century, book categories were more a literary convention among publishers and booksellers than a data-driven metric. Publishers' book categories only begin to settle into their current shape in mid-century, partly under the influence of the Dewey decimal system and the Sears categorization system developed for libraries in the twenties and thirties, but mostly because the book industry finally got serious about standardizing and rationalizing its business after the Second World War. And it's not until the 1990s that a trade association, the Book Industry Study Group—through its subdivision, the Book Industry Systems Advisory Committee (BISAC)—developed standardized subject categories, its BISAC codes, to help publishers organize their research and information processing.

My father's book-lined wall, in other words, was his interpretation of an ideal Jewish bookstore as that ideal existed in his mind and through his discovery of the famous bookstores of his era. If that interpretation inside our family seemed an imprisonment of sorts, its design nevertheless resonated with Jack's customers, just not always in the way or for the reasons he thought it should.

"I moved to Los Angeles, California in early 1979 which is when I began visiting the La Cienega shop," Meisha Leibson wrote me. She was a student at the University of Judaism up on Mulholland Drive, today the American Jewish University, studying for her teacher certification.

> When the shop was on La Cienega I would visit about once a month or so. When the shop moved to Pico I visited there about two–four times a semester. The location at the latter I found too busy. I loved the home feel of the first store. It seemed stacked with goodies to find. The second location was a bit more organized. It felt more like a regular shop versus the old-fashioned nickel and dime store where one often felt like they had just stumbled upon an unknown goodie long lost by or misplaced by another! . . . The customer service [at the La Cienega store] was comical. Sometimes at the first store I felt like I had fallen into family interactions and whatever was happening was happening. At the Pico establishment the customer care was professional and exacting. While warm, it was not quite as "hamisha." . . . The second store had the ambiance of a book store—with sometimes a semi hushed sound.

Customers like Leibson saw how Jack's design transitioned from a homey to a more "professional" guise, how the scholarly aspect of the store was made fine. The one constant, for her and others, was that the store's book-lined walls stocked everything from religion titles to "knick knacks that were well worth dreaming about, though, unreachable on a student's budget." Altogether, "the Jewish world seemed to be safe within those walls."

As the Pico store settled into its retail life, reactions to its style and feel focused more and more on its aesthetic refinement. "I'm only sorry I didn't have more time to linger in your beautiful shop," wrote the author Faye Moskowitz to Jack on stationery from the Westin Bonaventure hotel in 1985. That year the new librarian at Temple Beth Am wrote about the Pico store in the Association of Jewish Libraries of Southern California newsletter: "[It] was so bright and cheerful that I thought the sun had come out. Everything was clean, and the books were displayed neatly, allowing easy access to all of them." He lauded Jack, of course, for his hand-selling prowess and for the diversity of his subject categories and stock that made the store, he said, "one of the best sources I have seen for books on Judaica." Around the same time, the *Jewish Journal* astutely observed "the very British-looking sign across the Pico Boulevard side of the store" in its short piece about "fads and fancies in Jewish book buying," which according to Jack included books on intermarriage and the Holocaust. He admitted in the feature that he wasn't related to Philip, Henry, or Cecil Roth, but if he could choose, he'd prefer Cecil, the general editor of the *Encyclopaedia Judaica* who was not only a real Oxford don but also a Fellow of the Royal Historical Society and the Royal Society of Literature.

Jack liked and his bookstore attracted the Jewish intelligentsia, so I wasn't surprised that the sharpest observations relayed to me about the book-lined walls of J. Roth Bookseller during its golden age came from the anthropologist Riv-Ellen Prell, a loyal customer in those years. The participants in *havurot*, the "fellowships" of countercultural Jews creating new communities of Jewish religious renewal that were the subject of her first book, had turned her on to the bookstore back when it was located on La Cienega. The beauty, cleanliness, and welcoming atmosphere of the Pico store, however, impressed her as special, particularly in contrast with the unaesthetic and religiously intimidating stores on Fairfax. The space was airy, light, and comfortable, and Jack never talked down to anyone or made them feel as if they didn't belong there.

Most importantly, from her perspective, the bookstore's visual appeal and solicitous service to all who entered, whatever their degree of observance or knowledge, tapped into the contemporary *havurah*-inspired interest in beautifying the mitzvoth, celebrating Jewish ethnicity, and taking Jewish cultures seriously. Customers could find both everyday items and aspirational goods, exquisite things that they might one day afford. And the span of its book selection across the religious, cultural, and political spectrum perfectly served the fast-growing aesthetic of do-it-yourself Judaism and Jewishness.

Listening as Prell talked, I was reminded again of the book-lined wall's multi-sided nature, that just because it fosters the suspension of disbelief doesn't mean that the belief it does foster is always and suspiciously some form of false consciousness. A usable myth may sometimes be just what we need to find our better selves.

That's why after leaving Children's Book and Music Center, and then discovering that teaching first-year composition courses would still leave me too broke to eat regularly and well, I joined the congregation over at Book Soup on Sunset Boulevard. Once more, I had to explain to the owner, Glenn Goldman, why I wasn't working at J. Roth Bookseller, but he, too, was okay with my evasive answers and was glad to have both a native bookseller and a literature graduate student to help burnish his bookstore's already formidable reputation. Besides, I understood exactly what Goldman was aiming for, wittingly or not, when in 1985 he built his consummate version of Book Soup a block down from its original location. His new store boasted the same narrow aisles and crowded floor plan, the same towering bookcases and piles of books that I remembered from Foyles. The visual signification here was a busy-looking "privacy," a literary hideout for personal contemplation.

What especially made the store stand out was that, following the vogue in architecture and design for postmodern quotation, the shelves were painted black and the store's steel-and-concrete facade was constructed in a way and in a color (forest green and industrial gray) that didn't so much re-create as pay homage to the mullioned display windows ubiquitous among the little bookshops around the British Museum. I laughed in recognition, but I felt a keen desire to work there too. It was so cool.

And that was the essence of the store's belief system. Its architectural pretense and deference to the past, the expensive hardwood floor in the front of the store, the glass-fronted custom cabinetry at the back, the whole studied look was a praise hymn to style and, especially, to the attractions of celebrity. This was even reflected in decisions about which books to face out on the shelves. All the clerks were highly proprietary about this responsibility in their sections, and while I touted my own stars in poetry—Czesław Miłosz, Muriel Rukeyser, Yehuda Amichai, Robert Pinsky, Carolyn Forché, Bob Kaufman—other clerks promoted Sanford Meisner, or Jim Thompson, or Cindy Sherman, or Gabriel García Márquez, or Angela Davis, or Nick Tosches. The hip quotient of one's stable of faced-out authors was a key part of the sales staff hierarchy; those at the top always exhibited a careful balance between fame (Joan Didion, M.F.K. Fisher, the Marquis de Sade) and obscurity (Vicente Huidobro, Mikhail Bulgakov, Uta Hagen).

Most of the thrift store–clad staff also cultivated an attitude of mild scorn toward the agents and producers trolling the new fiction section, and indifference to the actors, musicians, screenwriters, and novelists who frequented the store. In part this was because they themselves were aspiring actors, musicians, screenwriters, and novelists, and in part because in Los Angeles acknowledging celebrity is an admission that one lacks it—and that would demean both clerk and store. To me, the store's calculated atmosphere was less a social minefield and more a happy confluence of my own past and present. I thought it a clearer projection of my father's ideal bookstore, on the one hand, and, on the other, another kind of graduate education. Where else could I have met Allen Ginsberg and William Matthews, Bette Midler and Muhammad Ali, Mick Jagger and Madonna, to whom I sold an art book and a pack of trading cards featuring great Jewish rabbis of the twentieth century. (Me: "One of them married my mother and father." Madonna: "That must have been awkward.")

For the average Book Soup customer, unaware of Foyles or Hatchards of Piccadilly, much less Scribner's, the store exuded a contradictory but appealing sense of cutting-edge timelessness. Shopping at the store was to be in the know, which lent a winking glamour to the ample, smartly chosen stock. Its book-lined walls were seductive lures to them, just as they were to the snobbish, book-addled clerks like me who staffed the store and to a Hollywood crowd that basked in such a well-realized set—the perfect backdrop for author readings. It was the literary version of Beverly Hills' Via Rodeo, a faux Italian mini-mall, and Universal CityWalk's simulacra of a downtown. But for me it was also, and at just the right moment, a refuge in which I might escape my disappointment in Jack's treatment of my brother and learn how to be my own, better version of a Jewish bookman.

Coming to terms with Jack took a long time. No doubt that informs my pocketful of disenchantments and skeptical nostalgia for the book-lined wall. And my impulse to judge it, too. Working as I do now at a job that puts a book-lined wall on one side of me and a desk on the other, I've staked out a place in between my old wonder and my current suspicions. I'm just close enough to the shelves that I feel a pressure akin to backlighting—a sense that the illumination behind me has itself become a presence, a character whose charismatic glow throws other characters into relief. But I'm far enough away to be aware of how easily that feeling turns all the objects on and in front of the shelves into suddenly tangible subjects that seem to bring the intangible to life.

Another way of putting this is that the book-lined wall reminds us of how the bookstore is a well-designed stage on which we can rehearse the bookish consumer's desire that books deliver to us both psychological insight and embodied experience, thought and action, *at the same time*. The sense of possibility we have in a bookstore is that handling and browsing the books in them might lead to our being intellectually raptured, to merging our selves with spirit. I think it no accident that we often speak of losing ourselves in a bookstore for an hour or two, as if it were possible to dematerialize while our bodies remain in plain sight.

In the end, though, the only loss I can verify with scholarly certainty is time. Jack visited the Scribner's location on Fifth Avenue shortly after it was converted to a Benetton clothing store in 1996. The Benetton Group had meticulously restored the building and its retail space, peeling off layers of paint from the imported stone walls, refurbishing the grand stairway and the skylight over the mezzanine, and pulling up carpeting to reveal the original marble floor. Wandering around the sales floor, my father was busy taking it all in when a clerk asked him if he needed help.

"No," he replied, as he looked straight up. "But let me ask you. Can you see the letters *CS* on the ceiling above you?"

"Yes."

"Do you know what they stand for?"

"No."

"Charles Scribner. This used to be a bookstore. Did you know that?"

"No."

"Well it was. This was one of the great bookstores in the city." In my father's telling the clerk has nothing much to say about that. For the clerk, the building was now just as it had always been, a monument to fashion with or without its book-lined walls, and the only testament to change was this old man in front of him.

I returned to Foyles in 2007 with a family of my own in tow. It was utterly changed. But why should I have been surprised that after its 2004 renovation it looked like any Borders or Barnes & Noble, five floors of well-organized sections, functional blond wood bookcases, and movable tables. There was the requisite music CD section too, as well as a bustling café with, what else, jazz performances. The closest approximation to the store I remembered was in a separate room on the third floor, "Unsworth's Antiquarian Books at Foyles." Clearly, my father's version of Foyles was itself antiquarian, even if, as Unsworth's boutique suggested at the time, it remained marketable on a small scale.

Sitting in the well-stocked children's section as my son Jonah read to himself and my wife, Mary, flipped through her haul of literary fiction, I realized that the vague sadness I felt was not disappointment at the changes that undermined my father's views on bookstore design and bookselling. It was awareness that his views had been a passing fashion and my internalization of them merely a childhood echo of his hero worship. The year 1974 was long gone; the quiet little boy reading there was not me. All that endured in that moment was the solace of public communion with a famous brand name and with the final incarnation of its book-lined walls before that flagship store was moved to a new location in 2014 and then sold, along with the brand, to Waterstones in 2018.

And also this paradox: The mythology of the bookstore, in the Anglo-American and Ashkenazi Jewish versions that nurtured me, has implicit in it the premise that we can think our way out of that very mythology. It masquerades as an intellectual escape hatch leading out of the materiality of modern consumer society to the safe haven of the ideal. Customers need not actually read any of the books on the book-lined wall to make real their getaway. Simply standing amid such a display of books becomes the physical manifestation of this flight to nowhere. Reading is almost beside the point. It's the environment of the books, what I used to call when I was a clerk "textpaper"—a cerebral version of wallpaper—that makes the bookstore such an alluring meeting place between the headspace of ideas and the hard copy of lived experience. That many never do feel an urge to escape this type of commodification may have something to do with the way memory gets inextricably bound with things like books—or typewriters, records, CDs, shoes, kitchen appliances, and French Impressionist posters.

For me, anyway, the book-lined wall functions no differently than it did for the students in my friend's graphic design course. It's still my first-thought element too, the staple background against which most of my life has played out. I use it as a visual shorthand for the promise that one day I'll see illuminated against it an understandable pattern and clear judgment about my growing up at J. Roth / Bookseller of Fine & Scholarly Judaica.

CHAPTER 7

The Shipping Room (*sound*)

I did eventually go back to work for my father. I don't remember when or how I returned, but I do recall that it was a gradual reappearance starting around 1988 or 1989. I was drawn back, I think, not just by the cooling of my anger or by the realization that I could make easy money working both with him and at Book Soup while I finished my dissertation. I was pulled in, too, by the memory and allure of certain sounds that my father and the bookstore trained me to hear, the bookstore's soundscape. The multilingual conversations of customers, publishers' representatives, and staff, the thud of book boxes being piled atop each other, the mechanical staccato of our billing machine and typewriters, the happy chings of the cash register—these were the things that attuned my ways of listening, swayed my liking for certain sounds over others, and helped me make sense of my noisy world.

Such polyvocal and eclectic sounds suffused the store, and if you were a customer walking into that soundscape, you'd likely think they were all just business as usual for a bookstore that served the Jews of Los Angeles. You might not hear, as I eventually did, how each added another layer of meaning to the store's presentation of Jewishness. Some of these sounds, say of Hebrew and Yiddish, seemed to harmonize with each other—ah, yes, Jewish languages you'd say as you wandered around the sales floor—yet for Jack and others with experienced ears these languages could also resonate with more than a few notes of cultural dissonance between them, especially in talking about home. Other sounds seemed to conflict directly with each other—the cantorial music Jack was fond of humming to himself versus the American folk music–inspired melodies from the Jewish Renewal movement wafting toward you from the store's tape player. These, however, could end up allied as two cassettes—Jan Peerce's *The Art of the Cantor* and Debbie Friedman's *Sing unto God*—in one customer's bag.

The puzzling and often contradictory social and cultural affiliations that these sounds conveyed created mini-soundscapes among the various nooks and spaces of the store. But it was the shipping room that provided my most important lessons in how to parse sound in my father's bookstore, and so became for me a metaphor for such perplexity that only amplified my willingness to return. That room was an assembly place for the objects, stories, and memories that defined American Jewish sounds for me. It figured, in small, the various ways these were shipped into and out of the store and how they orchestrated the soundtrack of my relationship with Jack and to bookselling. It's a room, too, that helped me recognize how the bookstore's cultural commerce escaped the store's physical boundaries in so many ways. True, that happened as well through my father's collecting and through the emotional turmoil that jumped the store's banks and flooded our family. Sound, though, led me farther afield and down a number of unexpected paths that intersected with our family's rising economic class, other ethnicities, and the fast-changing social reality of Los Angeles. It's not just that the sounds in the shipping room re-routed and re-rooted my understanding of Jewishness and bookselling. It drew my attention, as well, to other sounds outside the store that were also, and equally, a part of the store's inside.

When Jack showed up at the La Cienega store in 1966, there was no shipping room and no back door for deliveries. The boxes were brought in through the front entrance. Freight trucks and delivery vans parked or double-parked as close to the doors as possible, their drivers rolling hand trucks full of cardboard boxes into the store, my father helping out if the shipment was a big one. The only space you might call a shipping room in that store, which is to say the place where shipping materials were kept, was a cramped room tucked behind the back wall of the store. It was used mainly as a storage area for the shipping supplies and for a few select stacks of boxes and textbooks, but everyone called it the lunchroom since that's where Jack hurriedly gobbled his down when he had a chance.

When in 1968 he took over the rent on the beauty shop next door, broke through the wall to expand the store, and changed the store's name to Harelick & Roth, the first real shipping room was not an actual room but rather the open area along the back wall of the new addition, next to the filing cabinets, office desk, and billing computer. It was really just a designated space. And while there was now a back door that opened onto a narrow driveway between our building and the next, both the door and the driveway were too small to accommodate large trucks and shipments.

That's the space where I met Edsel, the first shipping clerk that I can clearly remember out of the nine who worked for my father over the course of his nearly thirty years in business. Edsel was a Filipino immigrant, lanky and jean-clad, with glossy black hair worn longer than my parents allowed me and my brothers. He was a student at Hamilton High School, and his girlfriend, Loreta, had been hired to run the IBM billing machine. I don't think he was a full-time employee; he may have just come in when Jack needed a hand in the early years, around 1967 or 1968. He was also an aspiring car designer and fond of drawing cars in his free moments, superbly drafted as Jack recalled, but I can't remember anyone remarking on the appropriateness of his name (even if it was one of Ford's least successful models), the sound of which mystified me at the time. My mother says he and Loreta spoke Tagalog, so I probably thought "Edsel" was just an unfamiliar example of their language, no different than "Aryeh" or "Davida," which sometimes threw non-Jews for a loop.

One day, I must have been eight or nine, I was sent along with Edsel on a quick delivery of a few books to one of the synagogues nearby. My father let him use our powder blue '65 Plymouth Valiant. Edsel was the first person I ever saw use the transmission shift on the steering column like a stick shift, guiding it smoothly at just the right intervals from first to second gear to Drive. Was that how you were supposed to use it? Both my father and my mother just put it in D and pressed the gas pedal. Edsel seemed to know something they didn't. And he spoke to me as he drove (about what, I don't remember), but that was also something my father and mother didn't do.

When we returned to the store, I struggled with a new insight that was related to mechanics but not limited by it. I had traveled with someone who was like us, a trusted employee of my father's Jewish bookstore, whom they let take me for a drive, who would later marry Loreta and come with her as family friends to Al's bar mitzvah. Yet Edsel was unlike us not because he looked different, spoke with an accent I'd never heard before, and professed a different faith, but because he *drove* differently, an action I never imagined had variations, much less sounds of its own: the click of the transmission shift, the revving of the engine upward and downward depending on the shift, the gravelly squeal of rubber as the tires took a firm turn around a corner, the sigh of brake pads bearing down on the brake drums as we came to a full stop at each red light.

These sounds were what first made me aware of all the practices and identities that the store accommodated, that there were different and unexpected ways to be "us" not necessarily related to religion. Edsel made delightfully audible a range of associations and ideas connected to the bookstore that had been inaudible to me only an hour before. From then on, the shipping room and the clerks in it always connoted for me that aspect of the store, a space where things unfamiliar and perhaps not even technically Jewish, but still part of our family's Jewish enterprise, gathered in and around the doorway.

Not that this type of thinking obviated the shipping room's other reverberations that echoed the manual labor and machinery of late twentieth-century Jewish bookselling. The sound, for example, of Jack endlessly reminding us about how difficult it was, and how hard he worked, to make order out of the chaos of shipments that overwhelmed his store before Hanukkah and Passover, and during July, August, and September when all the textbooks arrived from New York. One of his favorite anecdotes was about the time the Behrman House, UAHC Press, and KTAV textbooks were delivered on the same day. "Where's your loading dock?" one of the truckers asked. "You're standing on it," Jack replied. The street resounded with the bang of latches and locks being undone and the scrape of cardboard sliding across the truck and delivery van beds as the boxes were unloaded, resulting in more than 360 cartons lining the sidewalk in front of the store. Working in his shirtsleeves, Jack spent the whole night bringing them in using the store's rattling old hand truck and piling them up in the shipping room and in every corner he could find, including on the sales floor, leaving barely any room to walk around them. Then, after midnight, the *shoosh, shoosh, shoosh,* of the push broom as he swept the place perfectly clean (this last detail being the most important in his telling).

These large shipments, which could overwhelm even the Pico store's larger space, were why having a designated shipping room was essential for him when he moved there in 1979. There were two entrances into that back room from the sales floor, each flanking one side of the store's central stairway. If you walked through the left entrance and passed between the shelves for miscellaneous Hebraica and the *sifrei kodesh* and went about nine or ten steps straight forward, you'd hear the noise of boxes being torn down or filled up and, if the back door facing Elm Street was open, an idling engine or the footsteps of Jewish and non-Jewish passersby as you stood at the far-left end of the shipping counter, which ran the entire length of the back wall.

If you walked through the right entrance, between the ArtScroll section on your left and the pass-through to the back office on the right, you'd hear the billing machine's rhythmic typing, my first introduction to the sounds of bookselling. Straight back from there you'd be at the other end of the shipping counter, where the water cooler dispenser and the door to the bathroom would be to your right—both liminal places themselves between physical activity and social space. Running horizontally between the two entrances and the shipping counter and creating a small aisle within the room was a rough, handmade bookcase, open to both sides, with oversize shelving that looked more like storage bins through which you could carry on a conversation. This was where the textbooks were stocked, their stacks of twenty-five or thirty making a satisfying thunk as you shoved one against another on the shelf, their storage here making it easy to box them up and carry them out to the freight truck or UPS van. Around 1984, though, when Jack's retail trade really expanded, he decided to cut out dealing in textbooks. The publishers only discounted them 20 percent and he had to pay the freight, which was always about 10 percent, so they had become more than just a pain in his back and a thump on the floor. When he told Bernie Scharfstein, the owner of KTAV Publishing House, that despite doing over $75,000 a year with him on textbooks he was done with them because he'd made no profit, Scharfstein replied, "But I did." The storage bookcase was a bit quieter from then on, filled mostly with paperbacks and trade books.

Above the shipping counter was a shelf of shipping tools, mailers, and small cardboard boxes broken down and laid flat; underneath it were neat piles of large cardboard boxes broken down and laid on their ends, like very thin books. This is where many of my father's disquisitions took place, such as the one demonstrating that he was the resident expert at packing orders, something he'd learned and perfected while working at Jonathan David as a teenager and then at Behrman House.

"Laurence, look, when you put them in the box you have to arrange the books so that one spine faces away from the one below and they lay flat in the box, just like when you pile them in a display." As he explained this, he'd begin packing the order I was supposed to be working on.

"If you have a big order of workbooks or paperbacks, arrange them in groups of five so you can easily count them out when you pack and unpack them. Then if you have any space between each pile," holding a book in his hand, he'd scan the box, "you slide a book or books into it, *always spine down*!" and in the book would go, "or," he looked over at the order sitting on the shipping counter, scanning for just the right sized book and grabbing it, "between the books and the side of the box—see how this fits perfectly?" "And then you take a few sheets of packing paper," the rasp of a large dun sheet of paper sliding off the others below fills the air as he pulls it from its place below the shipping desk, "and you stuff it into all the empty spots," a crackle of stiff paper settles into the box, "and then put a layer on top so that when you close the flaps," which he did, "they're protected if the box is thrown around, because those *bulvans* at UPS just toss them off the truck, and also from the knife when the customer opens it, but you know you never extend the blade all the way, you just use the tip to open a box, right?"

Right. Without stopping, he leans over and pulls down on the lever of the packing tape dispenser, and with a tinny ping and long *sheesh* the tape runs off the spool and over a wet brush that applies a thin coat of water to the gummed side of the tape. He begins to seal the box. I'm still standing next to him, wondering if I'll ever get a chance to do my job.

"Now when you tape it up, make sure that first you put a strip from side to side, pulling the flaps right up against each other." With his hand holding the top down flat he quickly pulls the lever again, the clank of its mechanical return echoing off the walls as he pulls off another longer strip.

"And then tape it up from end to end. Last," he makes a quick pull on the dispenser, *shush-clunk*, "you take a shorter piece and you lay it over the box end and seal the edges." One, two, three, four, and he's done. "Laurence, there's a customer at the counter up front. Go see what she wants."

And we're done, but lesson learned: No one fills a box or mailer with such geometrically tight and securely sealed precision as he does; no one wields packing tape or address labels as dexterously, skills he took pains to teach each shipping clerk, and me.

As with the sounds of Edsel's driving, the sounds of the bookstore and of my father making order and affirming his control over it also taught me how to listen or, more accurately, taught me what listening entailed. Standing with my father at his little Sinai of rule-giving, I also agreed to *na'aseh v'nishmah*, to do and to listen, as the Israelites exclaimed when Moses brought the commandments down from the mountaintop. And so, at first, I simply copied his motions and performance. But in that shipping room I began to appreciate that listening is not the same as hearing. To hear connotes mere audible reception, a simple taking in of sound, says Jonathan Sterne, a sound studies scholar; to listen means paying close and active attention to what's being heard. It's a cultural practice.

This is also the case in rabbinic commentaries about the Israelites' pledge, where *nishmah* is interpreted as "understanding," achieved through study and questioning and deep reflection on one's doing and then on the words in the sacred and legalistic texts that proscribe that behavior. That's why doing has to come first, so there's something on which to reflect. And for the rabbis too, hearing is passive, a simple form of obedience; listening is learning how to interpret and comprehend the actions and language encountered amid the clamor of the Torah.

Yet listening, like anything else, is as much a practice as it is a method. And my practice was intermittent and often in need of tutoring, according to my father, just as in the shipping room. There were other languages to listen to in other parts of the store that competed for my attention with their own sounds and demands, more implications, I discovered, that I needed to understand.

It's tempting to assert that Yiddish was the common Jewish language of my father's bookstore simply because it had been Harelick's favored means of Jewish cultural expression and Jack's childhood vernacular at home and at Yeshiva Torah Vodaath. I enjoyed it too and missed its familiar cadences while working in the all-English environs of Children's Book and Music Center and Book Soup. Yet English, shot through with various words, phrases, and ideas from Yiddish and Hebrew, is what I heard most often at J. Roth Bookseller.

"It's a *shanda* what they're doing, but *lo nachum hashem derech eretz p'lishtim*. They'll regret it those *ameratzim*."

That mixture of languages, in a single sentence or throughout a conversation, is called code meshing, and it's why the hum of English in the store produced a chorus of meanings. Did that make English a Jewish language too? In the bookstore, sometimes yes and sometimes no. It depended on the particular sales situation and the way Jack might need to treat English, the way many Jews have in the United States, as a malleable form of multilingual communication, switching from English to Yiddish to Hebrew to inform or regale his customer or audience.

"This biography of Golda Meir is by Marie Syrkin. Do you know her? Her father was Nachum Sorkin, a famous Zionist, a socialist, from Lithuania."

"Our family is from Lithuania."

"Is that right? Syrkin was a real *Litvak* and a *lamdan* too. Once when he was giving a speech a group of *frum* protesters started yelling, 'Lo nachum hashem! Lo nachum hashem!,' and he thundered back, 'Derech eretz p'lishtim!'"

This was code switching, adapting his language and style of speech to make whomever he was talking to feel more comfortable or included, an especially important sales technique in his version of Jewish bookselling to the widest swath of Jewishly affiliated customers. It was also another example of how the store mashed up Jewish and non-Jewish sounds.

Yiddish, though, was a close second in the early years at Harelick & Roth, and it was there that I noticed its specific tonal and cultural effects. Whereas at home my father's Yiddish crashed against the walls or snuck about in whispers, at work it was more jovial, more complicated, and the words longer and multisyllabic. On the phone with a New York Orthodox publisher, he'd shrug and gesture with one arm as he unspooled a long declarative-sounding sentence, looking up at the ceiling and then down at the floor, tracking the voice on the other end as it whirled through the receiver, tossing out his lines like movie dialogue, it seemed to me, and usually ending his exchange with a guttural punctuation and a laugh.

"Shulem aleichem, Jack," a customer would call out upon walking in, his pronunciation sounding off to me, but he's an adult so of course he must be right. "Aleichem sholem," Jack would respond, already beginning to smile in anticipation of some entertaining tidbit or kooky story I might dimly grasp through my father's tone and body language: the upward vocal lilt whose meaning I took as "Of course!" followed by his arms opening wide or crossing in front of his chest; the singsong of Talmudic recitation accompanied by his index finger making an exclamation point high in the air; or the plaintive downbends in his sentences as he nodded and started to inch away, as if there were something important that needed his attention back in the shipping room. Some of these Yiddish speakers struck me as seedy, partly because my father trained me to see poorer religious Jews that way, but also because those he tried hardest to avoid, "the sick ones" who always made straight for him as if they sensed he could cure their psychological or existential ailments, were usually older men dressed, to my child's eyes, shabbier than the other customers. They wore heavy shoes, and dandruff powdered the shoulders of their cheap suit jackets; there was conspiracy in their voices. They grasped my father's arm at the elbow and hung on to make their points. Jack would look over at me, roll his eyes, and I'd be embarrassed. Didn't he realize the poor fellow could see him doing that?

He was far more solicitous of older Yiddish-speaking women. They knew what they wanted. "Balabustas," Jack called them, using the word for women who were sharp-witted and well-organized homemakers and business people, but making clear by the note of weariness in his voice that he didn't mean it as praise. They were often educators and tended to be exacting shoppers less susceptible than the Yiddish-speaking men to Jack's customer flatteries. He would follow them around as they checked out the display tables, lowering his head a bit and putting his hand up, palm out, as if to say, "Trust me," and then calling out, "Laurence, can you get me an order form?" I'd pass it over to him, and as the woman pored over a book that he'd just handed her, he'd roll his eyes again. I was old enough to file this away as yet another of his digs at strong women, but young enough to still wonder: When would I have the confidence that Yiddish appeared to confer on adults who demanded things and those who, like my father, found comedy in serving them?

After the move to Pico Boulevard, the Yiddish speakers from birth seemed older, like Mr. Rubin. He was from Poland, although I don't recall if he was a survivor or if he had immigrated to the States before the war. His thinning white hair was carefully combed, and he used an elegant wood cane to help him walk. Despite his slow speed he had a courtly manner, and his well-tailored sports coats looked to be from the same department stores we shopped at. Jack would show him the rare books and fine editions, and, as they bantered, the sound of my father's Yiddish would morph into something more articulated, the vowels carefully pronounced, the fricatives softer, the modulation less broad. When he left, Jack would always say to me, "Did you hear his Yiddish? You don't hear that kind of Yiddish in America. Very literary, very fine. He's *edelkeit—refined*," his index finger rising as teacherly pointer.

Yiddish, as I learned, connoted both the coarse and the dignified, business and banter, the strange and the homelike. That and the fact that all the people who spoke it were, at the time, at least my father's age or older helped to associate it in my mind with a literate and worldly Jewish adulthood. I also associated it with those customers who had what seemed to me a closer relationship to Jack, or at least one less businesslike. Yiddish, then, was the language of a particular kind of Jewish insiderness, one predicated on familiarity with that important part of my father's (and before him, Harelick's) magic circle. On another level, however, because it was as broad in terms of class as English and so welcoming of personal idiosyncrasies, it was at the same time a language of Jewish outsiderness, of those who belonged with other Jews culturally perhaps but not always socially. In that sense, it resembled those sounds I discovered through Edsel and the shipping room in that its speakers did "us" differently too.

Wouldn't this have been attractive to those American Jews who, like me, felt themselves to be insiders/outsiders too? In fact, this was precisely what happened among Jews my age who in the 1980s and 1990s came to the store asking for Yiddish primers and David Mendel Harduf's *English-Yiddish, Yiddish-English Dictionary*, adding their halting pronunciations to the store's soundscape. Like them, in college I could have easily asked a relative, my father, to teach me, or "borrowed" one of the old, sky-blue copies of Jean Jofen's 1962 workbook *Yidish far onheybers*, or *Yiddish for Beginners*, that Jack found now and then and resold in the store. In graduate school I took a class on Yiddish poets with Janet Hadda, but not her Yiddish-language course, which she first offered at UCLA back in 1973. I could even have attended the summer program at the Yiddish Book Center in Massachusetts that was fast attracting young, secular Jews passionate to rediscover the *mameloshn*.

It didn't seem necessary, I suppose. Everyone brought something a little different to the meanings in the store's soundscape, myself included, and for me it was Mr. Eisenstein, my second-grade Bible teacher at Hillel Hebrew Academy. Short and thickset standing in his uniform of dark blue polyester suit, white shirt, and firmly knotted tie, he had a broad face under slicked-back dark hair covered by a blue knit kippah. To my immature ears, his thick Eastern European accent and Ashkenazi pronunciation lent a note of religious authenticity to the Hebrew of Genesis that he was reading out loud, bolstered even more by the disgust he radiated at my class's inability to impress him as Jewish scholars. When I raised my hand and asked how we know that the snake could speak, his already compact body compressed itself even more as he leaned forward over the teacher's desk and delivered a sneering invective in Yiddish whose exact meaning was lost to me but whose import was that I was a troublemaker, an unbeliever who had some kind of chutzpah asking a question like that. Yiddish, I thought, didn't include me. And then my parents divorced and stopped speaking Yiddish at either of their homes, and as the years went by, those older Yiddish-speaking kibitzers at the store inevitably faded away. It was mostly the black-hatted Orthodox customers who spoke the language then, wielding Yiddish like street slang and mixing it into their English with impressive fluidity. I admired their linguistic confidence but had no interest in joining that speech community.

The upshot was that I never dared try sputtering anything in Yiddish at the bookstore. As a salesclerk, however, I felt confident enough stumbling through my childlike Hebrew with the religious clientele and with any Israeli customers that came in, taking my cue from Jack. Even I could tell that his Hebrew was also an improvisation, albeit of an older, formal Ashkenazi style whose Biblical vocabulary fell like overripe fruit from his mouth. Helping immensely with both of our performances was that the store was once again in the right place at the right time. After the 1967 Six-Day War, Hebrew in its Israeli-Sephardic pronunciation resonated with a more tuneful cultural literacy among American Jews, powering the store's sales of primers like Christian Castberg and Lillian Adler's *Reading Hebrew: Sefardi*. By the 1980s, the number of courses in modern Hebrew at the colleges and among adult learning organizations around town had significantly expanded, and we often sold students assigned texts such as *Ivrit Alfon* by Lois Rothblum, Bella Bergman, and Ora Band. I also needed Hebrew more than Yiddish to do my job, to greet customers, wish them a joyous holiday, or help them find a title they were asking for among the *sifrei kodesh*.

Which is to say that Hebrew was the crucial language of our everyday bookselling, whether up front at the sales counter or back among the textbook bins. It was a national language, literally and figuratively, and even before Yiddish receded, Doppler-like, from the sales floor, Hebrew was well on its way to superseding it on La Cienega Boulevard as the store's second most heard language. Hebrew, too, conferred a sense of belonging, but it firmly yoked that performance of Jewishness to the religious literature and Zionism sections and to the educational subject categories. Even when Jack gave up his textbook trade at the Pico store, Hebrew was still a visually loud presence on the shipping room's storage shelves. And not only because of the prayer books and Bibles but also thanks to the hundreds of copies of *The New Bantam-Megiddo Hebrew & English Dictionary* that Jack sold and Alfred Kolatch's very popular *Complete Dictionary of English and Hebrew First Names*.

The store's soundscape bounced back to my father the postwar and post-Zionist reality of Hebrew's ascendancy as the most in-demand Jewish language and identity for American Jews. It echoed as well their perception of it, as Hana Wirth-Nesher says in *Call It English*, as the "original" Jewish language, their linguistic home. Ironically, as Wirth-Nesher adds and all the primers and dictionaries we carried attested, these predominantly native English speakers were identifying "with a Hebrew alphabet that is as foreign as it is 'home.'" Like Yiddish, Hebrew, too, sounded contradictory meanings—ones both imported and naturalized—and the "us" it articulated was heard differently depending on the type of self to which those books were being shipped.

These ironies and verbal performances of Hebrew and Yiddish in turn peppered customers' aural shopping experience at the bookstore. They might be a satisfying affirmation of being among kindred spirits, or an alluring invitation to come learn, or simply an unremarkable part of the commercial noise of Jewish bookselling. From where I stood on the sales floor, though, these two languages were the bass notes of the bookstore's soundscape, pulsing beneath the sounds in English that it accompanied and anchoring the time passing measure by measure: the cyclical time of the Jewish calendar with its Sabbath sundowns, pilgrimage festivals, and memorial fasts; the time fast running out for an aging generation of Los Angeles Yiddishists; the time about to arrive of an increasingly neo-traditionalist clientele; and the limited time remaining for me to work in the bookstore despite my return and self-serving intentions. Because thanks to Hebrew and Yiddish it eventually dawned on me, with the same rueful clarity I experienced in the wake of Mr. Eisenstein's harangue, that I'd always be a child among the adults in my father's bookstore and never fluent enough to keep its conversations going the way Jack did. As much as I was drawn back to the store by its hubbub, sound also helped me to realize that perhaps this wasn't going to be the business for me. Perhaps, for better or for worse, I was destined to be a Jew mostly in English.

Other languages circulating among L.A.'s Jews were periodically shipped into the store too: Russian, Persian, French, Arabic. The bookstore's soundscape always included the surrounding ruckus of the city and the mélange of communicative and ambient noises that tumbled in through the open front and back doors of the shop. There was the din of the Rapid Transit buses braking at the bus stop in front of the Pico store, the gear-driven slaps of their doors opening and closing, the faint tinkling of change dropping into their fare boxes. Or the chatter of English slang traded between people walking by, the wail of police and fire sirens, the radio of the UPS delivery truck blaring Kool & the Gang's "Celebration" or Dolly Parton's "9 to 5." There was also another prominent city sound that was integral to L.A.'s soundtrack but so often dismissed by my Westside ears that it generally faded into audible irrelevance. That was Spanish.

I barely remember during our first years in Los Angeles, when I was still discovering my new hometown, how Spanish first floated by me in snippets. I caught it as I walked on the street or strolled by the door to the stock room at the back of the supermarket on the corner of La Cienega and Pico, or as my father dialed through stations on the car radio. Driving east on our way to tour the Barnsdall House, or maybe to take in the shabby-looking downtown and its historic city hall building, I heard the wind rushing through the open car window. My face just barely rising above the lower edge, I watched the words on the storefronts change to Spanish as their doorways gave up brief yelps of trumpets and, for me, incomprehensible words.

But Spanish flowed all around us, and not just in the parts of L.A. we occasionally visited. It was in the very names of the boulevards on which the bookstore was located. Pico was named after Don Pio de Jesús Pico, the last governor of California under the Mexican government, who was swindled out of his extensive real estate holdings in Southern California by the lawyer and land speculator Bernard Cohn, who infamously kept two families, one German Jewish and one, secretly, Mexican Catholic. La Cienega, "the swamp," was named after Rancho Las Cienegas, the land grant that was given by the Mexican government in 1823 to Francisco Avila, a cattle rancher and former mayor of Los Angeles, and that spread out over grasses and marshy wetlands from the area around the La Brea tar pits south to the Baldwin Hills and west from Mid-Wilshire to Beverly Hills.

How could Spanish not have seeped into the bookstore in one way or another? Yes, the most obvious route was through the inventory. Jack would sometimes stock a lone prayer book in Spanish should a rabbi at a local congregation have need for one. And he always carried a Spanish-language Passover Haggadah, which he displayed as part of his unrivaled array of diverse Haggadahs for sale in the city. And the shipping room was also and again a kind of VU meter here. In the 1980s Jack hired a new shipping clerk at the Pico store, Ernie, who, like Edsel, helped me hear another voice that was both "us" and not us. His uncle Chouie was a butcher at Doheny Kosher Meat Market down the street. Chouie confided in Jack, a longtime customer at the market, that his nephew Ernie had joined a gang and the family was increasingly worried about him and his future. I didn't know it at the time, but the crack cocaine epidemic was gathering steam across the Southland and violence among L.A.'s street gangs was on the upswing, eventually culminating in the horrific bloodletting and brutal police crackdowns of the early to mid-nineties. Uncle Chouie thought that a job at my father's bookstore would keep Ernie close by and safe.

I don't remember hearing Ernie speak Spanish, though his speech reflected a sort of singsong rhythm of a Chicano English I mostly recognized from movies and television. As with Edsel, it wasn't just his ethnicity or how he spoke that announced his difference from us. Ernie's appearance stated it most clearly: a sharply edged buzz cut, immaculate khaki long shorts, crisp white T-shirts, and tattoos on his arms. Despite the stereotypes about gang members that dogged my thinking about him, the sounds of his working in the shipping room and his management of that space added to the overarching language of inclusivity that helped advertise the store's wide and various inventory of books and people.

And if the soundscape in the store reflected what was outside it, what was inside also reverberated outward. Spanish filtered through and beyond the bookstore following another route, one that well described our family's privilege as upwardly mobile and Anglo-adjacent Jewish Angelenos.

"She was perfect and I loved her," my mother says to me on Zoom, recalling Regina Betancourt, our longest-employed maid, who, altogether, spent seven or eight years with us. "You three boys were like her family." Maybe, although from my perspective she was more like a family member for hire. It was Jack's business, after all, that brought her to our house. Rochelle, who grew up with the occasional maid in her house, tells me that Regina first came to work for us while we were still living on Olympic Boulevard and that she found her through an agency that specialized in placing domestic workers. My first memory of her is trying to pronounce her name, which in the Spanish pronunciation began with a rolled *r* and proceeded to a gentle fricative at the back of the throat for the *g*. Unable to roll any letter and knowing only one kind of fricative from my Hebrew lessons, I pronounced her name as "Re*kh*ina," as if her name were spelled with the Hebrew letter *cheth* rather than a *g*.

Regina was of medium height and had bobbed, dark brown hair, tired eyes, and a sharply angular face. Rochelle never knew her age, but she did know that she came from Mexico. From where, she couldn't say. This was the late 1960s, early 1970s, so Regina may have been one of the many Mexican immigrants who came over then to take advantage of the mid-century boom in manufacturing and manual labor jobs that opened up in Los Angeles. As the sociologist Mary Romero says in *Maid in the U.S.A.*, that opportunity to make a better future for themselves was part of the continuing urbanization of Chicanos in the United States that started at the turn of the twentieth century. And, as she goes on to point out, domestic employment was certainly better than many of the dehumanizing jobs in which immigrants like Regina could have ended up. It offered a safer environment and at least some possibility of negotiating a reasonable working schedule. Regina's was a five-day workweek, and then she'd return weekends to South Central, I think, because Al remembers once dropping her off somewhere around there toward the end of her time with us, when he had his driver's license. Neither he nor Rochelle can summon a street name or address from their memories, perhaps because Regina primarily took buses to go to and from work.

When we moved to Encino, Rochelle gave her the fourth bedroom on the far south side of the house. Located just past the bathroom that we boys used, it opened onto a short hallway where the washing machine and dryer also lived and that led to the fifth bedroom that Jack eventually turned into his wood-paneled library. Regina also went home for Easter and Christmas, though Rochelle always put a little Christmas tree in her room so she'd feel more at home during the holiday season. Regina cooked, cleaned, and was our nanny while Rochelle worked at the La Cienega store. As my mother tells it, she taught Al arithmetic and would look over his shoulder at how he carried his tens.

Rochelle also claims that Regina quoted Shakespeare to Al, which suggests that her English reading and speaking skills were quite good, if not fluent. She must have had a solid education, whether formal or self-taught, yet unlike Al and Ben, I don't recall her speaking that much or to me. There certainly was no need for any of us to learn Spanish, and the little I did speak with Regina never progressed beyond perfunctory phrases like "por favor" and "gracias." The only time Spanish made a conspicuous appearance in our home was on Passover when Regina, sitting at the small breakfast table in the kitchen as we sat at the expandable table in the formal dining room, flipped through the Spanish-language Haggadah that Jack brought from the store just for her. "She was part of the family," Rochelle sighs, though I can't recall her ever eating with us at the same table.

Nevertheless, one day Jack told her to let Regina go, perhaps as yet another consequence of their never-ending power struggle. "And it was painful what I did," Rochelle says to me, "but I listened to your father. In those days I did whatever he said." My mother's regret is palpable, even if her remorse about the loss of Regina is deeply bound up with her remorse over her subordination to Jack. "I miss her, I'm sorry. It was stupid of me to listen to him. But the way I was brought up, he was my husband."

Her attitude about domestic service was also part of the way she was brought up, and it reflected as well how that service was an extension of the bookstore's human resources. Rochelle placed a high value on friendship, caring, devotion, and loyalty as *the* constituent parts of our family's terms of employment, illustrating what Romero calls the "maternalist" perspective on the employer–domestic worker relationship. That perspective enables subtle and not so subtle manipulation by the employer, and in her own book on domestic workers in L.A., Pierrette Hondagneu-Sotelo says it's also indicative of ambivalence or even guilt about the "master-servant" relationship being enacted by the contracting parties. These experts have a compelling case for how to frame Rochelle's sentimentalism about Regina, even if Rochelle wouldn't see it that way. I can only agree with them that our family's rise into L.A.'s upper-middle class and consequent ability to hire domestic workers and gardeners who invisibly scrubbed our home and magically mowed the lawn so that it appeared well manicured to guests and neighbors—and to me, for I have no memory of those sounds—without question turned 4645 Noeline Avenue into a gleaming symbol of the economic and social success of the man of the house, Jack Roth.

You might say, then, that Spanish was the sound of that success, even if it makes me uncomfortable to put it that way. If employing a domestic worker is a way to reproduce the patriarchal social arrangements and class structure of the privileged White capitalist family—at the expense of the worker's own family, which is expected to mirror and play second fiddle to the boss's—couldn't you say that our arrangement was a form of Jewish social reproduction? That is, those who worked for us helped to sustain the family enterprise and reproduce, for me and my brothers' sake, our way of life as social-striving Americans in return for our sustaining them courtesy of that enterprise too. It's how we reproduced and enlarged our Jewish family at work and at home within the confines of the dominant culture and its ideologies. That's my cultural rationale, anyway, for our maternalist *and* paternalist perspectives on employee relations.

Still, listening to Edsel, Ernie, and Regina taught me that peoplehood—the sum of how we define, delimit, or expand "us"—is and should be a flexible conceit open to multiple voices. And also that no family or community is entirely open or totally self-aware. Spanish helped me to hear that and to recognize the bookstore's complex trade in sound, which was, for me, intimately connected to my childhood and so a compelling reason for my wanting to work there. Yet that trade always depended, like it or not, on my father's good graces and willingness to pay attention.

Nothing got Jack to take notice of something quicker than music did. He was addicted to *chazzanut*, cantorial music, always singing something during our half-hour drive from Encino to Hillel in the early seventies.

"Listen," he'd say from the front seat, and off he'd go trying to familiarize us with a particular melody or beautiful phrase.

"Turn on the radio!" we'd yell from the back seat, me on the left behind Jack, Ben in the middle, and Al on the right.

I saw his eyes scan us in the rearview mirror, a look of weary disappointment crossing his face, but he dutifully clicked it on. I'd still hear snippets of my father's low humming between Badfinger, John Denver, Melanie, or Marvin Gaye.

At the store, he loved talking shop with cantors, and he might even be coaxed into a call and response with one, each showing the other a musical detail that the leaden ears of congregants or other customers would never catch. Jack always carried a few cassettes and vinyl albums by famous cantors, including one by my uncle Jacob Konigsberg. For the students at Hebrew Union College, he kept Debbie Friedman's catalog in stock, and there was always a copy or two of Abraham Zvi Idelsohn's *Jewish Music in Its Historical Development* on the shelf in the Philosophy/Jewish Thought section.

When did I discover how music might turn that focus on me? We were driving down Wilshire Boulevard on our way to Hillel one morning in the late winter of 1971, KHJ serenading us as usual, my father lost in some obscure liturgical melody. The DJ cued up some ads, after which the station jingle played, signaling the start of a new set. And then the radio blared:

"JEREMIAH WAS A BULLFROG!"

Jack startled so hard I thought he would lose control of the car.

"What? What did he say?" Jack was looking at the radio as if it might answer him, but Chuck Negron just continued singing about some mighty fine wine he was drinking, while my brothers and I looked at one another with glee. Did he say Jeremiah was a *bullfrog*? Can you say that about a Jewish prophet? Because I knew that Jeremiah was Jewish, but I couldn't figure out what the song was trying to say about him. What did he have to do with cars and bars and fish in the deep blue sea? I was confused, mostly because I was trying to square the connection between the dour and frightening Biblical figure I knew with the absurd and joyful song that had just snapped my father out of his world and into mine.

A mile or so later we pulled up in front of Hillel, and I jumped out the rear door and into the school's side entrance thinking about my music and my language—rock 'n' roll, English—one of which my father couldn't control and that had the not-so-secret power to shock him into full attention, finally.

Music, I learned, was one more way in which to find a place in my father's magic circle, another way to claim a piece of the Jewish collection the store offered. It, too, was part of the transactions that the store promoted if a customer wanted to purchase a sense of belonging, but you had to get to know Jack to know that. Which made music perhaps the most personal of sounds circulating in the store because its meanings and affiliations were especially contingent on self-discovery—of both the owner's private passions and of your own.

Here again the shipping room was my tutor and sounding board for testing that insight. I remember in the summer of 1982, before Ben got ill, Jack gave me a key to the Pico store, a mark of his trust, though it was Al who suggested how we should really use it. It was the summer after I had finished at Berkeley, when Jack locked me into a rental agreement on a $625-a-month apartment across the street from Stoner Park in West L.A. and then made me a salesclerk at the Pico store so I could pay for it. When Al found out that I got a key, he made the case for my letting us in after-hours so we could secretly use the shipping room at the rear of the store to play our guitars through a couple of cheap amps turned way up. I didn't need much convincing.

By the fall I was bringing my own group of friends to join me in my substitute garage for our band. We moved quickly so the neighbors down the block on South Elm Drive wouldn't see us. Loading in through the back door, we set up our equipment among boxes of *Basic Judaism*, *Reading Hebrew*, *When a Jew Celebrates*, *A Maimonides Reader*, *Everyman's Talmud*, and *To Be a Jew*. We were all Jews too, of one stripe or another, and inevitably someone would swipe a kippah from a recent delivery and perch it on his head as we launched into Elvis Costello's "Pump It Up" or the Stooges' "I Wanna Be Your Dog." Looking back, I'd say the irony we rehearsed was largely a by-product of the beer we also brought along, but at the time it seemed to us a naturally funny paradox: Jews who rock? And then we'd look at one another and laugh because *we* were the joke.

The comedy here was entirely contextual. Most of my bandmates at the time learned about Judaism and Jewish cultures in Reform synagogues and Sunday schools, their families leniently observant of the major Jewish holidays but staunchly supportive of Israel, a few major Jewish charities, and delis like Canter's, Langer's, Factor's, Nate and

Al's, Junior's, and Jerry's. Musically, our influences were typical of our time, place, and class: initial exposure to and love of the Beatles, early immersion in 1960s Top 40 pop and rock music, later absorption of 1970s album-oriented rock, progressive rock, and punk–new wave courtesy of KMET, KLOS, KROQ, and KXLU. The bands we liked skewed heavily male, as did the playlists on the stations we listened to.

Jewish music, if it came up in conversation at all, was cordoned off as either the dull, incomprehensible congregational singing and choir music of mid-century liberal Jewish synagogues or the repetitive Israeli folk and dance music that sounded to our mass media–trained ears like elementary school pabulum. Playing the songs that we championed staked our musical identities as a dismissal of any Jewish musical tradition, which we thought of (if at all) as homogeneous and uninspiring. Sure, we took ironic pride in name-checking famous Jews in rock—Bob Dylan! Paul Simon! Neil Sedaka! Carole King! Neil Diamond! Gene Simmons! And Doug Fieger of the Knack!—but our Jewhooing was no assertion of some ethnic subgenre to which we aspired. It merely placed metaphorical yarmulkes on a few famous heads.

The songs we played in the shipping room were yet another riff on the contradictions that accompanied the sounds in my father's bookstore. You might call what we produced there non-Jewish Jewish music, but maybe our assemblage of American Jewish sounds in that space is better interpreted as a product of its liminal character, that the shipping room and, by extension, the store itself encouraged trade, transition, and self-expression. Didn't the workbooks we thumbed through with mock incomprehension set the scene for how to learn music, by copying it and through rehearsal? The kippahs on our heads, worn with a wink, were as much a costume as the bowling shirts and black jeans I bought at Jet Rag over on Melrose. But wasn't that juxtaposition just as much a declaration of my mutually perplexing affiliations as it was of knowing irony? The bookstore, I'd argue, helped to make such confused self-awareness audible and actionable for me and, more importantly, for customers too. Its configuration and soundscape gave them cues for how to rehearse their own version of indie Jewishness—or permission to simply play the hits and enjoy a few classical performances.

Jack saw my contradictory attachments and cultural mash-ups in part, I think, because of music, that it was something else I wouldn't give up, like Al and the store's familiar comforts, its solace of sounds. I don't remember Jack ever asking me why I returned to work for him, only that he welcomed me back and on my terms. Besides, there were other things vying for his attention.

Not long after I began clocking in as a semi-regular employee, another sound of the city rumbled through the Pico store. The 1989 Loma Prieta earthquake did no direct damage to the place, but it did reveal the necessity for the seismic retrofitting of all buildings in Los Angeles, which the state mandated. That summer, the Pico store's landlord, Nemat Novian, began work on the property and the bookstore reverberated with the clang of sledgehammers and the metallic whir of concrete mixers. And then it went silent. Novian and his contractor became locked in a dispute, and while the construction was stopped, breaches in the building's structural integrity invited two burglaries and caused major inventory damage after a torrential rain. Jack estimated his loss of profit during this period was $150,000. On top of that, his rent on the store had risen steeply during the 1980s, from $2,972.75 to $4,625.00 in 1986, and then to $4,902.50 in 1989. It was set to go up again, to $5,100.00, in 1990. All that tumult and dust and the looming increase in his operating costs was just too much chaos for Jack's finely tuned sense of order.

At the same time, the book business changed yet again, sending different but equally unsettling reverberations through the book market and into the store. In the 1980s, S. I. Newhouse and Rupert Murdoch were transforming publishing in America, merging older houses and ruthlessly demanding that every title pull its weight in profits. More important, by the mid-1980s the mall bookstore chains—Waldenbooks, B. Dalton, and Crown Books—reached the limit of their expansion. They were sold off to outfits like Kmart and Barnes & Noble, which recognized, according to Jason Epstein in *Book Business*, that the "surviving independents had shown that extensive backlist inventories attract customers to large freestanding bookstores, which often cost less per square foot to occupy than comparable space in high-rent malls." My father heard this rumble coming and understood that these new book superstores, as they came to be called, could and would undercut his prices. He especially understood how attractive a target his well-curated backlist presented to them.

So Jack thought he was making a smart decision when he moved in May 1990 from the mess on Pico to larger quarters in Beverly Hills, despite trading a corner property on a busy retail street for a location (formerly a carpet store) in the middle of a block populated by professional offices and with almost no pedestrian traffic. As he saw it, 9020 West Olympic Boulevard was adjacent to Beth Jacob Congregation and its wealthy congregants and Hillel Hebrew Academy with its students and their parents' pocketbooks. This quieter yet still very Jewish neighborhood better fit his dream of running "a first-class operation" in a higher-prestige zip code. And with five thousand square feet of space he could also mimic a superstore model, even though at its height the bookstore carried no more than twenty thousand volumes while superstores boasted inventories of one hundred thousand volumes or more.

Taking his cue from the superstores' extensive nonbook inventory, he decided to expand his small collection of fine art and, for the first time, to stock a full line of ritual items, greeting cards, and gifts. That was shocking to me, because in trying to outflank the competition, Jack was acknowledging the staying power of the Jewish bazaar and its bookstore model, that he could clean it up but not push it aside completely. It was a tactical retreat that revealed his dawning recognition about where the Jewish book business was headed in a tougher marketplace, one that would have been familiar to the booksellers on the Lower East Side. In any event, with all that new space to fill up and pay for, Jack finally couldn't afford not to sell tchotchkes like the bookstores on Fairfax, although he believed his were at least tasteful. The store added to its register of sounds the periodic bleat of rams horns, the tinkle of little bells on the silver spice boxes, the click of ceramic and wood mezuzahs being laid out for inspection on the sales counter, and the muffled whump of prayer shawls being shaken out and tried on.

He made a break, too, with the store's previous appearance, turning away from the look and feel of the "Old World" bookstores that had served him so well. Was it that the superstores had recalibrated his taste because their style set a new standard for success? Or was it, as I discovered on my tour with him years later of where Jewish bookstores in L.A. had been, that he was then, as always, committed to clearing out the past the better to free up the present? He, of course, believed it was another step up in the store's evolution, a more up-to-date packaging of the sophistication and dignity he craved for the Jewish book. Jack's architect-contractor, Yehuda Lavi, designed the new store in thrall to the indiscriminate rage in the city for a so-called postmodern style—clean lines, synthetic materials, sharp angles, cool pastel colors, and quoting historical design elements in unexpected ways. As Lavi's vision took form on West Olympic, Jack nervously realized it was too bold by far for his customers and the Jewish community. He fired Lavi midway through construction and had a contractor recommended by the building's owner, Grace Fleming, finish it off. Nevertheless, the result was a store strikingly different in aesthetic and in its soundscape from the Pico store's bookish ambience.

In preparing the essentially rectangular space, my father had workers remove and refinish the wood bookcases from the Pico store that Mr. Brockway had previously recycled from the La Cienega store and install them in the new store against the long wall to the right of the entrance, which itself was on the right-hand side of the storefront. Those cases remained the same dark chocolate color but with a new blond wood trim that ran across the top, on which were printed the subject categories. The dark wood show tables were repurposed with new hexagonal tops covered by blue-gray plastic laminate and with that blond wood trim lining their edges. Gone were the old wire display racks that rattled when empty of paperbacks. In their place were custom-made wooden A-frame display cases, solid and silent. These were chest-high, and their end supports were also painted blue gray with tan plastic subject category signs affixed at their apex.

Against the left wall were glass display cases for the giftware, with waist-high glass jewelry cases in front of them, and these summoned the regular jingle of the keys that had to be brought over to unlock their sliding doors, another new sound in the store. Following these cases was the long white greeting card display rack, like the type you find in fancy card stores, and in the back left corner was the fine art room, whose paintings you could see from the sales floor through a strategically placed glass window. At the back center of the store was the passageway to the shipping room, which was similar in its layout and sounds to the one in the Pico store, if without as much textbook and overstock storage. The back door there led to a few dedicated parking spaces in the alley behind the building, so that if the door was open, you could hear when a car turned sharply into one of the spaces—a customer was coming. In the back right corner of the sales floor next to the *sifrei kodesh* was the entrance to the billing office, and through it you'd reach the sanctum sanctorum of Jack's private office, now hidden from customers and a bastion of silence.

My father still had the sales counter in the center of the store, but this one was covered in that blue-gray plastic laminate, with blue carpeting covering the outside lower half of its base. The floors were beige carpeting, which helped muffle footsteps and the echoes of loud conversations. All the bare walls were painted a light pastel blue, as were the support posts in the store. The biggest visual change, which was Lavi's doing, was the decorative wooden beams sporting the signature blue-gray color hanging from the ceiling at odd angles and at three different heights, which seemed to quote . . . what? I couldn't tell. More familiar were the two "J. Roth Bookseller" signs that used to grace the west and south facades of the Pico store and that now hung on the slip of bare wall above the long bookcase on one side and the glass giftware cases on the other. The background of the main store sign, the one made by Josef Pelzig, was switched from dark chocolate to blue gray and its gold letters repainted silver, its half-moon design fastened onto the red brick of the storefront at eye level just to the right of the entrance.

The cumulative effect of the new colors, layout, and sounds rendered the Olympic store modern, boxlike, and cold. I had returned to work for my father in part out of an attraction to its soundscape—a soundscape intimately tied to my youth—but to me the new space didn't promote the same sonic energy that had circulated in the Pico store. All its sounds seemed dampened. And then, soon after the move, customers started to drop away. For this was also and unfortunately just when the resurgence of Orthodox Judaism, the burgeoning *ba'al teshuva* phenomenon ("born again" Jews whose return to a strict interpretation of faith was part of a national trend), and political developments in Israel turned the question of "Who is a Jew?" into an international Jewish brawl. Books were on the front lines of this fight. As Haym Soloveitchik observed about American Jewish life in the late eighties and into the nineties, the shift of religious and cultural authority from collectively practiced communal norms to selectively approved Jewish texts and "their enshrinement as the sole source of authenticity," potentially a boon for my father's business, instead provided a warrant for the newly religious to create litmus tests discriminating between authentic and inauthentic texts. The 1990 National Jewish Population Survey, with its report of American Jews' high rates of intermarriage, only fanned the flames. Though it was just six blocks from the old location, the bookstore now seemed to some, especially to the strictest among the Orthodox, whether born again or born *frum*, as too upscale and bereft of its former Jewish *tummel*, its familiar Jewish racket.

Perhaps, too, like all soundscapes, the specific version that these customers missed, and that I grew up with in my father's bookstore, had a limited shelf life. It's not that Yiddish and Hebrew were no longer spoken in the store or that the usual quotidian sounds of bookselling disappeared. It's that the timbre of Jewishness and bookselling changed, as they always have and always will. In the Olympic location, Jack got on board with having background music for his shoppers, just like the superstores and other contemporary retailers, playing the cassettes he carried to drum up their sales. This repeating playlist could often be numbing. Tanja Solnik's *From Generation to Generation: A Legacy of Lullabies* was a pleasant enough take on the contemporary hunger for traditionalism, yet it was in the cassette deck so often and in such a desperate attempt to appeal to the grandparents and young Westside Jewish mothers who still supported the store that I couldn't bear hearing it. And anyway, I no longer used the shipping room as a rehearsal space, so the bookstore was a little less central to my aural universe.

While I can and do replay—in digital format or only in my mind—some of the American Jewish sounds with which I grew up, I realize that at this remove from the shipping room, they no longer have the same visceral hold on me. Their contexts have faded. What they continue to exert on second listen, however, is the power to increase my understanding, because they highlight how a bookstore's soundscape can both anchor and unmoor a sense of self and belonging. We return to a favorite, or stop patronizing it, based sometimes on whether it sounds like "us." That's an important part of what makes a bookstore feel like home, a place in which to linger and read in quiet, which in that commercial space is not the same as silence. It's simply our kind of quiet. For me, what felt in the bookstore and in our home like the din of an extended Jewish family resonates now like the distant clatter of neighbors. Those old sounds are still nostalgic, sure, but also a reminder of what it was like to lose touch with what were once some of the most integral parts of my childhood identity, and to recognize that those parts weren't natural or predestined or permanent, but arranged, practiced, and performed to harmonize with the people accompanying me and with my father's direction of the bookstore's class and cultural productions.

It also finally occurred to me that I'd never asked Jack whether he knew that my friends and I were playing music and partying in his shipping room at night.

"Absolutely I did," he said. "Why not? You needed a place to rehearse, and the neighbors didn't complain."

Here's to the neighbors, then. May they always take that kindly to our noises.

CHAPTER 8

Collection's End (*networks*)

No business is damage-proof from the financial and social tremors that eventually knock them down. Whatever their neighbors may feel about them, bookstores are little different, and in many ways are even more vulnerable. Their profit margins are thin, and the products they sell appeal to highly subjective and idiosyncratic tastes, some shaped by unpredictable sociocultural trends and obsessions, some stubbornly resistant to any changes at all. As social hubs, bookstores intimately feel the political storms that blow up communities and friendships. As retailers, their competition is not just other stores but the book industry itself, always on the lookout for a more lucrative form of distribution. And their collections are, at best, indicative of their owner's calculated gamble that they know the market and their customers well enough to predict which titles lie in the sweet spot where both will profitably meet. At worst, they reflect good intentions gone bad, a mismatch between an owner's magic circle and an endlessly fickle public. Whichever the case, no bookstore's collection lasts forever.

Jack's collection was both his source of pride and the bookstore's Achilles' heel. That's because as a Jewish bookstore his collection was expected to speak to and for the notoriously unstable subject category Modern Jewish Literature. The large and varied selection of books my father sold over the years—the best sellers, the midlist mainstays, the hard-to-finds, the facsimile editions and collectibles—made clear that such a category is never simply a canon of works produced at a particular moment in history for this or that audience, or even produced strictly by Jews. As I learned growing up amid the store's book-lined walls and their steadily shifting subject categories, what's modern or Jewish about this literature emerges in the ways that new writing stakes or is denied a claim in an owner's collection and among that owner's cultural, social, commercial, and political networks. Bookstores have long mediated these claims and relationships, and not only between books and readers, but also among writers, publishers, cultural institutions, and communal leaders.

In our family's literary business, the flux and flow of these interconnections was evident in the ways that new titles and the people who made, circulated, or read them, who curated, archived, or regulated them, and who championed, rejected, or remained blind to them, reshaped the existing network of relationships between the frontlist and backlist titles. Jack's work as an owner meant keeping an eye not only on writers and publishers. He also had to keep tabs on copyright issues, transportation systems and supply chains, the media, educational organizations and institutions, and the politics of his customers and their denominations. All of these had an impact on the bookstore's collection. Down on the sales floor, how that network of relationships played out should be familiar to anyone who has patronized or worked in a bookstore: You like that? Then you'll love this! Dislike that? How about this instead? We don't have that, but this is similar. Customer service is network service, directing flows of interest and information back and forth between various locations in the collection, increasing traffic here, decreasing it there.

The store's backlist titles included not only classic Jewish texts and rabbinic responsa but also medieval Jewish travelogues like *The Itinerary of Benjamin of Tudela*; Jewish mystical writings and the gentile interpretations inspired by it during the Renaissance; Yiddish *tkhines*, Jewish women's folk liturgy; works that illuminated the ragged edges of Jewish affiliation like Uriel Acosta's *Exemplar Humanae Vitae* or Spinoza's *Tractatus Theologico-Politicus*; and works by non-Jews that claimed to describe Jews, such as Jean-Paul Sartre's *Anti-Semite and Jew*—or even *The Protocols of the Elders of Zion* and Hitler's *Mein Kampf*, both of which my father kept in a drawer of his desk available for sale, should someone ask for them. New titles materially and conceptually reassembled the bookstore's collection and literary networks, both expanding and contracting the store's definition of modern Jewish literatures year by year, sometimes month by month.

Still, J. Roth Bookseller had its limits; it could only stock so many books. It was not, and my father never intended it to be, a Jewish version of Jorge Luis Borges's Library of Babel, that famous metonymy for the world's collective but inscrutable mind wherein every book from history's polyglot human civilizations was gathered and preserved for eternity as if that library were the main hub in a centralized network for the human imagination. As a going concern, the bookstore was subject to the commercial and cultural marketplace, which is to say to the regularly conflicting demands of all the networks related to the Jewish book trade. It was therefore liable to competition and to public statements of discontent with the bookstore's interpretation of Jewish literatures, such as when certain customers felt compelled to turn Lev Raphael's *Dancing on Tisha B'Av* face down on the new-book table because its frank portrayal of gay Jewish life offended them. That was an omen. Remembering it now, I see how it revealed the store's vulnerability and historical contingency, foreshadowing its demise.

Moving to the Olympic location and making leasehold improvements to the property had upended the store's operations for close to eight months, from April to December 1990. In a "statement of financial condition" that Jack and his wife Elana wrote up in June 1993 as part of an appeal to select investors for a $300,000 capital infusion loan to stave off closure (they offered their house as collateral), Jack claimed that he forfeited two major sales seasons while customers navigated the disruptions and he worked to replenish and expand the store's stock: "April through May (Passover, Yom Hashoah, Israel Independence Day, Shavuot, Mother's Day, Father's Day and Graduation) and . . . September through December (High Holy Days, Sukkot, School orders, and Hanukah)." The bookstore lost around $150,000 in profit for the period. On top of that, Jack had taken out a leasehold improvement loan of $225,000 to be repaid over a four-year period through monthly payments of $4,000, "which completely debilitated product purchasing."

Withdrawing Elana's retirement savings and sinking $40,000 into "quality Judaic giftware" was their strategy to increase the store's bottom line in light of Jack's increasing struggle to maintain a robust book inventory and keep it competitive. The profit margin on giftware was 100 percent of cost, whereas the average profit margin for books was 28 percent, so adding giftware raised the overall sales profit margin from 28 percent to 36.8 percent, "a key factor in sustaining the bookstore," they wrote, and in keeping alive Jack's facsimile of a Jewish superstore.

Unfortunately, the corporate owners of the superstores—at the time Crown Books, Bookstar, Borders, Barnes & Noble—had already paid Jack their own kind of compliment in return. As I was standing behind the sales counter one day in the winter of 1993, I watched two young men come in, one with a camera and the other with a clipboard. The one with a clipboard headed straight for me, while the photographer began taking pictures of the sweep of bookcases along the wall to the right of the entrance.

"We're doing a piece on the bookstore," clipboard man said cryptically, though I don't recall that he mentioned working for any publication to back up his assertion. "If you sign here, with your permission, I'll just wander around the store."

Alarms went off in my head as I realized that the photographer was far too close to and focused on the shelves to be shooting anything that might accompany a feature story.

"No, I'm sorry, you can't photograph anything, and I'd appreciate it if you both left right now. If you want to do a story, you'll need to call the owner and come back later."

And without any complaint they exited the store. Who were those guys? Crown Books had been in L.A. for a while as a chain, but I knew they and Borders were eyeing the city for new superstore locations. Borders would eventually open its first superstore in Southern California in Mission Viejo on Labor Day 1994 and had already announced in 1993 that it planned to open one in Westwood. Would Borders' minions really have the temerity to come into the store and try to catalog its backlist? Maybe I was just being paranoid. My father's worry about finances and customers had clearly affected me too.

Yet I could see for myself that the customers were thinning out and drifting away. The quiet stretches in the store were getting longer and longer. Jack was right. He was losing his retail book trade, but it wasn't only because of the rise of superstores, his cash flow problems, or his shrinking inventory, which had for years been one of the pillars maintaining a vibrant culture of Jewish reading and learning in the city.

He was losing it, too, because of the store's complex position among Jewish networks in Los Angeles and nationally. On the one hand, J. Roth Bookseller functioned as a hub among these networks, with the store playing "a role in more than one cluster of nodes," to quote Caroline Levine's definition of the term in *Forms: Whole, Rhythm, Hierarchy, Network*. On the other hand, it also functioned as a hinge, a node connecting "otherwise separate networks," in this case, separate religious, social, cultural, and political communities. The bookstore profited from its multiple positions, but that also opened it to an even greater number of potentially destabilizing social forces. I like how Levine puts it: "We may have become accustomed to thinking about communications, transportation, and economic networks as powerful connectors that consolidate nations or enable globalization, but a formalist approach reveals many opportunities, large and small, to hamper networks and their coordinating power." Sometimes a single person with a complaint about service, who feels overlooked and undervalued, can undermine a network that seemed unassailable. Other times, and despite how robust the support of other nodes and networks, people just quietly refuse to connect. "In any network, nodes can be replaced," Levine writes, "and they can gather links to new nodes." Jack couldn't stop that, even if he had understood it in those terms.

Networks also fall apart because of a lack of trust between the participants, by the suspicion that a network can't or won't deliver on the goods they want. By 1990, the *ba'al teshuva* movement and the First Palestinian Intifada were splintering Los Angeles Jewry into competing and often contemptuous assemblies, each intent on exerting their own kind of order and control over the multiple identities of Jewish Angelenos. When Israeli Prime Minister Yitzhak Shamir visited Los Angeles in mid-November 1991 to receive an honorary doctorate from Hebrew Union College–Jewish Institute of Religion (HUC-JIR), Rabbi Sanford Ragins of Leo Baeck Temple, a loyal customer of J. Roth Bookseller, wrote a public letter to the president of HUC-JIR, Alfred Gottschalk, another good customer, protesting the institution's bestowing an honorary award on Shamir, given his government's brutal treatment of Palestinians. Both the *Los Angeles Times* and the Jewish Federation–funded *Jewish Journal*, publications in which Jack had run ads for years, ran parts of the letter. Herb Brin, another customer, who was the publisher of *Heritage*, an independent Jewish weekly where Jack also regularly ran ads, wrote a blistering editorial denouncing Ragins and his "idiot letter." He reported that "Rabbi Morton Wallack, one of the leading Conservative spiritual leaders in the West (at Adat Shalom Congregation in Westwood), described the Ragins letter from the pulpit on Saturday as a *chilul haShem*—an offense against the Name of God." Wallack, needless to say, was a customer too.

More concerning was the increasing combativeness of strictly observant, neo-traditionalist Jews about the books and writers represented on the store's shelves and where "their" books were located. "Why are all the *chumashim* in the back of the store?" a religious customer once asked me after browsing our selection of Pentateuchs. "Are you embarrassed?" Another time, one of the high school girls that Jack hired to help at the store on Sundays and weekday afternoons explained to me how a teacher at her Orthodox day school taught her that a passage in the Bible (I no longer remember which one) legitimized the Jews' sovereignty over all of Eretz Yisrael, including Judea and Samaria. I brought over Yeshayahu Leibowitz's book *Judaism, Human Values, and the Jewish State*, of which I was a fan, and explained that according to Leibowitz, a scientist, philosopher, and Orthodox himself, putting land before people was akin to idol worship. The next time she came into work she told me her teacher said that Leibowitz was not a legitimate interpreter of scripture and that his book was irrelevant. A few weeks later the girl stopped working for us, but whether it was because of our interaction or some other anodyne reason, I can't say.

By then, anyway, the interconnections on the sales floor and among those within its ambit were sending out danger signals. As religion reasserted its preeminence as a Jewish way of being, in Los Angeles and nationally, the shared interest and assent necessary for communication between networks became a scarce commodity. To keep these lines open, Jewish Angelenos needed to see themselves as connected in some way to others claiming a similar identity, either by agreeing to be counted as part of the faithful in the communities adjoined by that identity or by finding a common ground among the beliefs on offer in all of them. They needed to see all those communities' reason for being as integral in one way or another to their own spiritual sustenance and social desires. If any community saw only its own dedicated network as worth its attention and trust, there was little reason to talk to anyone outside the fold. Which led, inevitably, to the Jewish commercial market fracturing along religious lines. This opened up new business opportunities for ambitious Orthodox entrepreneurs and offered another incentive for neo-traditionalist consumers to shop for what they considered appropriate Jewish books only among their kind of Jews.

On Friday, November 22, 1991, in the same issue that featured Herb Brin's editorial attacking Rabbi Ragins, *Heritage* ran a story that shocked many of Jack's longtime customers. Titled "The Trials of a Bookseller," it began with a quotation from Rabbi Larry Goldmark of Temple Beth Ohr, a Reform congregation in La Mirada, praising Jack as "a local treasure, if not a national treasure." "He is the personification of the merchant we all dream about when we enter a store: someone who is honest, caring and knowledgeable who always has time to spend with his customers." It went on, however, to report that some in the Jewish public had turned against Jack and "his internationally patronized Jewish bookstore" out of ideological hostility to the store's collection and to Jack's secular appearance:

> The Problem, as it came to be called, was a tightly held secret, shielded from all but Roth's most intimate associates. Essentially, it was a bizarre boycott threat—that arguably worked for a while—engineered by what Roth refers to as "a fringe group."
>
> The first thing that must be known about the slightly-built Roth, one of California's best-dressed merchants, is that, above all, he is a man of immense pride. Friends say he values his pride and integrity more than profit.
>
> The so-called fringe group that reportedly orchestrated waves of complaints against Roth charged that he wasn't stocking enough texts to satisfy their far right-of-center Orthodox tastes and was "hiding" rather than prominently displaying the volumes he did have.
>
> "I felt demeaned, hurt," Roth said softly one recent morning in his private, back-of-the-store office. "Blood, sweat, tears, for 25 years—then to be accused of neglect."

> He came to the third and final accusation as he traced activities that some have called "terror tactics" by perpetrators out to wreck Roth's enviable business reputation, shaped over the last 25 years.
>
> Roth was berated by various members of the "fringe" group for "not looking religious enough" since he did not wear a yarmulke.

In the article Jack blamed the lack of Orthodox titles in the store on the move to Olympic Boulevard and the financial pinch it put him in. He didn't have to say it, but I knew the stock was low in other sections, too. As for wearing a yarmulke, on that he was willing to give, telling the reporter, Ari Noonan, that he had begun wearing one to work every day, noting that it would have pleased his father. As a matter of style more than observance, donning a yarmulke was a simple fix for him, even if visually it was a significant change. It acknowledged he was being watched now in a way he had never had to worry about before.

It's revealing, though, that Jack doesn't address the charge that he hid the religious literature in the back of the store. He was hiding nothing, of course. What his accusers had touched, it seems to me, was the third rail in any discussion with my father about his governance of the collection: his right to organize its appearance on the sales floor as he saw fit. It was bad enough, as Jack points out to Noonan, that these troublemakers wanted him to remove all the books that didn't accord with their view of Judaism, which they thought represented the only authentic version. "We haven't been oppressed enough?" Jack asks. "Now we have to be ordered by fellow Jews to burn our books?" Yet what was most threatening about their demands was that it would disappear "tomes on Biblical criticism, scientific studies and prayer books by Reform and Conservative scholars" and require that he rearrange the floor plan so that the *sifrei kodesh* and religious literature were up by the entrance. This would have shredded his prerogative as owner to shape the narrative of his store and would have undermined the carefully crafted one that welcomed all customers, no matter their network affiliation, to follow Jack's floor map of Jewish education and history. "He sees his 5,000 sq. ft. store as 'neutral ground,'" Noonan writes, "where Orthodox and non-Orthodox rabbis and leaders can discourse with each other, since they won't visit each other's synagogues."

These rabbis and leaders, representing all Jewish denominations in the city, rallied to Jack's defense. They urged their congregants and constituencies to shop at the store and to show their support in recognition of all the years my father had supported them. Calling him in the *Heritage* article "a literary mirror of Jewish life," Rabbi Harold Schulweis, a leading theologian in Conservative Judaism (and the rabbi at Valley Beth Shalom, our family synagogue when we lived in Encino), believed it important that Jack continue keeping the lines of communication between Jewish networks open, though he worded that perspective in the vocabulary of his time: "In a day when, tragically, everything we do is seen as sectarian—a Jew no longer marries a Jew but a particular kind of Jew—Jack has transcended that." He *had* transcended that. It just wasn't clear that he could much longer.

* * *

Ellis C. Berkowitz, M.D., Inc.
Otolaryngology
8631 West Third Street, Suite 410 E
Los Angeles, California 90048

Telephone 213/657-5806

November 18, 1991

Mr. Jack Roth
c/o J. Roth, Bookseller
9020 W. Olympic Blvd.

Dear Jack:

At our bible study group meeting this past weekend there was a rumor circulating that you were planning to sell the bookstore. Part of the reason for the sale was related to pressures exerted on you to keep certain "heretical" books out of sight in some back room.

Whether such rumors are true or not, the purpose of this letter is to express to you our gratitude for the many years you have helped guide us through the richness of Jewish literature. You have been for our group (and I am sure many hundreds of others) a constant resource, an advisor, and a good friend in directing us to Judaic materials for a variety of projects over the past fourteen years. Nearly all of us have built an enviable Jewish library that we use constantly in our studies.

It is indeed difficult to conceive of living in Los Angeles without the J. Roth Bookstore, and in particular, without you as the leading influence in the store. We don't visit your bookstore simply to buy books. We go to visit with you, and to enjoy the scholarly discussions on Jewish subjects, and to have you help us to find just the appropriate material we need for our study group. When I realize how much I have learned over the past fourteen years, part of the credit must belong to you.

Whatever happens, please know that you have our continued support and good wishes. We hope that you will have long years of service to the Jewish community. If you should choose to move to a new location, we will follow you.

With best personal wishes,
Ellis C. Berkowitz, M.D.

The rumors weren't entirely untrue. Jack was getting worn down by the stress of being underfinanced and under siege. The neo-traditionalists continued their boycott. And while he appreciated the loyalty of L.A.'s liberal Jews, he couldn't keep the store afloat with only their patronage. But he was ambivalent about getting out of the book business. Some days he'd look around the quiet sales floor and mutter something about closing up and walking away, or that he should have gone to work for the State Department when he was younger. Negotiating with foreign countries would have been easier than negotiating with his fellow Jews. Other days he'd be energized by his customers, telling them that he wasn't going anywhere and joking that he'd have to be carried out of the store feet first. It wasn't an idle boast. During the 1992 uprising after the acquittal of Rodney King, Jack worried that the burning and looting would flow west on Olympic from Koreatown and onto his doorstep, putting him in the same boat as the Korean merchants who were abandoned by the police and had to protect their businesses by themselves. He didn't know that the Beverly Hills police had drawn defensive lines around that city and that the Los Angeles police had deployed in force to protect the majority-White Westside from the pent-up anger of those on the Eastside who had long suffered under L.A.'s geographic racism. He stayed in his store anyway.

Clearly, the bookstore still meant too much to him. He couldn't just walk away; as the *Heritage* piece revealed, Jack had too much pride for that. He decided instead that he had no choice but try to restore the Orthodox networks that had disconnected from J. Roth Bookseller, so he fell back on his greatest strength: his knowledge of and abilities at collecting. With the money coming in from his supporters, he added more Orthodox and traditional Jewish materials. He invited an Orthodox silver wholesaler and an Orthodox sofer, a scribe and rabbi, to set up their shops within his store. He put the sofer behind the glass wall of the corner room that had originally separated his small collection of Jewish paintings from the book collection, thinking to show him off as evidence of his traditionalist bona fides and as a convenient publicity attraction too.

Was it a capitulation? A strategic one, yes. He was under surveillance, as verified by his black polyester velvet yarmulke, so he needed to figure out a concise way to visually signal that his store was *frum* receptive without compromising the rest of his collection. You must have everything, right? Then why not include more rather than move things around and ruin the order that took him years to perfect. He would simply add what amounted to two new sections on the sales floor, let's call them "Fine Silver Judaica" and "Scribal Arts," and a new subject category in the religious literature section, "Hashkafah." Jack was well aware that this translates as "world view" or "outlook," and that in Orthodox usage it refers to developing a correct Jewish ideological perspective that's firmly based on *halakhah*, the expression of God's will in law and rabbinic legal reasoning. Signal sent. What choice did he have anyway? He was yeshiva educated, he knew the texts they revered and was conversant in the varieties of Jewish religiosity these works had inspired as well as the passions they had provoked among those who saw themselves as trembling before God. He'd have to tremble a bit too if he wanted to blend in.

And for a while it worked. Both the silver dealer and the sofer brought a burst of customers and energy to the store, and Jack's socializing with the silver dealer in particular gained him some contact with a younger Orthodox clientele as well as inside information about the Orthodox synagogues and businesses back on Pico Boulevard. A few of them had started selling prayer books and religious goods.

Unwittingly, though, my father had turned his store from a busy network node and living library into a museum. Barbara Kirshenblatt-Gimblett's work on the use of objects in ethnography enabled me to see in retrospect that Jack's sofer exhibit and the scribe's performance of culture suggested that authentic Jewish tradition belonged, literally, to religious insiders, relegating nonobservant outsiders to the role of audience and cultural tourists. Despite Jack's attempt to update rather than rearrange his sales floor so as to recapture his centrality among L.A.'s Jewish networks, what had once seemed a hospitable and inviting space now appeared staged and contested. It discomforted some of his Reform and secular customers who were happy to support his fight against the neo-traditionalists' boycott but for whom the new store with its Orthodox set dressing no longer felt entirely theirs.

In any event, the solution didn't hold. Business was booming in the Orthodox sector and Pico Boulevard was its epicenter. The lease on Jack's old store there was taken over by a sizable kosher grocery, and by 1993 the street's financial lure helped unravel his arrangements with the silver dealer and the sofer. Doing well but ruing the lack of pedestrian traffic on Olympic Boulevard, the dealer decided he wanted his own retail location and opened Brenco Sterling Silver on Pico. He soon added Jewish books too. As for the sofer, he'd often stayed in the store after my father closed up for the night, working on Torah scrolls, tefillin, mezuzahs, and plans. Jack told me he knew the young rabbi was doing business on the side without him. When the sofer pulled out he, too, went to Pico and started his own bookstore, the 613 Mitzvah Store, which carried only "kosher" *sforim* and ritual goods.

"The younger Jews weren't buying at my store," Jack explained when I asked him what happened after that. "And my older clients weren't *frummies*," he added. "I was losing the retail trade."

He was also feeling pressure from other transformations in book retailing.

"Things were changing, getting to be on the computer," he told me, something I remembered vividly, because at the time I had tried to get him to see that computers weren't just for billing. For a few years already I had been using my Apple Macintosh Plus to design ads for the store and to type up and then print on my HP DeskJet some of my father's speeches and history talks that he regularly gave at synagogues, libraries, and Jewish professional conferences. Although he had helped me pay for these, he never used either and had no desire to purchase one for the store. What did he need it for if mine was available anyway? More importantly, I watched as Glenn Goldman at Book Soup invested in a new IBID Bookstore Management System to update his previous digital cash registers and to expand the database of titles he could access for his store. I insisted to Jack that this was the future of inventory control and he had to install a similar system, but the cost was too prohibitive for him. Neither of us could have predicted that Amazon and the beginning of online book retail would appear only two years later, in 1995.

If computer networks weren't within my father's grasp, he still had access to Jewish networks that might rescue his bookstore. He was put in touch with Lydia Kukoff, the author of *Choosing Judaism*, founding director of the Reform movement's Outreach Program, and at that time the North American director of the Avi Chai Foundation, a transdenominational philanthropy founded in 1984 by Zalman Bernstein to promote Jewish education and religious observance, especially among young American Jews. Kukoff visited the store and then requested an investment and outreach proposal that the foundation might fund, so Jack, Elana, and I went to work crafting a proposal. That was unfortunate, because none of us had ever written a grant proposal for a philanthropy and I, the designated copy writer, had no idea what Avi Chai's funding priorities or criteria were.

The result was a proposal that makes me cringe when I read it today. I recognize my bluster in the comparisons we made between our proposal and "the wonderfully prismatic world of the Jewish bookstores and cafes of Warsaw in 1928 and its panoply of thinkers, writers, and artists." We claimed that our purpose was "to provide marginal and unaffiliated Jews with an enticing five thousand square foot spiritual and cultural resource center and intellectual marketplace that will 'prime the pump' of Jewish creativity," and we essentially told Avi Chai that we wanted $352,400 in grant money for programming and products, including a restock of the book inventory. We explained how we would reconfigure the sales floor and add interactive multimedia, a meeting room, event space, and a coffee bar and kosher wine boutique (helped out again by my friend Jeffrey, who was by then working his way up in the restaurant business) and hire a program manager to run a children's storytelling series, a Jewish poets reading series, a Jewish movie night, information fairs on Jewish marriage, a lecture series on Jewish feminism, and an "Open poetry/folk music/singles night" once a month. We'd also finally purchase that IBID system.

It was a valiant but transparent attempt to bolster J. Roth Bookseller's market position as a Jewish superstore, but with enough education and outreach to make it attractive to the grantor. Our promised assessment of progress was entirely anecdotal. It doesn't surprise me that Kukoff never presented our proposal to the Avi Chai board in May 1993. Even if she had, the foundation was at the time shifting its funding focus to Jewish day schools and camps where they would have a direct impact on the next generation of American Jews.

Jack quickly turned our proposal into that appeal to investors for $300,000, which over the next six months fell on deaf ears. That signaled the beginning of the end for my father's bookstore, no matter all the kind words the Jewish communal establishment had heaped on it and on Jack. A bookstore can't survive on words alone.

"It's my child," Jack said to me one afternoon in the spring of 1994. We'd been talking in the shipping room and he had walked into the passageway connecting it to the sales floor, staring straight ahead at nothing at all. The store was empty. There hadn't been a customer all morning, and earlier the mailman had asked us if we were closing. Jack's reputation might have been intact, but not his credit with Jewish publishers back East. He had muddled along for another year thanks to a generous loan from his brother Rabbi Michael Roth and by selling off a few paintings from his private collection, including one by Issachar Ber Ryback and another by Emmanuel Mané-Katz. But now the shelves and tables were thinned out and filled with gaps, and those Jewish publishers, whose owners and sales representatives my father had treated as both business colleagues and friends, were refusing his orders. He'd been surviving on the few titles he could still afford to buy from the book wholesaler Ingram.

The store was his child? Did that make me its brother? As I waited for Jack to turn back to me, I remember thinking that I was going to lose the bet I had made with myself, that somehow Jack would turn things around and we'd eventually talk about these days as if they were just bad memories of a fleeting hard time. Now I knew that we were really finished. His child was lost, and I was going to have to watch the family dissolve once again.

Then the final blow: City National Bank (CNB), which had for years extended him a $100,000 line of credit, declined to renew that credit and demanded repayment of the $12,000 he still owed it. There were no options left; it was time to call it quits. He hired an attorney, who advised him to give the key to the store to CNB and do a reasonable commercial sale of inventory, on which CNB had a lien, to pay off the debt. The bank prepared to run the sale as an auction, with the highest bidder winning the store's remaining stock of books and Judaica.

Around that time, Moshe Gabay, the new Moroccan Jewish owner of the House of David bookshop in North Hollywood over in the San Fernando Valley, heard that the inventory was for sale. Avrum Schwartz, Jack's long-serving salesclerk, had gone to work for Gabay at his shop when Jack could no longer afford to pay him, and with Jack's blessing he let his new boss know about the opportunity and that the lease on the store might be available too. House of David had been the only real competition for Rochelle when she opened the second store in Encino back in 1973, and Jack had always viewed it as a minor outpost of the Jewish book and Judaica trade in L.A. But that changed with the arrival of Moroccan Jews to that store's neighborhood beginning in the 1970s. By 1990, when Gabay purchased House of David, their numbers had swelled. They had established new Sephardic synagogues in the Valley, according to Aomar Boum's mini-history "Little Jewish Morocco," and the Moroccan Jews living around Fairfax and Beverly Hills were growing in number too. The demise of J. Roth Bookseller offered Gabay both inventory and a convenient second location to serve a network of Jewish readers that the Ashkenazi Jewish booksellers had overlooked.

There was some hard-nosed negotiating at that point. While I was kept in the dark about the details, it created a rift between Jack and Elana for years after. Everyone involved was looking for an advantage, and Elana wasn't going to let anyone get the upper hand over her and Jack. Yet my father was still more concerned with his reputation. Having outmaneuvered Gabay during the auction but loath to fight the bank in court over the ramifications of Elana's shrewd bidding strategy (she submitted the winning bid of $5,018), Jack privately sold the inventory to Gabay for $25,000, used that money to pay off CNB, and got himself dismissed from the bank's lawsuit. In June 1994 Gabay took over the lease on 9020 West Olympic Boulevard, which became House of David. That location closed only a few years later, and Gabay consolidated the inventory back into his first store, now located in a larger storefront on Burbank Avenue in Valley Village.

Jack wasn't completely done with the store, however; his creditors remained unpaid. Although he could have declared bankruptcy, he instead worked out repayment schedules with each. He paid the last of them off ten years later, in 2004.

That was the finale, but not the whole story. The store's failure also vividly illuminated the double-edged sword of its success, which was partly due to the collection no doubt, but also and perhaps more importantly to all the networks it helped gather around and through the store. Their interconnections brought Jewish Angelenos into conversation with each other and brought what Jack thought it meant to be Jewish into association with a multitude of ideas, religiosities, people, places, and things in Los Angeles, America, and the world. These networks both enlarged and complicated the store's communal affiliations. Some of these were highly antagonistic to each other religiously and politically; all exceeded any one definition of "Jewish." As his daydream of working for the State Department suggests, Jack had long believed himself a diplomat of sorts. He had the unique ability to juggle relationships with people connected to a wide variety of community organizations and social circles. He implicitly understood what Laura Levitt would later describe when she writes that "Jewishness exceeds notions of ethnicity because there are multiple Jewish ethnicities and because it can include forms of religious expression beyond privatized faith. . . . The common rubrics of liberal pluralist difference—race, class, and gender and/or sexuality—just do not fit, nor does the overarching notion of religion."

This was good for Jack's business, even if the mix was highly volatile. The wider the definition of Jewishness and the greater the confusion over Jewish identity, then the more social and cultural networks would find their way through his sales floor. In return, the bookstore offered a commercial command and control system with which to manage the overdetermined nature of Jewishness and make its variable guises recognizable and discoverable to consumers. In that sense, it was a political business. It reflected and helped construct Los Angeles's fragile midcentury détente between all the disparate threads of Jewishness that described the warp and weft of Jewish life in the city and the region, when the one thing that everyone could agree on was the need to protect and maintain a fast-growing Jewish presence in a place where Jews could make a living, re-create themselves, or embrace the freedom to willingly disappear.

Leafing through the letters and documents my father sent me, and through the emails I've received through the years from former customers, I see now how its ability to serve and preserve these relationships gave form to the store's brand and reputation, how they were brought into being not only on the sales floor but also through Jack's involvement in community activities and politics, his servicing of the region's Jewish educational systems, and the store's coverage in public media.

All those boxed-up records that he sent me make this web of relationships briefly visible again. I spread them out on the floor of my study and consider the bookstore's importance to the networks that made up its cultural and intellectual reach as well as Jack's influence and legacy as a bookseller and collector. Trying to tease out all the good that the bookstore did for Jewish communities in the Southland and beyond, I realize there's one relationship still difficult to discern. It's the one describing my own inheritance from the store, my own "betweenness centrality," to borrow a term from social network analysis. I'm the bridge between all this information, between the competing narratives of Jack's failures and successes, between the store and you reading this book. I'm the one still distributing objects and information from my father's business, including some valuable things that belong to me yet aren't in the papers lying at my feet and that can't be seen anymore, at least not in the forms they first took. Placing everything back in folders that bulge like oversize wallets, I brood over where my father's legacy has gone.

* * *

Graduate Program in Religious Studies
Faculty of Graduate Studies
Mahidol University
Office 3 at Siriraj Hospital
Bangkok 7, Thailand

March 24, 1983

J. Roth, Bookseller
9427 West Pico Boulevard
Los Angeles, CA 90035
U.S.A.

Dear Mr. Roth,

As Director of the Graduate Program in Religious Studies at Mahidol University, I want to thank you for your special efforts in assisting us with the purchase of books on Judaism for our library. Dr. Marks informs me that you processed our order, with its unusual circumstances and conditions, in a particularly conscientious and understanding manner. I should like you to know that your work has greatly aided the development of the first Judaic Studies courses in Southeast Asia, which will certainly result in greater knowledge and understanding of Judaism and the Jewish people on the part of the people of Thailand and Southeast Asia.

Yours Sincerely,
Dr. Pinit Ratanakul

It's letters like this one that remind me how important the bookstore was to the development of Jewish studies in Los Angeles and around the Pacific Rim. Student and faculty desire for courses about Jewish life and practice aren't actionable without the books necessary to their syllabi and libraries. Whatever the precipitating incident was that successfully muscled those courses into a university's schedule, the most immediate task was always rounding up the learning materials. That may seem easy enough to those accustomed to the click of a mouse, the convenience of cell phones, and easy access to booklists, distributors, and publishers. In the days of parcel post and airmail, expensive long-distance calls on rotary phones, and hunting for books through catalogs and newsletters, however, it was a daunting challenge, especially if there were any oceans to cross. In that case, it was sometimes just easier to show up to the store in person. Jack recalled how one year when the German government was sponsoring a Jewish celebration in Berlin (he couldn't remember for what), a polite and well-dressed German gentleman came in and introduced himself. He said he needed tons of material, so Jack let him pull whatever he wanted off the shelves, and it came to over $5,000. He handed over a credit card and, much to Jack's relief, it went through.

It wasn't just academics or government emissaries who sought out the store as a resource for teaching and learning. Over the years, people formed many small study groups in Los Angeles inspired by the Jewish Renewal movement, or current events, or simply a hunger to know more about Jewish religion and cultures. They gathered in private homes and on weekends to learn together. I'm looking at a letter from a group of Los Angeles judges, including Judge Joseph Wapner, who presided over "the People's Court" on TV, thanking Jack for his help with and advice about their study of Torah and other Jewish subjects. It makes me wonder how their desire to learn more about Jewish religion, history, and cultures rippled into their legal reasoning, and I marvel at the role my father's bookstore played in inculcating Jewish thought into the professional life of the city.

These larger impacts of my father's influence on Jewish learning in L.A. are always gratifying to see, and when celebrity names light up a network, the store's reputation shines even brighter in their reflected glow. But I'm moved far more by the personal letters of those for whom the bookstore and meeting Jack were life-changing. These testified that the store's quotidian impacts had equally far-reaching implications that were often magnified by the customer's own focus on Jewish self-discovery. In one, a prize-winning journalist thanks Jack and encloses repayment for a gift of $100 that he gave him to attend graduate school for journalism. The writer makes a point of noting that he's remained involved in Jewish affairs by writing for Jewish publications and that he's lived a Jewishly connected life, as if this, too, were repayment for my father's generosity. These letters convince me that every transaction in the bookstore must have had a butterfly effect on future meanings of Jewishness, as do those letters thanking Jack for allowing marginalized streams of Jewish learning and religiosity—such as those dedicated to Jewish feminism—to use the bookstore as a venue for their events.

These private acts of public service are what cemented Jack's and his bookstore's public legacy, which is best summed up in the official tribute book printed by the Wagner Program of the University of Judaism (now the American Jewish University, or AJU) for a luncheon on November 27, 1990, celebrating Jack's twenty-fifth year in business and honoring him as a "distinguished Judaica book man" and "an essential educator of Southland Jewry." Founded by Betty Wagner Kramer, the Wagner Program served L.A.'s Jewish communities through various social support and outreach programs, but most notably through the Human Services Para-Professional Training Program, which would become the Wagner Human Services Paraprofessional Certificate Program at AJU.

The tribute book included well wishes from Temple Emmanuel, Beverly Hills; the University of Judaism; the libraries at Sinai Temple, Valley Beth Shalom synagogue, and Stephen S. Wise Temple; Dvorah Colker, president, Temple Beth Am; the Union of American Hebrew Congregations, Pacific Southwest Council; the education leadership at Adat Ari El; Temple Isaiah; Rabbi Chaim Seidler-Feller and the Hillel Council at UCLA; the Association of Jewish Libraries of Southern California; and Irene Fine, director, Women's Institute for Continuing Jewish Education, San Diego State University. Also wishing Jack well were the writers Faye and Jonathan Kellerman, Judy Zeidler, Sonia Levitin, and Dennis Prager, as well as publishers and other Judaica stores such as Mesorah Publications (the publishers of ArtScroll), Gallery Judaica, the UAHC Press, the Israel Book Shop, Carmi House Press, Kar-Ben Copies, and KTAV Publishing House. Forty-eight rabbis from congregations throughout the Southland sent their best to Jack.

Prominently displayed in the tribute book are letters of congratulations from the president of the Board of Rabbis of Southern

California, Rabbi Jack Simcha Cohen, and from the president of Hebrew Union College–Jewish Institute of Religion, Rabbi Alfred Gottschalk, and official citations from Allan Alexander, the mayor of Beverly Hills; Tom Bradley, the mayor of Los Angeles; Congressmen Anthony C. Beilenson and Henry Waxman; Senator Pete Wilson; and Governor George Deukmejian.

Most impressively, the "citations" section of the book culminates with a resolution from the State of California Senate Rules Committee, "By President pro Tempore of the Senate David Roberti; Relative to Commending Jack Roth":

> WHEREAS, Jack Roth, a distinguished bookseller, is celebrating his 25th anniversary of business in Los Angeles, and will be honored by the Wagner Program of the University of Judaism on November 27, 1990, and upon this occasion, he is deserving of special recognition and the highest commendations; and
>
> WHEREAS, Mr. Roth was born into a distinguished Eastern European family, and he spent 18 years studying in yeshivoth in New York; and
>
> WHEREAS, He attended City College of New York and worked part-time for the Jonathan David Company, a fledgling Jewish bookstore, which later became a successful publishing house; and
>
> WHEREAS, Mr. Roth served his country in the United States Army in Korea, where he received a citation for bravery; and
>
> WHEREAS, After his military service, he became general manager at Behrman House Publishers, where he served for 10 years; he brought his experience in Jewish book publishing to Los Angeles in 1966, with his purchase of the Michael Harelick's bookstore on La Cienega, and for 13 years Harelick and Roth was a major source for Jewish publications in Southern California; and
>
> WHEREAS, In 1979, Mr. Roth moved to Pico and Elm Streets, where J. Roth Bookseller became a center for Jewish bibliophiles and the largest and most complete Jewish bookstore on the West Coast; in May 1990, he relocated to 9020 West Olympic Boulevard in Beverly Hills, where he continues to make everyone comfortable "from Torah scholars to those who are just beginning to read Jewish books"; and he is noted for his acumen in finding rare Jewish books from around the world for first editions, autographed copies, and special bindings; and
>
> WHEREAS, He is a founder of the Hillel Hebrew Academy, and Member of the Western Association of Temple Educators, the Southern

California Jewish Historical Society, the Los Angeles Jewish Community Library, and the Wise Circle of Hebrew Union College Cultural Center of American Jewish Life; now, therefore, be it

RESOLVED BY THE SENATE RULES COMMITTEE, That the members take great pleasure in congratulating Jack Roth upon the occasion of his 25th anniversary of business in the Los Angeles community and his being honored by the Wagner Program of the University of Judaism on November 27, 1990, commend him for his illustrious record of personal and professional achievements, and convey sincere best wishes for continued success in his future endeavors.

Senate Rules Committee Resolution No. 2984 adopted September 20, 1990.

Jack was humbled by that recognition, writing in the tribute book's epilogue: "The friendships and good will of those I have met and worked with all these years, and who honor me today by sharing this meal together, are what I value most." Years later, he was honored again, but in a way that underlined how crucial friendships were to my father's impact on Jewish booksellers and bookselling.

In August 2013, I was in Jerusalem for the World Congress of Jewish Studies and Jack had joined me to make a family trip out of it. He had put M. Pomeranz Bookseller on our itinerary because Michael Pomeranz worked for him back in the late 1980s and he wanted to visit the Jewish bookstore that his friend and former salesclerk opened after making Aliyah in 1991. Pomeranz was an L.A. firefighter and policeman who became observant and quit his public-service job in favor of another kind of service: he wanted to open a store just like J. Roth Bookseller in Jerusalem.

Walking in, I had a moment of déjà vu. I saw the familiar wood sales counter in the center of the sales floor; the book-lined walls around it were stuffed with titles displayed in the neat, professional style I learned from my father, tightly stacked just as he liked on the new and featured books table right at the entrance. There wasn't a kiddush cup or tchotchke in sight. Jerusalem's largest English-language Jewish bookstore, M. Pomeranz exuded the same bookish gravitas and dense inventory that Jack's Pico store did. Here, though, the ArtScroll titles were up front along with the *sforim*, but spread out behind them was a wonderfully strong backlist of books from KTAV Publishing House, Jason Aronson, Feldheim Publishers, the Littman Library of Jewish Civilization, and university presses in the United States. The cookbook section featured Barbara Kingsolver's *Animal, Vegetable, Miracle*, and the front counter displayed *Intergalactic Judaism: An Analysis of Torah Concepts Based on Discoveries in Space Exploration, Physics and Biology* by David Lister. The wood may have been lighter in shade, but the stock was as eclectic as it was in Jack's store. There was even a second floor too, although Pomeranz's was devoted to books and not art, including a selection of the *American Jewish Year Book*. Piles of books lined the steps up to it.

I told the salesperson who Jack was, and she called Pomeranz right away. When she put Jack on the phone, I heard the two booksellers talk animatedly about the L.A. store and Pomeranz being in Israel for twenty-two years. They agreed to meet in person back at the bookstore after dinner, to catch up some more. When we returned around eight o'clock that evening the store was closed, but Pomerantz was waiting and opened up for us. I watched my father and Pomeranz fall together like long-lost brothers, each regaling the other with stories about books, authors, and the state of the business. Pomeranz told Jack that he started out with $20,000 worth of books, and they didn't even fill the shelves. He took a gamble, he said. My father was clearly proud and happy for him, and as they continued to talk I couldn't help but walk around the store again.

I relished feeling so at home there, and the memory of that enjoyment mixes with sadness as I sit here typing, having just discovered that Michael Pomeranz passed away in the summer of 2022, a beloved figure in Jerusalem bookselling, whose bookstore was considered one of the best in Israel and is now run by his two sons. They preserved his legacy. Mine was only discernable there through its echoes and in the description of Pomeranz in Alden Tabac's *Jerusalem Post* tribute as having "a customer-first orientation," a Jewish bookseller who was "nonjudgmental and treated everyone equally" and "everyone who came into his store was an honored guest." At least, I say to myself, my father's bookselling ethos lives on in Judaism's spiritual capital. Such open-minded service was integral to Jack's understanding of Jewishness, and its endurance in Jerusalem makes that perpetually contested city even more meaningful to me.

For a while after the store failed, Jack worked for an independent *mashgiach*, or a kosher overseer, who had been a customer, and then he leveraged his remaining business and social networks to launch himself as a full-time book and art appraiser. Still, he was essentially retired, and slowly the relationships he fostered through the store either disappeared through age and economic attrition or moved on without him. J. Roth Bookseller receded into Los Angeles's past.

I don't mean to bemoan the end of his store. Bookstores come and go; insolvency is an ever-present hazard of doing business. Even Crown Books and Borders went bankrupt and Barnes & Noble today plays second fiddle to Amazon. In April 2022, I read in *Publishers Weekly* that independent bookstores have made a slow but strong comeback from their nadir in 2009. Their intensive customer service and inventory curation, long-standing strengths, grew their loyal customer base, and the growth of e-commerce gave them a reasonable shot at competing with Amazon. The digitization of all facets of bookselling revolutionized not just their inventory management and point-of-sale transactions but also their ordering from publishers, document sharing, shipping, and customer relations. It's satisfying to note, I must add, that positioning indie bookstores as nonprofit literary-arts organizations with activities similar to those in Jack's Avi Chai proposal is a growing trend. All this simply underscores the one enduring aspect of the bookstore in general: it's a culturally invaluable space on which each generation projects its notions about writing and reading that both reflect and help assemble the networks always reshaping a society's understanding of literature and literacy. Bookstores aren't going to disappear any time soon.

American Jewish bookstores are no exception. We still need them for the readouts they relay about the meaning and makeup of contemporary Jewishness in the commercial marketplace and for the opportunity they afford us to make our customer requests heard in a private business that's crucial to the public sphere. Their book-lined walls are handy guides to identifying which writers are in or out and to observing what people are reading and teaching in Jewish homes and schools. They may not advertise or in some instances want to acknowledge it, but, as Jack knew very well, they're political spaces that help draw their patrons into the debates essential to the construction of contemporary Jewish cultures and identities. And they endure because they offer their customers the privilege of influencing and being influenced by their curator-owners' Jewish collections and the pleasures—existential, social, and material—of being seen by, as, and with Jews.

Back in 2014, I gave a talk about discoverability and Jewish bookstores, how their organizations and operations make the books we're looking for and those we didn't even know we wanted (which sometimes may not be, strictly speaking, Jewish books) visible and purchasable. One of the first responses from the audience was that my optimism about their continuing relevance in the age of the personal computer and mobile phone was "so twentieth century!" A mixed stock of Jewish and non-Jewish books? There wasn't a business model for what I was proposing, a famous Jewish historian insisted, though a British Jewish writer immediately offered the example of Joseph's Bookstore in Golders Green, London (where my Oma's sisters and their families had settled after the war), and its eclectic mix of British, world, and Jewish literatures. Thankfully, a brilliant Jewish linguist came to my rescue with the point I should have made at the start: that if supporters of new Jewish music have invested in the commercial venues for that music, why shouldn't Jewish entrepreneurs, philanthropists, and communal leaders invest in the commercial venues for Jewish literatures?

I was pleased to have an ally, but let's face it, the Jewish book trade wasn't asking for my help. Its current investors believe they know exactly where customer demand is and what the American Jewish market will bear. That's why Jewish bookstores in America have reverted to the commercially and economically more feasible model of their late nineteenth- and early twentieth-century forebears, which is to say of those general Jewish bookshops with their crowded aisles and jumbled display windows that Jack associated with the Jewish bazaar and the clutter of the Lower East Side. No Jewish bookstore that I know of in the United States carries only books. All feature large selections of giftware and ritual goods that seem essential to their contemporary identity. The books they do carry organize modern Jewish literatures according to the habits and networks of a new generation of American Jews, and the vast majority put forward a definition of that subject category reflective of the tastes of those who currently wield the greatest desire for, and ascribe the highest value to, the religion section of their collections. Their frontlists are packed with *sforim*, rabbinic hagiographies, scholarship on spirituality and mysticism, kosher cookbooks, and guides for the perplexed.

The religion section dominates even online, as any scroll across the Internet reveals. Some bookstores even disable browsing on their sites during the Sabbath. And the market sectors to which these online shops appeal seem like safe bets. You'll find sites that specialize in hard-to-find or used Jewish books, or books in Spanish, Russian, French, Yiddish, and Hebrew, so the familiar multilingual sounds of Jewish bookselling now ring electronically. On BookTok, the bookish subcommunity on TikTok, the owners of Chai Books in Melbourne, Australia, invite Jewish viewers to treat their homes as "miniature temples" for "Torah books." They talk up the late Lubavitcher Rebbe's teaching that a Jewish home should be a *bayit malei seforim*, a house full of Jewish religious books. All of these sites help to describe digital Jewish bookselling as a series of network clusters connecting customers to subject categories like Chassidus, Halakhah, Ba'al Teshuva/Newly Observant, Bitachon and Emunah, Dating and Marriage, Musar, and of course Hashkafah. A far smaller number extend links to Jewish Queer Literature and Jewish Women and Feminism, whereas the global reach of Jewish bookselling is easy to see; Jewish bookstores abroad connect American Jews via computer networks to Israel, the United Kingdom, Australia, France, and Poland.

In its neo-traditionalist guise the brick-and-mortar Jewish bookstore remains a viable if always demanding proposition economically. Not every Jewish community in the United States has their own, and most didn't even in my father's day. Yet the number and location of those that do suggest that for many American Jews, bookstores are as necessary to a vibrant Jewish commercial and communal life as synagogues, day schools, kosher markets, and community centers. A quick search on Google surfaced forty-three Jewish bookstores in the New York City area, including eastern New Jersey; nine Jewish bookstores both in Los

Angeles and in the Miami area; three Jewish bookstores in Atlanta and in Kiryas Joel (a Hasidic village in upstate New York); two Jewish bookstores each in Boston, Philadelphia, Baltimore, Chicago, Detroit, Dallas, the San Francisco Bay area, and Portland, Oregon; and one Jewish bookstore apiece in San Diego, Honolulu, Phoenix, Houston, Nashville, Minneapolis, Milwaukee, Indianapolis, Pittsburgh, and Kingston, Pennsylvania (just across the river from Wilkes-Barre). That's a healthy number, and this informal accounting doesn't even include general bookstores, such as Dunaway Books in St. Louis, that carry large selections of Jewish books or those retailers operating out of their homes or off the grid. These are the stores changing Jewish bookselling simply by serving their customers, because it's through those interactions that its future will be forged.

Which returns me one last time to Walter Benjamin and the fleeting order that owners make out of the fundamental and timeless disorder of all collections. He understood ownership well; "inheritance is the soundest way of acquiring a collection," he wrote. "For a collector's attitude toward his possessions stems from an owner's feeling of responsibility toward his property. Thus it is, in the highest sense, the attitude of an heir, and the most distinguished trait of a collection will always be its transmissibility." My father did indeed possess the attitude of an heir, a sense that he had been entrusted with a responsibility to care for and preserve for future transmission his beloved Jewish book collection.

Yet there was blindness to this insight too. The transmissibility of a collection, whether personal or commercial, may be its most distinguished trait—precisely through those networks that made my father's bookstore such an important relay in Jewish Los Angeles and in American Jewish history—but it's not a given. Yes, parts of the store's collection were physically transported elsewhere before and after its close, and I imagine that books with my father's price tag stickers or his penciled-in prices can still be found on a few bookshelves. One of his chocolate brown gusseted bags with the store's logo and address printed on them in gold, which he debuted at the Pico store's grand opening and of which he was so proud, ended up in the Lee L. Forman Collection of Bags at the University of Akron. And given the recollections that occasionally arrive in my inbox, I know that a network of memories continues to exist circulating my father's tastes in and ideas about the Jewish book trade.

But if a collection or parts of it are no longer attractive to buyers, if the market dries up or moves on, then, trust me, the collection will be broken up and lost. If some people, because of who they are or what they believe, refuse or are denied access to a collection, then the networks that sustain it are weakened and fail. The collection will be alienated and devalued. If a collection like my father's, and by extension the definition of literature it described, is broken up and demarcated by publishers, retailers, and consumers into rigidly policed categories of classical and modern, traditionalist and secular, authentic and inauthentic, proper and improper, its purchase will be subject to availability.

And if the inheritors decline or lose their inheritance?

In 2009, as the U.S. economy imploded and my own financial resources deflated, I saw no other choice but to sell my Zhitomir Shas in order to put a badly needed new roof on my house. This set of Talmud, printed in the 1860s in Zhitomir, Ukraine, off of plates first ceremonially immersed in a *mikvah*, was the jewel among the books my father let me take when the store closed in 1994. I vacillated for months at the thought of selling off this patrimony. I had wanted to pass it on to my only child, and through that tangible object of Jewish spiritual and material values gift him with a kind of literary *yichus*, or "pedigree," a network of familial worthiness, that would attest to the distinction of the store and of his family's Jewish identity.

But each day as I stepped out from under the leaky skullcap of my house and into the overwhelmingly Protestant, White, middle-class community of the Pennsylvania countryside where we live, I realized anew the illusory nature of that desire. Back then, my son attended a public school, and his favorite books were from the Harry Potter series. His formal Jewish education was conducted at a once-a-week Hebrew school run by the local synagogue. That year they were reading Chaim Potok's *The Chosen*. Unlike the conflict in that novel, rebellion against the world of our fathers was not the issue out here, where there are few Jews and no Jewish bookstore framing our literatures in its show windows. It's a quieter problem that the poet Adrienne Rich memorably identified: "When there's nobody to 'inspire the behavior,' act out of the culture, there is an atrophy, a dwindling, which is partly invisible." Neither of us paid much attention to the Shas; there was no weekly Talmud study with us. I didn't fawn over it as my father did his statue of the burning scroll, and the fact remained that the set attested only to a certain guilt about its disuse and increasing irrelevance in our family library. That investment in Jewish identity had dwindled. Nevertheless, I still believed in the power of this talisman of Jewish authenticity and connection. Perhaps in a different materialization its spiritual magic might weather a little longer on, rather than in, my American Jewish home?

Jack offered to help me sell it and easily found an Orthodox dealer in rare Judaica and *sifrei kodesh* who was interested. He lived in New Jersey, so in May 2010 we arranged to meet in Manhattan for the transaction. I drove in from Pennsylvania and met my father at the Waldorf. The sale was the next day, so we had time to see the sights, which for Jack meant going to the Morgan Library & Museum on Madison Avenue. The book-lined walls there were suitably impressive and, for my father, set the perfect mood for our impending sale: quiet reflection in another bookman's sanctuary. Soaking up this other kind of *yichus*, Jack wandered off as I took in the ornate gold-, red-, and brown-hued library with its floor-to-ceiling art.

I appreciated that mood, too, if a bit more critically. Visiting a museum dedicated to books affixed us into a network of other bibliobsessives who manifested merit by understanding its value. This was where the Shas belonged if you believed that Western aesthetic prestige and J. P. Morgan's WASPish robber-baron tastes were the marks of acceptance into an American collection. And yet all I could think about was the impending loss of my family inheritance and how that would decouple me and my son in a very material way from a certain part of our Jewishness.

Maybe that thought was brought on by the way that the glass-fronted bookcases with their carved inlaid-walnut bookshelves were protected by diamond-pattern bronze grillwork, giving the appearance that Morgan's books were incarcerated. He was a master at avoiding loss. His collection was arrayed against the south and north walls of the library on three levels running across the two sides. These could be reached by staircases located behind the bookcases—you had to pull them open as in some horror movie. Anchoring the center of the east wall was a grand fireplace with a massive tapestry, *The Triumph of Avarice*, above it.

The point of such a formidable display was precisely in its materialization of Morgan's power to possess and of the multiple networks in his personal and professional lives that made possession possible. Banking, armaments, railroads, steel, politics, and art all interconnected in that room in various ways, some legal, some spatial, some physical. I couldn't exactly see those networks in their original configurations, but I could still palpably feel them in that library. Would I still feel the Zhitomir Talmud in my own library years later if I exchanged it for a roof?

Later, on our way of out Barney's department store, Jack said to me, "I think 'bohemian' is apologetic for not being able to afford top of the line. What you do is look at what they're showing and you go buy a cheaper version. That's what I used to do with my clothes." Which was just another strategy for redirecting a network into a different quality of connection. What I heard Jack saying was that I could have the affiliation I wanted for a more affordable exchange rate. That made me less apprehensive about the next day's sale.

As it turned out, we sold the Zhitomir Shas on the street—in Manhattan on Thirtieth between Seventh and Eighth Avenues, a block over from Penn Station and Madison Square Garden. Jack and I drove down the block looking for the buyer, who had told us he needed to make this fast since had to get back to New Jersey in time to prepare for the Sabbath. There were no parking spots, and it seemed most of the buildings on that stretch of Thirtieth were covered in scaffolding and under construction. After another go-around I double-parked, and my father got out and headed over to a late-model Lexus idling farther up the street. When he returned with the dealer, I handed a sample volume to the black-suited, trim fellow, who examined it as we loudly talked a bit more about the particular edition, trying to hear each other over the din of traffic and car horns. Then he nodded, removed a check from his coat pocket, and signed it quickly. When he looked inquiringly at me, I realized it was time, and I quickly began removing the boxed-up Talmud from my Element.

When I brought over the second box, I turned to him and said, "Listen, I didn't really want to sell these. I wanted them as *yichus* for my son, so when you sell them, I hope they go to someone who deserves them." He looked at me as if I were speaking in tongues and said nothing. Only then did I fully understand that this transfer was not going to result in anything like J. P. Morgan's library, that I had gotten it precisely backward. In their magnificence, Morgan's books expressed their converted value like little mirrors, each exclaiming him the most powerful person of all. My exchange of books for a new roof was not a form of transubstantiation but a networked transaction that forever detached me from my personal relationship with a magnificent example of Jewish book culture and to a material expression of J. Roth Bookseller's *yichus*. I should have paid more attention to my Torah study at Hillel; I had sold my patrimony for a mess of pottage.

After transferring the third box into his car's open trunk, I shook the dealer's hand and crossed back to my side of the street, and when I turned around, he was gone. It was ten o'clock in the morning. Jack and I considered what we'd like to do before lunch, and it wasn't much of a discussion. Manhattan Judaica was only fifteen blocks away, and I needed a few titles that I couldn't get in central Pennsylvania, so we headed off, me driving in silence, my father—ever the bookseller—happily dissecting the transaction.

Selinsgrove, Pennsylvania, 2021

"You don't remember the good things, Laurence, all the nice times we had."

Rochelle is unhappy that I can't remember going with Al and Ben to Tiffany's in Beverly Hills to buy Oma a gift for her seventy-fifth birthday.

"You three put all the money you'd saved on the glass counter," she reminds me, "and the saleswoman was absolutely thrilled. She had never seen anything like it." My mother is smiling with pride. "Do you remember Uncle Chaskel coming for Oma's birthday? Do you remember the party we had at the house?"

"No," I answer truthfully. "Did we put change on that counter or was it bills?"

"Laurence, that's the second time I asked you something both your brothers remember, and you don't. I think you have a mental block for certain things."

She's right about that.

"Al," I interrupt Rochelle on our weekly family Zoom call, "do you remember Uncle Chaskel coming for Oma's birthday?"

"Uh, no," he says.

"Al, how come you don't remember all the good things?"

He laughs. Al is a math instructor at a technical college in Seattle and has come to accept our family past. Ben remains noncommittal; he made a new life for himself with my mother in Israel. Rochelle, however, glares at me through her screen, and I can tell that she's very angry, but no angrier than I am that I need to defend my admittedly shaky memory from her critique. Is it my fault that what I do remember wasn't her or my brothers' or my father's happiest moments? We all hold on to those memories we most need to make sense of the past as we see it, and once we're gone much of that goes too, though no one's memories are disappearing faster than Jack's.

Back on the red sofa in my den, it's still January 2021, the middle of the COVID-19 pandemic, and Jack is staying with me because Elana was handling a family emergency and thinks he'll be safe (or at least safer) in Selinsgrove. He sits back easily, hands in his lap and fingers interlaced, watching me and Mary in the kitchen preparing dinner. I'm aware that these may be the final months when my father's mind can still summon up the charming proprietor and beloved uncle who lends everyone an ear and is quick to do a mitzvah, who my cousins love for his love of *chazzanut* and Yiddishkeit, for tearing up when a relative failed to act with *chesed*, loving-kindness.

"I could have gone on with just used books back on Pico," he says, "with periodicals and maybe a few new books, but I wouldn't have made a living at it."

For a moment I'm stunned. That was my idea. But I let it go. He's right again anyway, he wouldn't have made the kind of living to which he was accustomed running a used bookstore. Besides, we're at the end of our last real interview, and it's become clear that whatever I don't get now will be gone forever. Best just to let him vent.

"I was an upscale dealer. I had the floor washed once a month." Which store was that? La Cienega? Pico? "They all kept filthy stores."

After dinner he goes upstairs to our guest bedroom to read Gerold Frank's *The Deed*. A few days before, Jack had asked me for a book to keep him occupied. About a tenth of the books in my home library are from his, so I figured I'd find something he might have once enjoyed or kept in the store. Of course I walked him over to my shelves, just as he'd taught me, and as we looked over the titles on one—Isaac Babel's *The Collected Stories*, Cecil Roth's *Gleanings*, Cynthia Ozick's *Art and Ardor*, Sholem Asch's *East River*—he reached for the Frank book. My copy is a first printing from 1963, and on the flyleaf in my father's neat and precise hand is written "$20.00 O.P."

An interesting choice, I thought. He usually gravitated to biographies and histories. *The Deed* is a true-crime book about the political assassination at Cairo in 1944 of Lord Moyne, the minister resident for the Middle East. He was killed by two young members of the Stern Gang, an extremist right-wing Jewish liberation group (officially known as Lehi, the Hebrew acronym for Fighters for the Freedom of Israel) whose acts of terror against the British earned it both condemnation and a grudging respect among Jews in pre-state Palestine and worldwide. Perhaps Jack wanted something that would retell a story he knew from his youth.

A day or so later we're in my study talking about nothing in particular when he suddenly says, "I think they'll get away."

"Who will, Dad?"

"The two boys. I think they'll get away in the end. Don't you? I think they will."

I realize he's talking about *The Deed*. "Yeah, maybe," I lie.

Did he not remember how the story went? Yitzhak Shamir, the future prime minister of Israel, who took over from Avraham Stern after he was killed by the British, sent Eliyahu Beit-Zuri and Eliyahu Hakim to shoot Moyne. Both were hanged for it on March 22, 1945, each singing "Hatikva" before the trapdoor swung open beneath them. It was one of the most controversial events in Zionist history up to that time, and it ramped up the political bad blood between the Right and the Left among Israel's founders. Jack lived through the event. He was twelve when they died, thirty and working for Behrman House when Frank's book was published. How could he have not heard the story before?

And then it occurs to me that whether his unknowing was caused by his dementia or simply revealed an embarrassing gap in his literary and historical knowledge is beside the point. For my father, raised on the promise of a better future for himself and for Jews in America, the hope of averting a bad ending was and always would be evergreen. Notwithstanding his store's demise, and Lehi's noxious influence on Zionism and Israel, Jack's clinging to the better conclusion seems to me an essential part of his worldview, of his story. He worked hard, he raised himself up, he tried to make things better, cleaner, and more fit for his customers and his community. The past was to be respected, but it didn't get a veto. The present is just the future unfolding, and how one conducts oneself along the way is the true measure of one's worth. No matter that circumstances might lay out a hard road leading to a disappointing terminus. Meeting this with duty done and honor intact enables a final escape and the happy ending.

I wish I could believe in that kind of ending too, but I'm of a different generation. I tend to put quotation marks around many of the words so important to my father, and it takes real effort for me to understand, much less inhabit, his certitude about the world. Unhappy endings seem much more believable to me, perhaps because the store's failure was such an essential part of my life's education. It became the type of story I preferred.

When Jack finished *The Deed* and returned it to me, all he said was, "Very sad." Not long after, he left for Los Angeles, where for a time he stayed in an assisted living facility until he moved back home to be near the things that made him feel well-kept and comfortable. In Selinsgrove we spent days dissecting my father's long visit, and eventually Jonah offered me this interpretation of his *zeyde*'s story.

"All he cared about was presentation. He didn't care about money," Jonah insisted. "He'd have had to go backwards in time to keep up with the future. He didn't want to be Orthodox. He wanted to be upscale, dignified, and clean. And it defined his life."

I'm not certain about the money part, although the rest of it rings true enough. It chimes, too, with the larger story of American Jews in the mid-twentieth century striving for social acceptance and hustling to fit Jewishness into a White mainstream. That's one meaning of "upscale." Their story is almost over now, its characters steadily passing away each year, and most of the Jewish bookstores that once helped retail it have vanished. Sitting with my father and talking about the store and books and customers and conflicts and the stratagems needed to keep them all in line was in some ways an act of nostalgia, a chance to re-create one last time the soundscape of his sales floor through a conversation he'd often had there and with me. It allowed both of us to consider in our own ways, and for our own stories, the end of the order on the bookshelves of my father's generation of American Jews. Like his memory, that order was deconstructing in plain sight, and both of us knew it. For me, I realized that I'd reached a conclusion that was neither happy nor unhappy, but rather another beginning, the uncertain future of its retellings by my son and by those with whom I'll share it, in trust and in love.

And for my father?

"Hi, Dad, how's it going?" I'm on the phone checking up on Jack, trying to gauge if he's declined any further this week.

"Okay. You know, I do the best I can."

"That's good."

"I'm doing the best I can."

"Great. That's fine. And you're getting outside and walking?"

"Uh, outside? No, not so much. Some days I can walk, you know, around the, the, the . . ."

"Block?"

". . . block, but I do the best I can. I'm doing the best I can."

"Good."

"Okay. It's hard to hear you, so I thank you for seeing me and in the meantime, I'll do the best I can. Bye."

Having done the best he can is where we leave it then, he at home finally and me three thousand miles away still holding on to my cell phone and to everything left unsaid in our short call.

Locations and Dates in Operation

M. Harelick Books: 1948–1966
330 West Fourth Street, 1948; 228 West Fourth Street, 1949–1952; 4228 Melrose Avenue, 1952–1959; 1049 South La Cienega Boulevard, 1959–1964; 1070 South La Cienega Boulevard 1964–1966

Harelick & Roth Booksellers: 1070 South La Cienega Boulevard, 1966–1979
Encino branch store, 4847 Paso Robles Avenue, 1973–1974

J. Roth / Bookseller of Fine & Scholarly Judaica: 1979–1994
9427 West Pico Boulevard, 1979–1990; 9020 West Olympic Boulevard, 1990–1994

Acknowledgments

Writing about family is a daunting expedition, so it took time to find my way through its thickets. I'm deeply grateful to all those who helped me steer a path, who supported my research and writing, and whose insights, suggestions, and kind words encouraged me to finish the journey.

At Rutgers University Press, Christopher Rios-Sueverkruebbe proved to be the editor that I had always dreamed of working with. He not only understood exactly what I was attempting to write, he often saw it more clearly than I did. His wise counsel and perceptive edits were essential, and I can't thank him enough. My thanks as well to my next editor, Carah Naseem, who thoughtfully and caringly shepherded this book into print, and to the anonymous reviewers whose reports sharpened the final manuscript.

Three fellowships helped secure the time and intellectual engagement that made this book possible: the Charles W. and Sally Rothfeld Fellowship at the Herbert D. Katz Center for Advanced Judaic Studies, University of Pennsylvania, in fall 2004, where this book germinated as an essay for that year's fellowship volume; a fellowship at the Jean and Samuel Frankel Center for Judaic Studies, University of Michigan, in winter 2013; and the Ruth Meltzer Fellowship at the Herbert D. Katz Center for Advanced Judaic Studies, University of Pennsylvania, in fall 2020. To all my fellow Fellows, thank you.

Portions of this book appeared previously in the following publications: "Unpacking My Father's Bookstore," in *Modern Jewish Literatures: Intersections and Boundaries*, edited by Sheila Jelen, Michael Kramer, and L. Scott Lerner (University of Pennsylvania Press, 2011), 280–302; "Talmud on the Roof, or Materializing American Jewish

Literary Studies," *Studies in American Jewish Literature* 31, no. 1 (2012): 91–96; "Editor's Introduction: American Jews and Music," *Studies in American Jewish Literature* 38, no. 2 (2019): 93–100; and "The Storefront (*place*)," *Los Angeles Review of Books*, January 6, 2021 (yes, that January 6).

This book's epigraph comes from *Illuminations* by Walter Benjamin. Translated by Harry Zohn. English translation copyright © 1968 by Harcourt Brace Jovanovich, Inc. Originally published in Germany by Suhrkamp Verlag, Frankfurt a.M. copyright © 1955 by Suhrkamp Verlag, Frankfurt a.M. Used by permission of HarperCollins Publishers.

My thanks to Eddie Lee, old friend and teammate, for permission to use his wonderful, keenly observed photos of the store's 1979 "grand opening"; to Ellen Berkowitz for permission to reprint the letter from Ellis C. Berkowitz; to Pinit Ratanakul for permission to reprint his letter; and to Ari Noonan for his permission to quote at length from his article "The Trials of a Bookseller," *Heritage* 5752, no. 12 (Friday, November 22, 1991): 7, 19, 24.

For inviting me to speak about my project as I developed it, I'm grateful to Laurence J. Silberstein and the Judaism and Postmodern Culture Colloquium at the Berman Center for Jewish Studies, Lehigh University; Jeffrey Shandler and the Scholars Working Group on the Jewish Book at the Center for Jewish History, New York; Carolyn Starman Hessel and Anita Schmidt at the Sami Rohr Jewish Literary Institute in Irvington, New York; and Adam Shear and the Jewish Studies Program at the University of Pittsburgh, who made possible a wonderful evening at Pinsker's Bookstore in Pittsburgh.

I'm fortunate to have found an academic home at Susquehanna University in the Department of English & Creative Writing. Surrounded by talented and passionate colleagues, I was constantly encouraged to stay the course with this book no matter where it led or how long it took to complete. In administration, thank you to Jonathan Green, Dave Ramsaran, L. Jay Lemons, Linda McMillin, Valerie Martin, and Laurie Crumpacker, the dean who helped set me on my academic path. To all the students who took my course "Unpacking the Bookstore" over the years: your questions, conversations, and projects were profoundly helpful as I developed my thinking about book retailing. So too were the mini-grants from Susquehanna University's Committee on Faculty Scholarship that supported my research. A very early version of my story about J. Roth Bookseller was presented as the John C. Horn Distinguished Scholarship and Creative Activity Lecture at Susquehanna University in March 2006.

This book is evidence that research and writing are always collective endeavors sustained by solidarity, collaboration, and kindness. No one was more influential in getting me started and helping me learn how to write about my father's bookstore than Mark Fertig z"l, whose graphic design assignment inspired my reflections on the book-lined wall. Our friendship was once in a lifetime, and I miss him—as well as his sharp edits and blunt advice—every day. For preparing and formatting the photos included in this book, and for her sage design advice, my deepest thanks to Amanda Lenig. For reading, commenting on, and improving various chapters, a special thank you to Lila Corwin Berman, Susan Bowers z"l, Riv-Ellen Prell—who also generously recalled for me her experiences as a customer at the store—and Glen Retief. Deborah Dash Moore has been a rock of support who not only read and critiqued several chapters but also offered incisive suggestions for shoring up the book's structure and getting it published. And Laura Levitt was there from the beginning, inspiring me with her unflagging belief in the project and steady stream of invaluable insights and direction.

I'm especially indebted to these colleagues, friends, mentors, relatives, and correspondents for sending me documents, resources, recollections, and answers and for countless discussions that enriched my thinking and writing: Arnold Band z"l, Samantha Baskind, Cornel Bonca, Zachary Braiterman, Marc Caplan, Michael Casper, Nick Clark, Alanna Cooper, Kathy Dalton, Carol J. DeMars, Laura Eckstein, Dean Franco, Jonathan Freedman, Jennifer Glaser, Pete Groff, Patrick Thomas Henry, David Hirsch, Rabbi Chaim Hisiger, J. Andrew Hubbell, David Imhoof, Karla Kelsey, Arthur Kiron, Shirley Klein, Cantor Josh Konigsberg and Meri Glasgall, Markus Krah, Michael Kramer, Josh Lambert, Louie Land, Erika Lehrer, Masha Leibson, L. Scott Lerner, Julian Levinson, Jeremiah Lockwood, Sherry and Larry Lockwood, Patrick Long, Caroline Luce, Rabbi Nina Mandel, Rick Meschino, Sheilah Miller, John Moscowitz, David Myers, Anita Norich,

Monica Prince, Alan Rosen, Evelyn "Chanie" Roth, Lynn Roth, Michael A. Roth, Rabbi Michael Roth z"l, Tracy Salkowitz, Larry Scher, Nicole Schmidt, Maeera Schreiber, Ben Schreier, Michelle Schwartz, Hasanthika Sirisena, Ilan Stavans, Britt Tevis, Nadia Valman, Crystal VanHorn, Betsy Verhoeven, Jennifer Weis, Richard Wellerstein, Beth Wenger, Terry Winegar, and Reed Wilson. To anyone I forgot to mention, know that you too have my deepest thanks.

Over most of the time in which this book is set and during the years I readied myself to write it, I was accompanied by my oldest friend, Jeffrey Best. He and his brothers, Steven and Charlie, were also part of the life of the store, and the myriad hours I spent with Jeffrey trying to make sense of our families and what it means to be Jewish and Americans are the foundation on which I built my story. I am forever grateful.

To my family, and to my father foremost, I hope that my love is recompense enough for the information, encouragement, interpretations, empathy, and patience you have shown me. This book wouldn't be as thorough without my mother's recollections and corrections, and I'm blessed that Rochelle Roth gifted me with an ardor for truth and music. Elana Cohen Roth has stood by my father for over forty years, and her children, Elise Grace and Marc Cohen, experienced the store too, each in their own way. For all the documents, photos, and memories she shared with me, I'm extraordinarily thankful. Al and Ben, this book is for you.

And Mary and Jonah, how could I have done this without your love and inspiration? Mary, you read every word; without your ear for honest prose, I would have been lost. You talked me down from my worries, pulled me up when I needed it, and let me know when I was fooling myself. Jonah, the future of this story, you reminded me to laugh, and watching you with your *zeyde* recalled for me the words of *Mishlei*, that those who pursue goodness and loving-kindness will find life, prosperity, and honor. May it be so for us and for all families.

Works Cited and Consulted

SOTHEBY'S, MANHATTAN, 1985

Important Judaica: Books, Manuscripts and Works of Art, New York, Monday, November 25, 1985. Sale 5402. Sotheby's, 1985.

CHAPTER 1 GRAND OPENING (*OBJECTS*)

Anzaldúa, Gloria. *Borderlands/La Frontera: The New Mestiza*. Spinsters/Aunt Lute, 1987.

Benjamin, Walter. "Unpacking My Library." In *Illuminations*, edited by Hannah Arendt and translated by Harry Zohn, 59–67. Schocken Books, 1969.

Bernstein, Robin. "Dances with Things: Material Culture and the Performance of Race." *Social Text* 27, no. 4 (Winter 2009): 67–94.

Brown, Bill. "Thing Theory." *Critical Inquiry* 28, no. 1 (Autumn 2001): 1–22.

Buzbee, Lewis. *The Yellow-Lighted Bookshop: A Memoir, a History*. Graywolf Press, 2006.

Carrión, Jorge. *Bookshops: A Reader's History*. Translated by Peter Bush. Windsor, Ontario: Biblioasis, 2017.

Haskell, David A. "J. Roth Bookseller." *Judaica Book News* 9, no. 2 (Spring/Summer 1979/5739): 36–38.

Latour, Bruno. "Why Has Critique Run Out of Steam? From Matters of Fact to Matters of Concern." In *The Norton Anthology of Theory and Criticism*, edited by Vincent B. Leitch, William E. Cain, Laurie A. Finke, John McGowan, T. Denean Sharpley-Whiting, and Jeffrey J. Williams, 2111–2136. 3rd ed. W.W. Norton, 2018.

Oldenburg, Ray. *The Great Good Place: Cafés, Coffee Shops, Bookstores, Bars, Hair Salons, and Other Hangouts at the Heart of a Community*. Marlowe, 1999.

Palmer, Alex W. "The Case of Hong Kong's Missing Booksellers." *New York Times*, April 3, 2018. https://www.nytimes.com/2018/04/03/magazine/the-case-of-hong-kongs-missing-booksellers.html.

Pels, Dick, Kevin Hetherington, and Frédéric Vandenberghe. "The Status of the Object: Performances, Mediations, and Techniques." *Theory, Culture & Society* 19, no. 5–6 (2002): 1–21.

Roth, Laurence. *Inspecting Jews: American Jewish Detective Stories.* Rutgers University Press, 2003.

Seierstad, Åsne. *The Bookseller of Kabul.* Translated by Ingrid Christophersen. Back Bay Books, 2004.

Sonny Alexander Florists. "About." Accessed June 11, 2013. http://www.sonnyalexanderflorists.com. [Information no longer on website.]

Winship, Michael. "'The Tragedy of the Book Industry'? Bookstores and Book Distribution in the United States to 1950." *Studies in Bibliography* 58 (2007–2008): 145–184.

CHAPTER 2 THE INVENTORY (*COMMERCE*)

Abramovitsh, S.Y. *Tales of Mendele the Book Peddler : Fishke the Lame and Benjamin the Third.* Edited by Dan Miron and Ken Frieden, Schocken Books, 1996.

American Book Trade Manual. R. R. Bowker, Office of *The Publishers' Weekly*, New York, 1922.

Bakhtin, Mikhail. *Rabelais and His World.* Translated by Hélene Iswolsky. Indiana University Press, 2008.

Book Peddler: Newsletter of the National Yiddish Book Exchange. "Jewish Bookstores of the Old East Side." 17 (Summer 1992): 20.

Brooklyn Eagle. "In Bankruptcy." February 15, 1910.

Bulletin of the New York Public Library. 17, no. 1 (January 1913).

Bush, Lawrence. "September 17: Benjamin the Bookseller." *Jewish Currents*, September 17, 2010. https://jewishcurrents.org/september-17-benjamin-the-bookseller.

Caspar's Directory of the American Book, News and Stationery Trade, Wholesale and Retail. Milwaukee: C. N. Caspar, 1889.

Clegg, James, ed. *The International Directory of Booksellers and Bibliophile's Manual, Including Lists of the Public Libraries of the World.* James Clegg, Aldine Press, 1903.

Clegg, James, ed. *The International Directory of Booksellers and Bibliophile's Manual, Including Lists of the Public Libraries of the World.* James Clegg, Aldine Press, 1914.

Cooperman, Isidore. *The Jewish Book Shop: Its Organization and Operation.* 1947. Reprint, New York: Jewish Book Council of America, 1953.

Directory of Booksellers, Newsdealers and Stationers in the United States and Canada. Minneapolis: H. W. Wilson, 1908.

Directory of Booksellers, Stationers, Newsdealers, and Music Dealers and List of Libraries in the United States and Canada; Complete to November 1st, 1870. New York: John H. Dingman, 1870.

Friedman, Lee M. "Wills of Early Jewish Settlers in New York." *Publications of the American Jewish Historical Society*, no. 23 (1915): 147–161.

Goldman, Yosef. *Hebrew Printing in America, 1735–1926: A History and Annotated Bibliography.* Edited by Ari Kinsberg. 2 vols. Brooklyn, NY: YG Books, 2006.

Goldstein, Eric. "A Taste of Freedom: American Yiddish Publications in Imperial Russia." In *Transnational Traditions: New Perspectives on American Jewish History*, edited by Ava F. Kahn and Adam D. Mendelsohn, 105–140. Wayne State University Press, 2014.

Gordan, Rachel. *Postwar Stories: How Books Made Judaism American.* Oxford University Press, 2024.

Grannis, Chandler B. "More Than Merchants: Seventy-Five Years of the ABA." In *Bookselling in America and the World*, edited by Charles B. Anderson, 65–108. Quadrangle/New York Times Book Co., 1975.

Highland, Kristen Doyle. "In the Bookstore: The Houses of Appleton and Book Cultures in Antebellum New York City." *Book History* 19 (2016): 214–255.

J. Levine Books & Judaica. "J. Levine Co.: A Modern Tradition, 'Judaica Book News, 1981.'" August 10, 2005. http://www.levinejudaica.com/catalog/moderntraditions.php.

Jacobs, Maurice. "Generations of Jewish Literary Labor: Sixty Years of the Jewish Publication Society of America." In *Essays on Jewish Booklore: Articles Selected from the Jewish Book Annual, 1942–1971*, edited by Philip Goodman, 224–235. New York: KTAV Publishing House, 1972.

Jefferson, Rebecca. "Isaac Pinto and the First Jewish Prayer Book in America." *Special & Area Studies Collections Blog*, Smathers Libraries, University of Florida. Accessed March 5, 2015. https://ufsasc.domains.uflib.ufl.edu/isaac-pinto-first-jewish-prayer-book-published-america-ufsasc/.

Katznelson, Ira. "Two Exceptionalisms: Points of Departure for Studies of Capitalism and Jews in the United States." In *Chosen Capital: The Jewish Encounter with American Capitalism*, edited by Rebecca Kobrin, 12–32. Rutgers University Press, 2012.

Kurinsky, Samuel. "Gomez House The Oldest Jewish Residence in the USA." Fact Paper 30. Hebrew History Federation. Accessed July 9, 2012. https://hebrewhistory.info/factpapers/fp030_gomez.htm.

Leiman, Shnayer Z. "Montague Lawrence Marks: In a Jewish Bookstore." *Tradition* 25, no. 1 (1989): 59–69.

Levine, Yitzchok. "Glimpses into American Jewish History (Part 24): The Gomez Family." Accessed July 9, 2012. http://personal.stevens.edu/~llevine/gomez_part_%2024.pdf.

Madison, Charles A. *Jewish Publishing in America: The Impact of Jewish Writing on American Culture*. New York: Sanhedrin Press, 1976.

Miron, Dan. *A Traveler Disguised: The Rise of Modern Yiddish Fiction in the Nineteenth Century*. Syracuse University Press, 1996.

Publishers' Weekly. "Jammed into a Bookcase." No. 1904 (July 25, 1908): 201–202.

Reform Advocate. Judah Meir Katzenelenbogen obituary. April 24, 1920.

Sarna, Jonathan. *JPS: The Americanization of Jewish Culture, 1888–1988*. Philadelphia: Jewish Publication Society, 1989.

Shandler, Jeffrey. "Keepers of Accounts: The Practice of Inventory in Modern Jewish Life." David W. Belin Lecture in American Jewish Affairs 17. Frankel Center for Judaic Studies, University of Michigan, 2010.

Stern, Madeleine B. "Henry Frank: Pioneer American Hebrew Publisher." *American Jewish Archives* 20 (1968): 163–168.

Tebbel, John. "A Brief History of American Bookselling." In *Bookselling in America and the World*, edited by Charles B. Anderson, 3–25. Quadrangle/New York Times Book Co., 1975.

"The Spectator," *The Outlook*, 82 (March 24, 1906): 639–641.

Wilson, H., comp. *Trow's New York City Directory*. New York: John F. Trow, 1860.

Wilson, H., comp. *Trow's New York City Directory*. New York: John F. Trow, 1876.

CHAPTER 3 THE STOREFRONT (*PLACE*)

Bourdieu, Pierre. *Distinction: A Social Critique of the Judgement of Taste*. Translated by Richard Nice. Harvard University Press, 1984.

Brook, Vincent. *Land of Smoke and Mirrors: A Cultural History of Los Angeles*. Rutgers University Press, 2013.

Cohen, Hagit. "Foreword," *Bechanuto shel mocher hasfarim: Chanuyot sfarim yehudiot bemizrah eropa bamachatzit hashniya shel hame'a ha-19* [At the bookseller's shop: The Jewish book trade in Eastern Europe in the nineteenth century]. Translated by unknown. Hebrew University Magnes Press, 2006.

Dave in Northridge for Readers and Book Lovers Community. "All Things Bookstore: Bookselling in Los Angeles before 1910." *Daily Kos*, October 1, 2013. https://www.dailykos.com/stories/2013/10/1/1242463/-All-Things-Bookstore-Bookselling-in-Los-Angeles-before-1910.

Davis, Joshua Clark. *From Head Shops to Whole Foods: The Rise and Fall of Activist Entrepreneurs*. Columbia University Press, 2017.

Davis, Mike. *City of Quartz: Excavating the Future in Los Angeles*. Vintage Books, 1992.

Dawson, Ernest. "Los Angeles Booksellers Fifty Years Ago." *Quarterly: Historical Society of Southern California* 29, no. 2 (June 1947): 84–92. https://www.jstor.org/stable/41168126.

Find a Grave. "Michael Harelick." Sholom Memorial Park, Sylmar, CA. Accessed January 5, 2017. https://www.findagrave.com/memorial/158184658/michael-harelick.

Franco, Dean J. *The Border and the Line: Race, Literature, and Los Angeles*. Stanford University Press, 2019.

Harelick, Michael. Certificate of Death, March 27, 1972. County of Los Angeles, Registrar-Recorder/County Clerk.

Heimann, Jim, and Kevin Starr. *Los Angeles: Portrait of a City*. Taschen, 2009.

Hernández, Kelly Lytle. *Bad Mexicans: Race, Empire and Revolution in the Borderlands*. W. W. Norton, 2022.

"Hugh Gordon, circa 1930." Miriam Matthews Photograph Collection. UCLA Library Digital Collections, 2019–2024. https://digital.library.ucla.edu/catalog/ark:/21198/z1bs0987.

Kanellos, Nicolás. "Spanish-Language Anarchist Periodicals in Early Twentieth-Century United States," In *Protest on the Page: Essays on Print and the Culture of Dissent since 1865*, edited by James L. Baughman, Jennifer Ratner-Rosenhagen, and James P. Danky, 59–84. University of Wisconsin Press, 2015.

Kayembe, Astrid. "13 Historical Sites That Made Central Avenue the Cultural Lifeline of South L.A." *Los Angeles Times*, February 28, 2023. https://www.latimes.com/entertainment-arts/story/2023-02-28/south-central-los-angeles-mapped-black-history-behold.

Klapper, Melissa. "The Great Adventure of 1929: The Impact of Travel Abroad on American Jewish Women's Identity." *American Jewish History* 102, no. 1 (2018): 85–107.

Klein, Norman M. *The History of Forgetting: Los Angeles and the Erasure of Memory*. Verso, 2008.

Kushner, Sherrill. "The Solomon Family of Boyle Heights." Jewish Genealogical Society of Los Angeles, edited by Nancy Holden. Accessed February 11, 2016.

Los Angeles Daily Times. Lazarus-Kremer wedding announcement, 1882.

Los Angeles Public Library. "Historic City and Business & Phone Directories, 1873–1970." ResCarta-Web. https://rescarta.lapl.org.

Los Angeles White Pages. Central Area, June 1956. Library of Congress United States telephone directory collection.

Los Angeles Yellow Pages. Central Area, December 1949, August 1952, and August 1959. Library of Congress United States telephone directory collection.

Luce, Caroline. Email message to author, December 2, 2016. Sent with six attachments: "Brooklyn Avenue Addresses"; "Fran Oberman Interview"; "Kapshut Manischewitz Orders"; two photographs of Kapshut and his bookstore; and one Yiddish-language advertisement.

Luce, Caroline. "Reexamining Los Angeles' 'Lower East Side': Jewish Bakers Union Local 453 and Yiddish Food Culture in 1920s Boyle Heights." In *Jews in the Los Angeles Mosaic*, edited by Karen S. Wilson, 25–42. Autry National Center of the American West in association with University of California Press, 2013.

Luna, Claire. "Alfred Ligon, 96; Started Oldest Black Bookstore." *Los Angeles Times*, August 16, 2022.

Magonista.org. "1906–1907: Hiding in LA." Accessed August 30, 2017. https://sites.google.com/site/magonistaorg/1906-1907-hiding-in-la.

Moore, Deborah Dash. *To the Golden Cities: Pursuing the American Jewish Dream in Miami and L.A.* Harvard University Press, 1994.

Oliver, Myrna. "Bernice Ligon of Early Black-Owned Bookstore Dies." *Los Angeles Times*, November 10, 2000.

Ravitch, Melech. "Yehoash." *Encyclopaedia Judaica*, Vol. 16, 727–730. Keter Publishing House Jerusalem, Third Printing, 1974.

Scher, Larry. Email messages to author, October 1, 2, 4, 6, and 7, 2020; Zoom interview, October 6, 2020.

Soja, Edward W. *Thirdspace: Journeys to Los Angeles and Other Real-and-Imagined Places*. Oxford University Press, 1996.

Starr, Kevin. *Material Dreams: Southern California through the 1920s*. Oxford University Press, 1990.

Stern, Norton B. "Pincus Lazarus: Report of an Interview with Mr. Arthur P. Lazarus, 930 West Santa Ynez Avenue, Hillsborough, California April 28, 1967." *Western States Jewish History* 41, no. 3 (Spring 2009): 517–520.

SurveyLA: Los Angeles Historic Resources Survey. "Los Angeles Citywide Historic Context Statement: Architecture and Engineering/Period Revival; Housing the Masses/Period Revival Neighborhoods." Prepared for the City of Los Angeles, Department of City Planning, Office of Historic Resources, January 2016. https://planning.lacity.org/odocument/5997064e-8a5b-4bd4-a26d-c6009582e847/PeriodRevival_1919–1950.pdf.

Tsing, Anna Lowenhaupt. *Friction: An Ethnography of Global Connection*. Princeton University Press, 2005.

Vorspan, Max, and Lloyd P. Gartner. *History of the Jews of Los Angeles*. Philadelphia: Jewish Publication Society of America, 1970.

GREYSTONE PARK, NEW JERSEY, 1935, 1940

Cook County, Illinois, Marriage Index, 1914–1942. Michael Harelick, Flora Sawburg. Ancestry.com.

District Court of the United States, Eastern District of New York. Naturalization Records. Petition for Naturalization, file no. 73149, March 31, 1927, for Michael Harelick. Ancestry.com Library Edition.

Klein, Shirley. Personal communication with author. Ancestry.com message, December 4, 2020; email message, February 16, 2021. Shared access to Klein family tree.

Moffly Media. "40 People Who Made a Difference: Dr. David W. McFarland (1858–1934)." Accessed June 9, 2021. https://ilovefc.com/2006/12/15/40-people-who-made-a-difference/.

New York State Census, 1925. Population Schedule for King's County, New York. Brooklyn, New York City, block no. 2, election district no. 30, assembly district no. 6, p. 26, dwelling 26 and 27, family 26 and 27, Michael Harelick, Flora Harelick. Ancestry.com Library Edition.

New York State Death Index, 1931. Flora Harelick. Ancestry.com.

Preserve Greystone. "History of Greystone Park Psychiatric Hospital." Accessed June 9, 2021. http://preservegreystone.org/history-html.

Town of Smithton, Smithton, New York. Certificate of Death, Flora Harelick, February 6, 1931.

U.S. Census, 1910. Population Schedule for King's County, New York. Brooklyn, New York City, enumeration district 814, sheet no. 3-B, dwelling 64, family 64, Gamlice Harelick. Ancestry.com Library Edition.

U.S. Census, 1930. Population Schedule for Fairfield County, Connecticut. Westport Township, enumeration district 1-222, sheet no. 2-A, dwelling 40, family 40, Flora Harelick. Ancestry.com Library Edition.

U.S. Census, 1940. Population Schedule for Morris County, New York. Troy Hills Township, enumeration district 14-89, sheet no. 54-A, dwelling 13, family 13, Michael Harelick. Ancestry.com Library Edition.

U.S. World War I Registration Card. Michael Harelick, September 12, 1918. Ancestry.com Library Edition.

U.S. World War II Registration Card. Michael Harelick, April 27, 1942. Ancestry.com Library Edition.

Virtual Museum, Westport Museum for History and Culture. "Sanitariums of Westport." Accessed June 9, 2021. https://virtualhistorywestport.org/exhibits/cure/sanitariums/.

Wikipedia. "Kings Park Psychiatric Center." Accessed June 9, 2021. https://en.wikipedia.org/wiki/Kings_Park_Psychiatric_Center.

CHAPTER 4 THE SECOND STORE (*GENDER*)

Bassett, Troy J., and Christina M. Walter. "Booksellers and Bestsellers: British Book Sales as Documented by *The Bookman*, 1891–1906." *Book History* 4 (2001): 205–236. http://www.jstor.org/stable/30227332.

Baumel-Schwartz, Judith Tydor. *The Incredible Adventures of Buffalo Bill from Bochnia (68715): The Story of a Galician Jew; Persecution, Liberation, Transformation*. Sussex Academic Press, 2009.

Berlant, Lauren, and Michael Warner. "Sex in Public." In *The Norton Anthology of Theory and Criticism*, edited by Vincent B. Leitch, William E. Cain, Laurie A. Finke, John McGowan, T. Denean Sharpley-Whiting, and Jeffrey J. Williams, 2450–2467. 3rd ed. W. W. Norton, 2018.

Breger, Jennifer. "Printers." In *The Shalvi/Hyman Encyclopedia of Jewish Women*. Jewish Women's Archive. Accessed April 22, 2019. https://jwa.org/encyclopedia/article/printers.

Butler, Judith. "Performative Acts and Gender Constitution: An Essay in Phenomenology and Feminist Theory." In *Performing Feminisms: Feminist Critical Theory and Theatre*, edited by Sue-Ellen Case, 270–282. Johns Hopkins University Press, 1990.

Cohen, Hagit. "New Trends—The Zuckerman Family vs. the Ahiasaf Publishers," in *Bechanuto shel mocher hasfarim: Chanuyot sfarim yehudiot bemizrah eropa bamachatzit hashniya shel hame'a ha-19* [At the bookseller's shop: The Jewish book trade in Eastern Europe in the nineteenth century], 69–84. [In Hebrew]. Hebrew University Magnes Press, 2006.

Dave in Northridge for Readers and Book Lovers Community. "All Things Bookstore: Bookselling in Los Angeles before 1910." *Daily Kos*, October 1, 2013. https://www.dailykos.com/stories/2013/10/1/1242463/-All-Things-Bookstore-Bookselling-in-Los-Angeles-before-1910.

Diner, Hasia R. "Editorial Introduction." In *Doing Business in America: A Jewish History*, edited by Steven J. Ross, Hasia R. Diner, and Lisa Ansell, ix–xxii. Purdue University Press, 2019.

Dworkin Andrea. *Pornography: Men Possessing Women*. Women's Press, 1981.

Epstein, Louis. Interview by Joel Gardner, 1977. UCLA Library, Center for Oral History Research.

Gries, Zeev. *The Book in the Jewish World, 1700–1900*. Oxford, UK: Littman Library of Jewish Civilization, 2007.

Gries, Zeev. "Romm Family." In *The YIVO Encyclopedia of Jews in Eastern Europe*. November 19, 2010. https://yivoencyclopedia.org/article.aspx/Romm_Family.

Kronzek, Lynn C. "Fairfax . . . A Home, a Community, a Way of Life." *Legacy: Journal of the Southern California Jewish Historical Society* 1, no. 4 (Spring 1990): 21–36.

Levitt, Laura. *Jews and Feminism: The Ambivalent Search for Home*. Routledge, 1997.

Los Angeles Jewish Journal. "Booksellers' Retrospective to Highlight Bicentennial Salute." April 6, 1981.

Los Angeles Times. "Harelick & Roth" advertisements. November 22, 1973, 389; November 29, 1973, 236. Newspapers.com.

Los Angeles Times. Lucille Blatt obituary. April 7, 2017.

Los Angeles Yellow Pages. Central Area, September 1938, December 1940, December 1943, June 1948, August 1953, August 1954, and August 1955. Library of Congress United States telephone directory collection.

Lowy, Melanie. *A Childhood Memoir: A Double Childhood*. Bloomington, IN: AuthorHouse, 2011.

MacKinnon, Catharine A. "Pornography, Civil Rights, and Speech." *Harvard Civil Rights—Civil Liberties Law Review* 20, no. 1 (1985): 1–70.

Phillips, Bruce A. "Not Quite White: The Emergence of Jewish 'Ethnoburbs' in Los Angeles, 1920–2010." *American Jewish History* 100, no. 1 (2016): 73–104.

Prell, Riv-Ellen. *Fighting to Become Americans: Jews, Gender, and the Anxiety of Assimilation*. Beacon Press, 1999.

Sedgwick, Eve Kosofsky. *Epistemology of the Closet*. University of California Press, 1990.

Seidman, Naomi. *The Marriage Plot: Or, How Jews Fell in Love with Love, and with Literature*. Stanford University Press, 2016.

Shavit, Zohar. Review of *Bechanuto shel mocher hasfarim: Chanuyot sfarim yehudiot bemizrah eropa bamachatzit hashniya shel hame'a ha-19* [At the bookseller's shop: The Jewish book trade in Eastern Europe in the nineteenth century]. *Haaretz*, Jan. 12, 2007. Accessed June 4, 2007. https://www.haaretz.com/2007-01-12/ty-article/a-bookstorehouse-of-knowledge/0000017f-f8b8-d887-a7ff-f8fc50ec0000?lts=1738432489907.

Starr, Kevin. "Opinion and the Aristocracy of Art: The Search for Common Ground in Emergent Los Angeles." In *Material Dreams: Southern California through the 1920s*, 305–333. Oxford University Press, 1990.

Wikipedia. "*The Bookman* (New York City)." Accessed 1 January 2019. https://en.wikipedia.org/wiki/The_Bookman_(New_York_City).

Winship, Michael P. "'The Tragedy of the Book Industry'? Bookstores and Book Distribution in the United States to 1950." *Studies in Bibliography* 58 (2007–2008): 145–184.

Winship, Michael P., and Jeffrey D. Groves. "The National Book Trade System." In *A History of the Book in America*, vol. 3, *The Industrial Book,*

1840–1880, edited by Scott E. Casper, Jeffrey D. Groves, Stephen W. Nissenbaum, and Michael P. Winship, 117–157. University of North Carolina Press.

Zollo, Paul. "Aaron Epstein." In *Hollywood Remembered: An Oral History of Its Golden Age*. 258–263. Cooper Square Press, 2002.

CHAPTER 5 THE SALES FLOOR (*COLLECTION*)

Babel, Isaac. *You Must Know Everything; Stories, 1915–1937*. Translated by Max Hayward. Edited, and with notes, by Nathalie Babel. Farrar, Straus and Giroux, Fifth Printing, 1980.

Benjamin, Walter. *Illuminations*. Edited by Hannah Arendt. Translated by Harry Zohn. Schocken Books, 1969.

Clifford, James. *The Predicament of Culture: Twentieth-Century Ethnography, Literature, and Art*. Harvard University Press, 1988.

Freehof, Solomon. *On the Collecting of Jewish Books*. New York: Society of Jewish Bibliophiles, 1961.

Goodman, Philip. *Essays on Jewish Booklore: Articles Selected from the Jewish Book Annual, 1942–1971*. KTAV Publishing House, 1971.

Greenberg, Sidney, and Jonathan D. Levine, eds. *Mahzor Hadash: The New Mahzor for Rosh Hashanah and Yom Kippur*. Prayer Book Press of Media Judaica, 1986.

Gumbrecht, Hans Ulrich, and Michael Marrinan, eds. *Mapping Benjamin: The Work of Art in the Digital Age*. Stanford University Press, 2003.

Lerer, Seth. "Epilogue: Falling Asleep over the History of the Book." *PMLA* 121, no. 1 (January 2006): 229–234.

U.S.S.R., 1976

Abrams, Elliot. "Lessons of the Soviet Jewish Exodus." *Jewish Review of Books*, Spring 2019.

Naor, Mordecai. *Israel's Cradle: The National Institutions Building*. Jerusalem: Yehuda Dekel Library—Society for Preservation of Israel Heritage Sites, 2020.

Newman, David. "Borderline Views: Remembering the Soviet Refuseniks." *Jerusalem Post*, April 22, 2013.

CHAPTER 6 THE BOOK-LINED WALL (*DESIGN*)

Adamich, Tom. "The Book Industry Study Group: Promoting Partnerships and Perspectives." *Technicalities* 34, no. 6 (2014): 15–18.

Barthes, Roland. *Mythologies*. Translated by Annette Lavers. Hill and Wang, 1979.

Byers, Reid. *The Private Library: The History of the Architecture and Furnishing of the Domestic Bookroom.* New Castle, DE: Oak Knoll Press, 2021.

Ellis, Estelle, Caroline Seebohm, and Christopher Simon Sykes, eds. *At Home with Books: How Booklovers Live with and Care for Their Libraries.* New York: Carol Southern Books, 1995.

Emblidge, David. "Scribner's Bookstore: All the Good Horses." *Logos: Journal of the World Publishing Community* 31, no. 4 (February 2021): 39–43.

Jewish Journal. "In the Beginning . . . : Rumors, Rumors Everywhere in Pico-Robertson; Fads and Fancies in Jewish Book Buying; It's Moving Month in the Rabbinate; AJC Congress Brings in a New President." April 22–April 28, 1988, 4–5.

Leibson, Meisha. Email message to author, January 1, 2021.

Martínez-Ávila, Daniel. "BISAC Subjects Heading List." In *ISKO Encyclopedia of Knowledge Organization*, edited by Birger Hjørland and Claudio Gnoli. Accessed August 21, 2020. https://www.isko.org/cyclo/bisac.

Miller, Laura J. *Reluctant Capitalists: Bookselling and the Culture of Consumption.* University of Chicago Press, 2006.

Moskowitz, Faye. Personal letter to Jack Roth, April 30, 1985.

Nelson, Stephen. "Where to Find What You Want." *Library Light* (Association of Jewish Libraries of Southern California [AJLSC]), April/May 1985.

Petroski, Henry. *The Book on the Bookshelf.* Alfred A. Knopf, 1999.

Pike, Stan. Stan Pike Designs. Accessed August 13, 2020. https://www.stanpikedesigns.com/cbmc.htm.

Prell, Riv-Ellen. Zoom call, November 5, 2020.

Pyne, Lydia. *Bookshelf.* Bloomsbury Academic, 2016.

Salkowitz, Tracy. Email message to author, January 20, 2021.

Time: The Weekly Magazine. "The Barnum of Books." 58, no. 6 (August 6, 1951). https://content.time.com/time/subscriber/article/0,33009,856910,00.html.

CHAPTER 7 THE SHIPPING ROOM (*SOUND*)

Epstein, Jason. *Book Business.* W. W. Norton, 2001.

Hondagneu-Sotelo, Pierrette. *Doméstica: Immigrant Workers Cleaning and Caring in the Shadows of Affluence.* University of California Press, 2007.

Jewish Museum of the American West. "Bernard Cohn: Pioneer Jewish Merchant & Civic Leader." August 21, 2012. https://www.jmaw.org/bernard-cohn-jewish-la/.

Kun, Josh. "White Christmases and Hanukkah Mambos: Jews and the Making of Popular Music in L.A." In *Jews in the Los Angeles Mosaic*, edited by

Karen S. Wilson, 75–89. Autry National Center of the American West in association with University of California Press, 2013.

Michelson, Alan. "Pico, Governor Pio, House #2, Whittier, CA." Pacific Coast Architecture Database, University of Washington Library, 2005–2023.

Nelson, W. David, trans. and ed. *Mekhilta de-Rabbi Shimon bar Yohai*. Philadelphia: Jewish Publication Society, 2006.

Romero, Mary. *Maid in the U.S.A.* Routledge, 1992.

Soloveitchik, Haym. "Rupture and Reconstruction: The Transformation of Contemporary Orthodoxy." In *Jews in America: A Contemporary Reader*, edited by Roberta Rosenberg Farber and Chaim I. Waxman, 320–376. Brandeis University Press, 1999.

Southern California Quarterly. "The Historian's Eye: What Does a Historian Notice in a Photo from the Past?" 104, no. 1 (2022): 128–130. https://muse.jhu.edu/article/850747.

Sterne, Jonathan. *The Audible Past: Cultural Origins of Sound Reproduction*. Duke University Press, 2003.

Thompson, Emily. "Sound, Modernity and History." In *The Sound Studies Reader*, edited by Jonathan Sterne, 117–129. Routledge, 2012.

Vorspan, Max, and Lloyd P. Gartner. *History of the Jews of Los Angeles*. Philadelphia: Jewish Publication Society of America, 1970.

Weingrad, Michael. *American Hebrew Literature: Writing Jewish National Identity in the United States*. Syracuse University Press, 2011.

Wirth-Nesher, Hana. *Call It English: The Languages of Jewish American Literature*. Princeton University Press, 2006.

CHAPTER 8 COLLECTION'S END (*NETWORKS*)

Ackerman, Ellen, ed. *The Wagner Program Honors Jack Roth, Bookseller*. Los Angeles: Wagner Program of the University of Judaism, 1990.

Barabási, Albert-László. *Linked: How Everything Is Connected to Everything Else and What It Means for Business, Science, and Everyday Life*. Plume, 2003.

Benjamin, Walter. "Unpacking My Library." In *Illuminations*, edited by Hannah Arendt and translated by Harry Zohn, 59–67. Schocken Books, 1969.

Berkowitz, Ellis C. Personal letter to Jack Roth. November 18, 1991.

Boum, Aomar. "'Little Jewish Morocco': A History of an Angeleno Settlement." In *100 Years of Sephardic Los Angeles*, edited by Sarah Abrevaya Stein and Caroline Luce. UCLA Alan D. Leve Center for Jewish Studies, 2020. https://sephardiclosangeles.org/portfolios/little-jewish-morocco/.

Brin, Herb. "Across the City Desk: An Attack That Backfired." *Heritage* 5752, no. 12 (Friday, November 22, 1991): 10.

Chazanov, Mathis. "Rabbis Condemn School's Plan to Honor Shamir." *Los Angeles Times*, November 14, 1991. https://www.latimes.com/archives/la-xpm-1991-11-14-me-2071-story.html.

Hanau, Shira. "Avi Chai Says Goodbye, but Not 'Mission Accomplished.'" Jewish Telegraphic Agency, November 13, 2019.

J. Roth Bookseller. Proposal, April 18, 1993.

J. Roth Bookseller. "Statement of Appeal," June 2, 1993.

Kirshenblatt-Gimblett, Barbara. "Objects of Ethnography." In *Exhibiting Cultures: The Poetics and Politics of Museum Display*, edited by Ivan Karp and Steven D. Lavine, 386–443. Smithsonian Institution Press, 1991.

Levine, Caroline. *Forms: Whole, Rhythm, Hierarchy, Network*. Princeton University Press, 2015.

Levitt, Laura. "Impossible Assimilations, American Liberalism, and Jewish Difference: Revisiting Jewish Secularism." *American Quarterly* 59, no. 3 (2007): 807–832. http://www.jstor.org/stable/40068451.

Moffet, Penelope. "Chain Reaction: Westwood Booksellers Warily Await Opening of Huge Store by National Rival and Wonder, Can the Independents Last?" *Los Angeles Times*, September 29, 1994. https://www.latimes.com/archives/la-xpm-1994-09-29-we-44200-story.html.

Noonan, Ari. "The Trials of a Bookseller." *Heritage* 5752, no. 12 (Friday, November 22, 1991): 7, 19, 24.

Ratanakul, Pinit. Personal letter to Jack Roth, March 24, 1983.

Rich, Adrienne. "Split at the Root: An Essay on Jewish Identity." In *Blood, Bread, and Poetry: Selected Prose, 1979–1985*, 100–123. W. W. Norton, 1986.

Rosen, Judith. "The Changing World of Bookselling." *Publishers Weekly*, April 19, 2022.

Roth, Laurence. "Networks." In *The Routledge Handbook of Contemporary Jewish Cultures*, edited by Laurence Roth and Nadia Valman, 195–209. Routledge, 2015.

Schrank, Andrew, and Josh Whitford. "The Anatomy of Network Failure." *Sociological Theory* 29, no. 3 (September 2011): 151–177.

Tabac, Alden. "Mourning Jerusalem Icon Machel Pomeranz." *Jerusalem Post*, July 16, 2022.

That Jewish Family. "Did you know there are THIS MANY Torah books?" TikTok, January 18, 2023. https://www.tiktok.com/@thatjewishfamily_/video/7190200256636701954?lang=en.

Torok, Ryan. "House of David Store Is a Family Affair." *Jewish Journal*, January 2, 2020. https://jewishjournal.com /news/los_angeles/community /309114/house-of-david-store-is-a-family-affair/.

Watts, Duncan J. *Six Degrees: The Science of a Connected Age*. W. W. Norton, 2003.

SELINSGROVE, PENNSYLVANIA, 2021

Golan, Zev. "Jewish Assassins in Cairo." *Jerusalem Post*, October 16, 2013.

Saidel, Joanna. "Yitzhak Shamir: Why We Killed Lord Moyne." *Times of Israel*, July 5, 2012. https://www.timesofisrael.com/yitzhak-shamir-why-we-killed-lord-moyne/.

About the Author

LAURENCE ROTH is the Charles B. Degenstein Professor of English and director of the Jewish & Israel Studies Program and The Build Collaborative (a project-based center for liberal arts, business, and creativity) at Susquehanna University. He is the author of *Inspecting Jews: American Jewish Detective Stories*; coeditor, with Nadia Valman, of *The Routledge Handbook of Contemporary Jewish Cultures*; and editor of *Modern Language Studies*, the scholarly journal of the Northeast Modern Language Association.